Muḥammad and the Golden Bough

Muḥammad and the Golden Bough
Reconstructing Arabian Myth

■

Jaroslav Stetkevych

INDIANA UNIVERSITY PRESS
BLOOMINGTON AND INDIANAPOLIS

The paper used in this publication meets the minimum requirements of American National Standard for Information Sciences—Permanence of Paper for Printed Library Materials, ANSI Z39.48-1984.

Manufactured in the United States of America

Library of Congress Cataloging-in-Publication Data

Stetkevych, Jaroslav.
Muḥammad and the golden bough : reconstructing Arabian myth / Jaroslav Stetkevych.
p. cm.
Includes bibliographical references (p.) and index.
ISBN 0-253-33208-7 (alk. paper)
1. Mythology, Arab. 2. Muḥammad, Prophet, d. 632—Legends. 3. Thamud (Arabian people) 4. Mythology—Comparative studies. I. Title.
BL1685.S74 1996
299′.27—dc20 96-12390

1 2 3 4 5 01 00 99 98 97 96

To Suzanne

This is the ʿAqīq, rein in
The amber camels in their rush!

ʿAlī Ibn al-Jahm

Contents

PREFACE

■ Myth as a constituent of Arab-Islamic culture has long been ignored or even denied. Prodded, indeed, irked, by this stance exhibited by scholarship on the one hand and by a dogmatic theology or ideology on the other, I attempt in this study, first of all, to demonstrate the existence of a culture-specific, coherent pre-Islamic Arabian myth—which deserves to be qualified as autochthonous—and, further, to engage that Arabian myth in the dynamism of subsequent Islamic myth-building and mythopoesis. The study first identifies as an autochthonous Arab-Islamic myth Muḥammad's unearthing of a golden bough from the grave of the last survivor of the divine scourge that destroyed the ancient race of the Thamūd. It then proceeds to establish a ground of comparison between this myth and the literary and religious traditions contained in kindred structures and symbolic systems that range from Gilgamesh and the Hebrew Bible to Homer and Vergil. On its concrete, traceable level, this study thus intends to introduce the corpus of largely unrecognized Arabian myth into the purview of a much broader comparative world of myth and symbol.

As its starting point the study takes an incident in the biography of the Prophet Muḥammad, in which, in the course of his raid against the Byzantine outpost in Northern Arabia, Tabūk, he discovered a bough of gold. It was unearthed from the grave of the last survivor of the Thamūd, an ancient Arabian people who once had prospered in their rock city of al-Ḥijr. The history of the Thamūd—apart from their myth—we can actually follow from as far back as the eighth century B.C. to the threshold (fourth/fifth century A.D.) of the Byzantine period. Myth and repeated qurʾānic notices, however, tell us that at a historically unspecified time they were smitten by a divine scourge for their iniquity and for having defied their prophet, Ṣāliḥ, and that their ultimate destruction was precipitated by their supreme abomination, the slaying of the

Divine She-Camel, known in myth more commonly as the She-Camel of Ṣāliḥ. In a direct way, Arabian myth makes Qudār, the "marked" champion of the Thamūd, the tragic perpetrator of this fateful abomination. Under the byname of Abū Righāl, this Qudār is then also identified as the one who was buried together with the golden bough of the Thamūd.

Various directions of inquiry have made possible the reconstruction of the underlying Thamūdic myth. They involved the drawing together of the lore of pre-Islamic Arabia, the Qurʾān, the Biography of the Prophet, and the Stories of the Prophets, the major Islamic works written in the manner of hagiographies. Once reconstructed, and deconstructed (chapter 6), this Arabian myth then serves as the basis for a comparative study of myth and symbol, beginning with the unearthed golden bough of the Thamūd itself (and with James G. Frazer's *The Golden Bough*), but moving quickly to a more focused literary discussion of archaic, classical primary, and classical secondary epic (Gilgamesh, Homer, and Vergil).

The Introduction argues in behalf of an Arabian mythology. For the most part it pursues the traces of the scattered morphology of myth in Arabic culture. Chapter 1 presents the essential textual sources for the unearthing of the golden bough—among them the Qurʾān, the Traditions of the Prophet, the Biography of the Prophet, the Stories of the Prophets, and encyclopaedic and exegetical compendia. On the basis of these materials, some of which offer no more than detached brief episodes or scattered tesserae of a shattered ancient verbal mosaic, we can reconstruct the overarching Arabian myth of the Thamūd—and within it begin to place the puzzle of the Thamūdic golden bough. Chapter 2 provides further background to the myth of the fall of the autochthonous Arabian race of the Thamūd to allow for the construction of a narrative around the mythic slaying of the She-Camel of Ṣāliḥ. Chapter 3 offers an interpretation of Muḥammad's raid on Tabūk as a reenactment of the trials of the Thamūdic prophet Ṣāliḥ. In Chapter 4 the bivalent identity of Abū Righāl, in whose grave the Thamūdic golden bough was discovered, is explored in terms of the ambiguity of totem and taboo. Chapter 5 demonstrates how in classical Arabic poetry the tragic dimension of the Thamūdic myth comes to the fore, as opposed to the exegetical moral dimension of the Qurʾān and qurʾānic materials. Chapter 6 presents the history—as opposed to the mythography—of the downfall of the caravan city of the Thamūd. Chapter 7 discusses the mythic and seismic aspect of the Thamūdic final "scream" that marked the moment of their destruction. Chapter 8 takes Frazer's *Golden Bough* as the starting point for an excursus into the comparative sphere of archaic and classical epic with a view to the further identification and interpretation of the symbol of the golden bough. Finally, the Conclusion places the Arabian golden bough at the core of an Arabian myth that produces a symbolic identification of Qudār, the slayer of the She-Camel of Ṣāliḥ, Ṣāliḥ, the Thamūdic prophet himself, and Muḥammad, the discoverer of the golden bough.

Acknowledgments

I wish to record my gratitude to Paul Friedrich for his generous reading of the manuscript and his thoughtful suggestions, and to Edward F. Wente for sharing his expertise on things Egyptian. Most of all, I thank Suzanne Pinckney Stetkevych for her help and support at all stages of this work.

Muḥammad
and the Golden Bough

Introduction

Reclaiming Arabian Myth

■ Arabic literary culture comes to us magisterially introduced by its pre-Islamic odes/*qaṣīdah*s, indeed by the entire classical Arabic poetic corpus, and by the Qurʾān. Western literary-critical culture has lived with that legacy in an unbroken, although fluctuating, dialogue at least since the late eighteenth century;[1] and our poetic culture, too, has lived off the legacy of that culture with a receptivity that was equally fluctuating—invariably between romantic enthusiasm and formalist hesitancy.

Our awareness of the mythic-legendary side of Arabic literary culture in poetry as well as outside it, however, has remained less well informed—as well as less receptive. First of all, too early in our contacts with the Arabian cultural legacy we came to assume that, outside certain mytho-legendary elements in popular Arabic literature, such as the *Arabian Nights,* there was little else of mythical, legendary, and, broadly speaking, symbolic source material to be expected from that legacy. The richly narrative Arabic "folk epics," such as those of *Zīr Sālim,* the *Sīrah of ʿAntar,* the *Hilālīyah,* and others, suffered an early linguistic-dogmatic (translated into ideological) condemnation by an intransigently classicist Arabic literary-historical "establishment." For various code-based reasons, which we now feel free to call summarily unliterary, that establishment, a true Arabic historical construct, chose to exclude from its legitimizing critical concerns all "popular" literary manifestations, that is, that kind of textuality that did not follow either the formal Arabic genre-code or, above all, the code of the ideological-more-than-linguistic construct of a "literary" language. Thus Arabic formal criticism and formal literary history well-nigh allowed Western interest in Arabic literature, and in the Arabic cultural legacy as a whole, to drift into almost pontifically handed-down fixed notions of Arabic literature and of the entire complex of Arabic cultural legacy—a situation that has only recently begun to change, as in both the East and the West the multidimensional richness of Arabic folk literature is being recognized and studied.

Regarding the traditional classical corpus, however, the literary-critical and cultural-critical "front" became (and largely remained) unified between the East and the West in matters of code inclusions and exclusions, recognitions and denials. In this picture, qurʾānic religious-dogmatic, as well as philological and cautiously literary, studies—always subservient to exegesis—came to hold an undisputed primacy. Myth and symbol were excluded from their hermeneutics.

The legendary, myth-forming potential of the many narrative incipiencies in the Qurʾān became a tempting, narratively expansive ground nonetheless. Throughout the classical Islamic centuries, narrative fragments of Qurʾān and Ḥadīth were picked up as mythopoeic spinoffs by historic-encyclopaedic compendia and florilegia. Together with much overlapping legendary material, they were culled from surrounding literate and oral cultures and shaped into coherent stories and ideo-units. Among other things, Arabic-Islamic legendary renditions of diverse prophetic life stories, known as "stories of the prophets" *(qiṣaṣ al-anbiyāʾ),* thus came into being.

An Arabic would-be hagiography, especially that part of it that touches upon materials other than those held in common with the Hebrew Bible, that is, those that drew on and grew around stories of prophets of Arabian legendary ancestry, thus became narrative structures falling somewhere between "catechism" and "permissible" *(ḥalāl)* new mythology. Here the interesting thing is that, although the catechismic purpose in this would-be hagiography claims, on the surface, to be the primary one, as a textual component it is, nevertheless, no more than the expression of an unconfessed "neomythography." No case is clearer than that of the people of Thamūd, their rock-hewn city of al-Ḥijr, their prophet Ṣāliḥ, and the divine scourge that befell them when they slew the She-Camel of God, which, together, offer not merely the setting but also an essential subject-component in the present book about the Arabian golden bough.

"One of the practical functions of criticism, by which I mean the conscious organization of a cultural tradition, is, I think, to make us more aware of our mythological conditioning." Northrop Frye thus readies himself for his study of the Hebrew Bible, the Old Testament, or, in Western cultural-historical terms, the Great Code.[2] Strongly agreeing with this premise (and dimension) of cultural and literary criticism, I nevertheless find it extremely difficult to approach the task of a "critical organization" of the Arabic cultural tradition and, in it, the place of myth. For, of its own volition and without shying away from the awkwardness of declarative rhetoric, Arabia and the Arabia-nurtured and Arabic-speaking world has most stubbornly denied itself the acknowledgment of a "mythological conditioning," that is, what we have termed here its "unconfessed neomythography."

Within the premises of this Arabian stance—begun with the Qurʾān's instant, and almost total, doctrinal impact—Arabic cultural history, with all its anthropological constructs, was supposed to have begun and thereafter forever to unfold in the clarity of broad daylight, as it were. All "falsehood" and all "truth" were forever absolutely differentiated into some timeless pre-revelation (the age of Jāhilīyah) that was followed by an equally timeless revelation (the Qurʾān), that is, into that which *exists not* and that which *exists*: *al-bāṭil* and *al-ḥaqq*. The former has not had or could not possibly have any cultural-historical continuum, whereas the latter, by being an immutable hermeneutical monolith, or an absolute "given," precluded in a starkly declarative manner even hermeneutics itself: It *was* (and *is*), and that was what it *was* (and *is*). An absolute binary breakdown of ideated time thus became instituted.

The knowledge of the communal Arabian past and its inheritors' creative and re-creative self-knowledge within it were definitely not furthered by the concrete, ahistorical, and anti-mythical doctrinal stance that relegated mythic materials to anecdotal and "catechistic" functions. An earnestness, and even somberness, of rigorous theological dogma came to reign with an almost puzzling, and, in its single-mindedness, unrippled march through more than a millennium of history. It succeeded from the first qurʾānic moment in almost suppressing or banishing into unusually reclusive layers of subconsciousness that part of the counterdogmatic Arabian cultural "self" which, under conditions of a less stable doctrinal rigor, would have had the strength to lead that culture to its remythologizing, or to an awareness of its "mythological conditioning."

In this respect even more inhibiting than the suppressions and condemnations that came forth from the doctrinal apparatus which had formed itself around the newly-arrived Arabian sacred text and which soon succeeded in forming its own cultural code was the co-optation by that new code of much of the most centrally autochthony-determining materials of the old code. This process began with the confrontation of the central values of the old ethos—those values that were embedded in the language itself. By this I mean those numerous cultural key words and concepts of the archaic Bedouin ethos and of its once comprehensive value system that found their way into the very core of the new ethos and code—whether through the inversion of their original meanings, or through a selective exception assumed toward them, or through their full, unqualified co-optation.

It would be too cumbersome to go through the most numerous co-optations and redefinitions of Arabian cultural key words through which the old code was brought to its knees and the new code was allowed to emerge. To stop over only a few, it is easily noted that some, such as the binary pairing *raghbah/rahbah* ("desire," "aspiration"/"awe"), came through the peripheral transferal of symbols from ancient, and not so ancient, empires and kingships in which these words, or concepts, had defined the relationship of the client to the sovereign. With this ritualized sense they found their way into pre-Islamic Arabic poetic lore and from there, or along the parallel tiers and variants of existing "scriptural sources," into the conceptualizing language of relationships in the Qurʾān.[3] Another term, *ghayb* ("absence," "hiddenness"), that is, everything "revealed but not fathomable or verifiable," had its semantic base in the terminology of the pre-Islamic Arabian hunt, where it meant "the hunter's invisibility to the quarry." In the Qurʾān, *ghayb* is zealously guarded as the sole domain of God; and only he can reveal it.[4] In the process of its co-optation, an important Bedouin term designating "blood kinship," *ʿashīrah*,[5] on the other hand, underwent no change that would be registered textually or in lexicons, although in its Qurʾān-initiated contexts it failed to maintain the intensity of its commitment to, and the implications of, old Bedouin custom.

Almost the sole word of the Bedouin Arabic specifically poetic and festive realm to become on the one hand qurʾānically rejected while on the other hand, and, as it were, in the same breath, co-opted into the Qurʾān's own mythic sphere of the Garden of the Blessed was *khamr* ("wine"). It is quite ironic that it was only by forbidding wine "on earth," that is, by making it inaccessible to mortals and then by transferring it to the place and the life "beyond mortality," that it attained in Arabic its "mythical transubstantiation." It became the analogue to the "nectar of the gods," a mythically conceived and represented human desire: "A parable of the Garden promised to the righteous, in it there are rivers of water incorruptible . . . and rivers of wine, a joy to those who drink. . . ."[6] Or again, "Truly the righteous are in bliss. / On thrones they look out [commandingly]. / You recognize in their faces the glow of bliss. / Their thirst is slaked with pure sealed wine [nectar], / whose seal is musk: and for this, let the aspirers aspire. / Its mixture is that of Tasnīm, / a spring from which drink the favored ones."[7] This wine thus became an enticement and, paradoxically, a form of moral compensatory currency that, in order to circulate "on earth," had to deny itself or to dematerialize, as it were, into earthly probity or, rather, submission to a law imposed without explanation or justification. No wonder that with so much built-in complexity and paradox, both "ancient" and "new" wine became almost the only denied/co-opted element not to have lost in Arabic cultural lore and social circumstance much, if any, of its hold on multiple levels of Arab mythogenic imagination—if not on its myth itself, certainly on much of its mythopoeia.[8]

Denied and made indispensable at the same time was the word *al-jāhilīyah* itself, which, in its new terminological usage evidenced already in the Qurʾān, had come to define the age preceding the coming of Islam as the *Age of Ignorance*. In the Qurʾān this term is found in diverse contexts, however. Thus, in arguing away the defeat of the Muslims in the Battle of Uḥud by the still "pagan" Quraysh of Mecca, it is used to explain the distress and loss of faith of the Muslim host after their previous excitement of near-victory (Qurʾān 3:154). It defines the judgment of the ungodly to be like that of *al-jāhilīyah* (Qurʾān 5:53). It occurs again as "the First Jāhilīyah," to be understood also as "the Jāhilīyah of bygone days" (*al-jāhilīyah l-ūlā*, Qurʾān 33:33). In that latter formulation, too, it thereafter becomes a "companion term" that stresses the remoteness, both temporally and morally, of the age before Islam; and, more than that, it also contributes to a conspicuously imprecise further subdivision of its own broader scope into two prophetic sub-ages, one from Adam to Noah or, equally likely, to Abraham, and the other from Jesus to Muḥammad.[9]

The most revealing qur'ānic occurrence of *al-jāhilīyah* is in Sura 48, of Victory *(al-fatḥ)*, verse 26, for there it stands introduced and, indeed, interpreted by another term of decisive significance, *ḥamīyah*[10] ("zeal, "heat," "heat of combat"), which, in turn, is the synonym of *jahl*, the etymon of *al-jāhilīyah*. Quite clearly, *jahl* also means "ignorance"; but more than "not knowing," it is "knowing no other [way]." In its pre-Islamic tribal and warlike contexts it is the Bedouin warrior's "intemperance," "fierceness," and even single-minded, self-sacrificial "heroism," which is not ethical, ideological, or devotional, but merely psychological and "adrenergic."

There was thus this earlier underlying sense to the new Islamic abstraction and conceptualization of *al-jāhilīyah* for it, as term, to have become fully meaningful as periodization. After all, "Islam" *(islām)* did not mean knowledge/*gnosis* to have produced as its antonym non-knowledge/ignorance/*agnosis*. Islam was "submission," and submission was *not* there to abrogate "ignorance." If its opposite was indeed *jahl*, that *jahl* of "non-submission," once again, did not mean ignorance. There had to have taken place, therefore, a semantic circumvention. Inasmuch as *islām* had an almost synonymic relationship to another Arabic cultural key term, that of *ḥilm* ("forbearance," "indulgence," "discernment," "gravity," "sobriety"), which was an object of full, positive co-optation by the Islamic ethos, and inasmuch as this *ḥilm* was the true antonym of *jahl*, this legitimately syllogistic equation was capable of producing the graspable binary opposition and semantic antonymy between *islām* and *jahl*—submission and non-submission—and, ultimately, the terminological antiposition between Islam, the creed, and al-Jāhilīyah, the non-creed.

Thus *jahl/jāhilīyah* had to have been a singularly important concept (or state) in archaic Bedouinity to have deserved such a stupendous "transfer" into its new terminological prominence—and into its paradoxical semiotic self-denial. We must, therefore, entertain the strong notion that its denial by the new Arabia that emerged with Islam also meant Arabia's denial of myth as its cultural, autochthony-defining ingredient. For myth, all myth—the epics it engenders and those from which it nourishes itself—not just Arabian myth, is hardly conceivable without the presence of *jahl* somewhere near its very core. This *jahl,* however, also in its archaic Arabic understanding, is above all that kind of heroism that also contains its own tragic flaw.

The pre-Islamic Battle Days of the Arabs *(Ayyām al-ʿArab)* were in the Arabic terminological sense paradigmatic manifestations of *jahl*. It is in such Days that the warfare between two brotherly tribes, the Banū Bakr and the Banū Taghlib, finds its legendary, epic, and even mythic expression. Begun with the slaying of the She-Camel of Basūs of the Banū Bakr and the counter-slaying of Kulayb, the imperious leader of the Banū Taghlib, the bloody fratricidal animosity continues for forty years, providing one of the most fertile sources for the lore of *jahl*.[11]

The mythic and strongly archetypal aspect of the War of Basūs is underscored further by the very semantics and semiotics inherent in the names of the two warring sides, the [Banū] Bakr and the [Banū] Taghlib. According to tribal genealogy, they are the descendants of the eponymic sons of Wāʾil, himself an eponymic progenitor. In the archetypal sense, however, what we ultimately come to know of the two respective tribes and their founders reveals itself to us first of all through the meanings of the eponymous tribal names: Bakr and Taghlib. And the essence of their legendary fratricidal war of forty years should also emerge as symbolically related to their names. For in archetypal terms, Bakr, the "elder," that is, literally, "the first-born son," the one endowed with the privileges of primogeniture (translated in the Arabian sense into privileged pasture grounds), is challenged and overpowered by his younger brother Taghlib. In symbolic terms this is borne out by the name of the second-born, *Taghlib,* which in personal terms means "*you* shall prevail," and, with reference to the tribe, "*it* shall prevail." It is here that the mythical Jacob and Esau archetype of succession-and-foundation finds its fulfillment. Of the two brothers/tribes, through their wars of mythical characteristics, such as the War of Basūs of forty years' duration, the younger of the two inheritors of the patrimony of the progenitor Wāʾil shall be "victorious": *taghlib*.[12] As for Wāʾil himself, his name, too, is symbolically significant. On the one hand it approaches being Abrahamic in its meaning of "refuge," while on the other hand it imprints on its eponymic bearer a mark of tragedy by also meaning "a great calamity."

Among Muḥammad's own warlike activities, still at the divide between the pre-Islamic and Islamic periods, the Battle of Badr and the Battle of Uḥud—each one in its own way, and each one depending on the perspective assumed, whether that of the new co-optation-through-inversion of *jahl* or that of its untouched inherited meaning—were, respectively, either the last acts of pre-Islamic *jahl,* or the first acts of its denial. In the Battle of Badr, due to unusual heroism of epic proportion, or, according to the new interpretive perspective, due to divine intervention, the small host of Muḥammad achieved a startling victory over a numerically overpowering army of the still "unbelieving" Meccan Quraysh. *Jahl,* then, was on the Muslim side, if viewed from the side of the Meccan unbelievers. In the Battle of Uḥud, however, those once-defeated Quraysh avenged themselves with a ferocity that only the purest *jahl* could have induced.[13]

Ignaz Goldziher, in his excursus on "What is Meant by al-Jāhiliyya," understood al-Jāhilīyah as denoting the Arabian "time of barbarism" and, especially in its primary terminological sense, as not at all being the time of a nondescript "ignorance." He saw furthermore that, inasmuch as *jahl* is opposed terminologically as well as broadly semantically to *ḥilm,* the adjectival *jāhil*—to him the terminological equivalent of "barbarian"—would thus be the antonym of the equally adjectival epithet *ḥalīm,* which he proposed should be understood as "what we call a civilized man."[14] Ultimately, however, this "barbarian"/"civilized" antiposition is to Goldziher not an antiposition in the sense of a mutually excluding, or repelling, polarization; for he recognizes that, precisely as *jahl* and *ḥilm* form part of the pre-Islamic Arab personal and communal ethos, both qualities, together, blend in quite equal measure into the Bedouin formation of the view of the *heroic*—for which another early term, that of "manliness" *(murūwah),* then emerges (and is duly recognized by Goldziher) as a figural galvanizer and an embodiment. With some hesitation in the face of a possible socio-ideological anachronism, albeit with appreciation of its basic analytical correctness, we have, therefore, to rise above Goldziher's barbarian/civilized, not entirely felicitous dichotomizing of the pre-Islamic Bedouin heroic *persona* into "barbarian" and "civilized."

Jahl and *ḥilm,* and their intertwined heroic coexistence in an implied *murūwah,* come to the fore in the following early anonymous lines:

> Although I be in need of *circumspection (ḥilm),*
> Of *fierceness (jahl)* I am at times in greater need.
> I do not fancy *fierceness* as bosom friend and fellow,
> But free rein I do give it when in straits.
> Should people [other warriors] say, 'In this
> there is accommodation,'

They'd speak the truth: Abasement is most foul
to one born free.
A horse I have for *circumspection* with
circumspection bridled.
Saddled with *fierceness,* for *fierceness,*
I have another horse.
To him that wishes me unbending, unbending I shall be,
But if he wants me crooked,
there's crookedness in me![15]

We know *jahl* from other mythological, epic-heroic, and legendary sources abundantly well. Thus in the *Iliad*'s Trojan War both Achilles and Hector represent *jahl*. The "wrath of Achilles" was *jahl*. His mad run around the walls of Troy in pursuit of Hector was *jahl*. Indeed, the entire Trojan War was a magnificent manifestation of *jahl*. In the European mediaeval epic, scenes of *jahl* are those poems' true mythic residue. The combat and death scenes in the *Nibelungenlied*—especially those of the death of Siegfried, Gunther, and Hagen—will be understood best through an understanding of *jahl*. The battle at Roncesvalles in the *Chanson de Roland* offers an almost single-minded focus on the psychology and the ethos of *jahl*. The *Song of Igor* and the pathos of Igor's host's defeat by the Polovcians with that prince's heroic escape are that epic's two faces of *jahl*. Above all, most closely qualified as *jahl* even terminologically was the Norse "berserker rage," the ability of Norse fighters to raise themselves to almost superhuman levels of strength and frenzied fury in battle.

Today *jahl* is only known to us as the momentarily triggered, ungraspable, and uncontrollable state in individuals and groups under special conditions of danger and stress. It is most consistently experienced in sports, where it may be referred to as "being in a phase." Regardless of the flippancy of its new television medium, in present-day science fiction *jahl* was correctly identified as an archetype and a new myth in the story/phenomenon of the "wrath" of the Incredible Hulk, the man who mutates metabolically when possessed by ire, reaching heights of power and size.

Having no use for the myth-forming capacity of *jahl,* the new ethos and order of Islam saw its states as dangerous, unpredictable, and ungovernable. In moral terms *jahl* was thus understood correctly, albeit still in the ancient tribal manner, as that quality that stands opposite *ḥilm*. No doubt strengthened by that context, the latter was, therefore, co-opted with double zeal, unrestricted and unchanged, while the former was exscinded as ethos and psychological dimension, and its time condemned to remain known, but not understood, as the Jāhilīyah.

In a more "storied," genre-determined understanding of myth and legend, other than that of "the myth behind the word"[16] which we have pursued so far, the Arabian memory of the past proved not to have been wholly subdued by the new canon after all—especially not by its co-optation into the new canon. Some mythic material escaped that new canon's rigor at least vestigially. It was still given to speak of portentous things gone by, things that had remained afloat in the collective Arabian memory, not always differentiated in their communal proprietorship and provenance. Such was the narrative mythic debris associated with the Hebrew Bible, or with the even vaguer sources that imaginatively and narratively had fed into the Hebrew Bible: the story of the Flood, the story of Joseph, the Solomonic mythic florilegium and sprouting mythopoeia of the Bilqīs legend,[17] and other, less evolved, or merely alluded-to mythical narrative residues or incipiencies. These, however, precisely through their narrative stinginess, if not altogether inadequacy, took care to remind us that in its recesses, outside its "text," the Arabian collective memory must have retained much more than it cared, or was allowed, to retell. In the "text" itself, Arabian myth lived mostly in echoes and off echoes.

The problem with a number of these nuclei of myth was that in their survival in the new code, that is, through their co-optation by the Qurʾān (and the subsequent dogmatizing tradition), they were put to the service of a rhetoric that was almost inimical to "narrative" itself—this despite the qurʾānic claim that there they are being told in the best of narrative ways. That is, in the Qurʾān, narrative, and indeed everything else, is subordinated to the overarching rhetoric of salvation and damnation.[18] Thus in the Sura of the Cave (18), after a narratively chaotic introduction (vv. 9-12) to the story of the Sleepers of Ephesus—which is due precisely to that story's total subordination to antinarrative rhetorical purposes—we are told that "We relate to you their [the Sleepers'] story [news] in truth: they were youths who believed in their Lord, and we increased them in guidance" (v. 13). Verses 14-15, and most of verse 16, then merely perpetuate the narrative disruption through indoctrinating rhetoric, and only verses 17-22 return us to the story—and there, too, in most uneven ways. Altogether the narrative is so strongly punctuated with the rhetoric of admonition that its flow may only be pieced together against the grain of its rhetoric.[19] In the Sura of Ṭāhā (20), which retells the story of Moses at length, that narrative concludes: "Thus do we narrate to you some stories [news] of what happened before, for we have brought to you from us remembrance" (v. 99). This is then followed by verses of admonitory rhetoric and eschatological drama, only to be structurally repeated, still in the same sura, in the "story" of Adam and Satan, and ending in an admonition of the necessity of "guidance" *(wa man ihtadā)* (v. 135). The story of Moses is told again in the Sura of the Heights (7), followed by a similar reference to, or admittance of, the virtue of storytelling, although there it is, more than anything else, a curious refrain to the strictly proverbial "example" of "the dog with the lolling tongue" (v. 176).

Rarely do we sense in the Qurʾān a self-sufficient and self-justifying joy in storytelling; indeed, rarely, if at all, does the Qurʾān allow for the formation of "themes" in the literary terminological understanding, that is, of descriptive (or imagist) units that possess their own formal and thematic circumscription and "sufficiency" and are not intruded upon by a stylistically disruptive rhetoric. Rather than "themes" in the literary sense, the Qurʾān, therefore, knows primarily rhetorically subordinated motifs.[20]

An exception to this is the Sura of Yūsuf (12), which presents a sustained story, even if it, too, is interspersed with predictable, and stylistically entirely Qurʾān-specific, admonitions and "self-exegetical" interjections. Furthermore, it is not told according to the narrative model of the Hebrew version. Unlike the latter, the qurʾānic rendition is not an ideology-saturated pretense of tribal history, and, for that reason, it is more detached and more archetypal—and thus closer to myth.[21] It is in this story alone (perhaps with the exception of one verse in the story of the Sleepers of the Cave [v. 19]) that the sense of the "joy of storytelling" is perceived in the Qurʾān. With at least an internal qurʾānic justification, therefore, its verse 3 opens the narration: "We narrate to you the most beautiful of stories . . ." *(naḥnu naquṣṣu ʿalayka aḥsana l-qaṣaṣi).* It is then not surprising that in the closure of the qurʾānic Joseph story (v. 111), too, we should be given another observation on the virtue of "storytelling"—that, when all is told, a narrative self-reflection should be perceived as necessary: "There is, in their stories, instruction for those endowed with understanding. It is not a tale invented, but a confirmation of what went before. . . ."

Despite the narrative inconsistency of the Qurʾān, we must nevertheless recognize its unflagging, almost compensatory capacity to generate textually secondary narrative mythopoeia. Of this expansive corpus of Arabic "neomythography," a most intriguing episode is that of the Arabian "golden bough" which the Prophet Muḥammad—as consistently retold in the context of the dissension-ridden march on Tabūk—unearthed from the grave of the last survivor of the divine destruction of the Thamūd. One source of this episode's allure is the narratological challenge of reconstructing the myth from the briefest of *ḥadīth*-references and their recontextualization; another is the discovery of a myth that incorporates the Biography (Sīrah) of the Prophet Muḥammad into autochthonous Arabian myth; and, finally, there is its compelling comparative mythographic potential.

1

The Textual Puzzle

■ In its own tangle of myth and legend, which is no less dense and dark than the "boundless forest" that lay before Vergil's Aeneas on his road to where his golden bough shone out amid the branches of the twofold tree,[1] there lies buried together with the last ancient Thamūdean the mysterious Arabic reference to a "golden bough." In its textual latency, it is only barely gleanable from such classical Arabic sources as al-Ṭabarī's (d. 310/923) *Commentary on the Qur'ān,* Ibn Kathīr's (d. 774/1373) *The Beginning and the End* as well as his *The Stories of the Prophets,* al-Thaʿlabī's (427/1035- ?) *The Book of the Stories of the Prophets,* and finally—or firstly—from its "validating," but entirely decontextualized and narratively bare, *ḥadīth* (prophetic traditions) locus.[2]

In spite of the parsimony of narrative context in the Arabic references to that golden bough, however,—a parsimony which is also characteristic of the style of the "sayings" and "acts" attributed to the Prophet Muḥammad (*ḥadīth/sunnah* and *akhbār*)—what emerges out of such isolated, if not altogether truncated, Arabic texts is nevertheless the striking, puzzle-like detachment and narrative unselfconsciousness of the manner in which the term "golden bough," i.e., *ghuṣnun min dhahabin,* is spelled out.

In the Arabic sources the "story" in these minimalistic references to such an arcane object is as follows: As the Prophet Muḥammad in one of his military campaigns was on the road to Tabūk, which at that time was the southernmost Byzantine outpost in Arabia, he passed by the ancient al-Ḥijr of the Thamūd, and a series of stories/*ḥadīth*s connected to the tragic fate of the Thamūd and to their city was told. Among these there was one which the Prophet himself volunteered, and which comes phrased in a narratively provocative, stylistically quite "folkloric" manner.[3] It goes that, as Muḥammad passed by a grave, he halted and said to those around him, "Do you know what this is?" and they answered, "Only God and his Prophet know for certain." "This," he replied answering his own question, "is the grave of Abū Righāl [Rughāl]." But they said, "And who is Abū Righāl?" "A man of the Thamūd," replied he. "He was in God's sanctuary, which protected him from God's punishment, but when he stepped outside it, there smote him that which had smitten his people. He was buried in this very place,[4] and with him was buried a bough of gold!" At this the Prophet's companions dismounted and hastened to dig open the grave with their swords, and they brought up the bough.[5]

But, whereas the "golden bough" texts in al-Ṭabarī and Ibn Kathīr end here, the text of al-Thaᶜlabī's more narrative work continues: "Then the Prophet muffled his face in his cloak and hurried on in his march till he had crossed the valley."[6] An inference of awe remains in the air after the brief story is thus told, planting in the reader's mind an awareness that it has touched upon some portentous events, and that the golden bough is somehow the sign of the mystery surrounding those events. Such a scene reappears also in the incident of the ring which one of the Tabūk raiders finds in the ruins of al-Ḥijr. Muḥammad orders him to throw the ring back, covers his eyes, and turns away in mysterious awe.[7]

This brings us to the broader contextualization of the Arabic "surprise" of the golden bough. Viewed properly, there are two contexts to be taken into account. The more immediate context is that of the time and the circumstance in which the finding of the golden bough occurs in the sources, that is, the events of the last military expedition led by Muḥammad personally, which is the raid on Tabūk (9/630). It was during that raid that Muḥammad and his followers passed by the old Nabataean-Thamūdic mortuary city of al-Ḥijr/Madāʾin Ṣāliḥ. But we shall not be able to understand the meaning of the Arabian golden bough in that context alone without first reaching further back into the pre-Islamic and pre-Arab—although not non-Arabian—past of the people of Thamūd and of their city of al-Ḥijr, the destruction of the people and of their city, and the city's rebirth as Madāʾin Ṣāliḥ in myth and in parascriptural tradition. This will be our second, less immediate, although, as concerns the recovery of the myth itself, primary context.

The original textual salvaging of the myth of the downfall of Thamūd takes place in the Qurʾān, where there are no less than twenty-one suras that make reference to the Thamūd as a people. All of these references, however, are built into the comprehensive rhetorical qurʾānic strategy of serving as *exempla* within the cyclic theonomous, rather than temporal, reappearance of recalcitrant nations, of prophetic stories of intercessions and warnings, and of the unfailing punishment of those nations or of their utter destruction.[8]

Because of the rhetorical subservience of the "matter" of Thamūd in the Qurʾān, only scattered fragments of it appear in any one segment of that text; and, furthermore, only four of the fragments extend beyond the scope of one to three verses. Thus the Sura of the Heights (7) contains seven verses (vv. 73-79), of Hūd (11) eight (vv. 61-68), of the Poets (26) eighteen (vv. 141-158), and of the Moon (54) ten (vv. 23-32). A further characteristic of all twenty-one of the qurʾānic occurrences of the topic of the Thamūd is that, with the exception of the single-verse references in the Suras of the Repentance and of the Pilgrimage, which are of the Medinan period, all the others are the product of the early Meccan, much more strongly mythopoeically swayed inspiration.

The story, as it appears in its characteristic qurʾānic disjointedness in the four major texts (The Heights, Hūd, The Poets, The Moon), is terse in the extreme: in their iniquity the people of Thamūd, who had once lived in opulence amidst their gardens, springs, and tilled fields, feeling secure in their skillfully executed, rock-hewn dwellings, had belied previous apostles [of warning], till God sent to them his "faithful messenger" Ṣāliḥ to admonish them against spreading "corruption in the land" (7:74; 27:48). The Thamūd, however, called Ṣāliḥ a simple mortal like themselves, or at best one "bewitched." They demanded of him a "sign" of God's power, if he were indeed "one of the truthful." As such a sign, but also "as a trial for them" *(fitnatan lahum)*, God sent to the Thamūd a she-camel. The trial was to consist of this: That the she-camel, which was also the explicit "She-Camel of God" *(nāqatu Allāhi)*—not "the She-Camel of Ṣāliḥ" of subsequent Islamic hermeneutical adjustment and mythopoeia—was to have the right of sole access to all the water of the Thamūd on alternate days. On those days the Thamūd would have to withhold their herds of camels [and flocks of other livestock] from all access to water and abstain from it themselves, awaiting their own respective alternate days; nor were they to touch the she-camel with harm, lest punishment of "a portentous day" befall them. But the Thamūd did not heed the warning. They hamstrung and slew the she-camel. The next day they were remorseful—but to no avail. The Prophet Ṣāliḥ gave them three days' respite to ponder, or rather, to "take pleasure" in their abode for those three days (*tamattaʿū fī dārikum thalāthata ayyāmin* [11:65]), after which a great "scream" *(al-ṣayḥah)* destroyed them.

Such is the extent of the qur'ānic use of the myth of the downfall of the Thamūd. Indeed, the opaqueness of its textually scattered segments almost fails to yield a composite narrative. And yet, defying its opacity and disjointedness is its employ in the Qur'ān as a "clear" *exemplum,* thus as something whose understanding is postulated on the prior knowledge of some broader framing sphere of an invoked, but not elicited, myth or legend. This myth, or legend, as it is recorded in the various extant texts, is, however, no longer easily datable to the age of pure oral lore before the advent of Islam, for it is to be assumed that along the centuries that led up to its collection and redaction it has undergone its own evolution not only as mythopoeia but also as a hermeneutic tool at the service of the qur'ānic text. It is, therefore, only as such, within this vague correlation of textual purposes, that we find embedded the story of the Arabian golden bough: hidden anecdotally within a myth. The myth itself is told, once again in a manner that begs for a cumulative retelling, in narrative as well as in exegetic sources such as the *Commentary* of al-Ṭabarī, the comprehensive history of "things first and last," that is, *The Beginning and the End*, of Ibn Kathīr, the encyclopaedic *Ultimate Aspiration* of al-Nuwayrī (d. 732/1332), the hagiographic *Stories of the Prophets* of al-Thaʿlabī, and, likewise, in the *Tales of the Prophets* of al-Kisā'ī, a not clearly identified author who must have written his work sometime shortly before A.D. 1200.[9]

The textual puzzle that results from the twin mythic contexts of the Arabian golden bough—externally, Muḥammad's discord-ridden march on Tabūk and, internally as well as necessarily implicitly, the destruction of the Thamūd—becomes even more clamant and challenging by the fact, in itself puzzling, that modern scholarship has entirely failed to even mention the Arabian "golden bough."

2

The Thamūdic Backdrop to the Puzzle

■ It is characteristic of all of these "reconstructive" texts that they are sustained in a rigorously mythologizing mode, not touching upon the actual historicity of the people called Thamūd, save for their name, their settlement in the rock city of al-Ḥijr, and their ultimate total disappearance. Above all, what we are not given even to speculate about—either in the Qur'ān or in the extra-qur'ānic myth—is the historical time of their sojourn and, especially, of their destruction. Only their myth remains, which is to say, only the ahistorical meaning of their existence has been propelled into historical time, with the purpose of interpreting other things, not itself. On such levels we may thus easily empathize with Jawād ʿAlī, the modern Iraqi historian of pre-Islamic Arabia, as he vents his uneasiness with the distinct ahistoricity of the postulation of the Thamūdic question evidenced in existing Arabic textual transmission. In his search for surefooted historicity, he calls this perplexing state of affairs "a lack of perception for either time or place."[1] But then, as Bernard F. Batto remarks, myth also "stands outside of time as we know it and serves as the *principle* or source of secular time and order." And, as such, a myth becomes "paradigmatic for the society in which that myth is operative."[2]

The mytho-qur'ānic story of the Thamūd does indeed possess its paradigmatic mythical time frame, for we know from the qur'ānic lineages of prophetic cycles and sequences that the Thamūd flourished and perished in that time of cyclic polytheistic rebellion and punishment that is flanked respectively by the even more enigmatic, myth-encoded, explicitly "archaic" peoples of ʿĀd and Madyan, and, as a secondary mytho-frame to those two (we should assume), in accordance with qurʾānic lineage, by the people of Noah/Nūḥ at the head of a separate mythical lineage and by those of Lot/Lūṭ at the tail. Only then does the Abrahamic/Ibrāhīmic mythos begin—in the Qurʾān as well as in the Arabic narrative and exegetic mythopoeia—but not without establishing a link across preceding prophetic cycles with the Thamūdic mythic matrix. Thus we read in the early, still highly mythographic layers of al-Ṭabarī's *History*, that Ismāʿīl, the son of Abraham, is said to have been buried beside the grave of his mother Hagar in no other place than al-Ḥijr of the Thamūd.[3]

The story of the Thamūd, especially up to the ominous "trial" *(fitnah)* of the she-camel, which al-Kisāʾī and al-Nuwayrī retell more exhaustively than the other mythographers, freely mixes a highly syncretic flow of the narrative with wholly decontextualized quotations from the Qurʾān. It begins with Kānūh, the high priest of the Thamūd, as he receives the signs of the coming of his son, Ṣāliḥ. The scene is distinctly one of "annunciation." Kānūh was in the temple of the idols "when the semen of Ṣāliḥ moved in his spine, giving a glow to his eyes. And he heard a voice calling: 'Truth has come and falsehood perished; surely falsehood is bound to perish.'"[4] Upon hearing this, Kānūh became frightened and turned to the "supreme idol," which spoke to him: "Why do you turn to me? One like you serves me, but the earth is radiant with the light of your face for the light which is in your spine."[5] Then the idol tumbled down from its throne, but Kānūh, still not grasping the implications of the "change of covenants," re-placed it there.[6]

When that which had occurred in the temple reached the ears of the king, he sank into deep gloom. His courtiers quickly put all the blame on Kānūh, accusing him of bad service to the gods. The king wished to kill Kānūh, but God hid the priest from his enemies' eyes; and when night fell and Kānūh was asleep, angels picked him up and deposited him in a distant valley. There Kānūh saw a cave in a mountain. He entered it to escape the rays of the sun, and soon fell asleep. His sleep lasted for one hundred years.[7]

The Thamūd now considered Kānūh lost and appointed another high priest to serve their idols. "One day they went out to celebrate one of their feasts, when the trees around them spoke, saying: 'O race of Thamūd, are you not going to give heed? God gives you a yield of fruits twice a year, yet you renege on his bounty and worship others than him.' And likewise spoke the cattle. But they [the Thamūd] turned on the trees and cut them down, and they slew the cattle. Then the beasts of prey spoke, calling down from the tops of the mountains: 'Woe to you, O race of Thamūd, do not cut down those trees, nor slaughter these cattle, for they spoke the truth!'"[8] at which the Thamūd set out with their weapons, and the wild beasts fled before them.

After one hundred years Kānūh's wife is visited by the Raven of Paradise, the same raven that had once instructed Cain on how to bury his brother Abel.[9] It guided Kānūh's wife to the cave and brought him out of his sleep. It was then that Kānūh lay with his wife, and she conceived Ṣāliḥ.

The appearance of the Raven of Paradise in the story of Kānūh at this point turns our attention to the Arabic symbolic, mythical, and then massively poetic lore of that bird as one of the Arabian imagination's richest poetic-elegiac motifs. In all its roles and exemplifications, however, the raven/crow *(ghurāb)* appears as a messenger; but its messages are diverse and even polarized. Thus, whereas in the Qur'ān's briefly retold story of Cain and Abel this raven, itself the inhabiter of Paradise and courier of God,[10] is sent out to instruct a murderous Cain in the necessity, and thus ultimately the rite, of burying the dead, in the Thamūdic mythopoeia this same Raven of Paradise is the messenger of resurrection, that is, of the awakening of Kānūh from his century-long sleep, an awakening that is not only a return to his own life but also an engendering of new life, that of the Prophet Ṣāliḥ. Viewed in a lighter vein, the Raven of Paradise plays in the Kānūh story the role of Cupid.

With Ṣāliḥ in her womb, Kānūh's wife returned to the Thamūd, and, in due time, on a Friday of the Inviolable, the first month of the year *(shahr al-muḥarram)*, the earth trembled, the wild animals fell prostrate, the idols tumbled to the ground, and Ṣāliḥ was born.

When Ṣāliḥ reached the age of seven, he addressed the Thamūd and manifested to them his lineage. His powers were recognized first when he freed his people from an invading king who every seventh year had been raiding the land. Ṣāliḥ's position was now that of savior and rival to the Thamūd's king. The king at first intended to kill him, but, realizing his power as "hallowed," let him walk amongst his people "venerated and exalted."[11]

Only upon reaching the age of forty years, however, did Ṣāliḥ begin his mission as prophet—and then very much as the precursor of Islam, i.e., establishing the "profession of the faith" *(al-shahādah):* "There is no god but God, and Ṣāliḥ is his Servant and his Prophet." And here, too, began his excoriations of the people's evils and his exhortations against those who "bring corruption to the land."[12]

But the Thamūd did not listen or obey—thus until Ṣāliḥ reached seventy years of age. Then divine patience ran out. "God turned their women sterile, their trees dried up and did not yield fruit, their cows did not calve, and their ewes did not lamb."[13] The Thamūd remained unrepentant, and their domain was turning into a wasteland. In despair over so much recalcitrance, Ṣāliḥ left his people and set out toward the wilderness. There he roamed on the slopes of a mountain until the coming of evening, when he found a fountain, performed his ablutions, performed a prayer, and, like his father before him, entered a cave. In the cave he found a lamp and a golden bed draped in silk. He climbed upon the bed and fell asleep for forty years. God then awakened him, and he returned to his people and to his temple-mosque, which had fallen into ruin.

Thus Ṣāliḥ's last reforming mission begins.[14] He faces the Thamūd and renews the *shahādah;* "There is no god but God, and I am Ṣāliḥ, the messenger of God"; and once again the people are perplexed, the idols fall to the ground, and the beasts of burden speak.[15]

Facing further defiance, Ṣāliḥ performs a miracle by causing a whole family to die in order to resurrect them thereafter. But the people's recalcitrance does not diminish.[16]

Prodded on by Iblīs, the Thamūd challenged Ṣāliḥ further. They demanded of him a miracle like those performed by Hūd and Noah.[17] Ṣāliḥ agreed. Together they went out to a valley where the Thamūd asked their idols for a miracle, and where Ṣāliḥ was to ask for one from his God. Their miracles, or "signs," failed them, however. Of Ṣāliḥ they requested the miracle/"sign" of bringing a she-camel out of a rock. Thus begins the actual story of the "She-Camel of Ṣāliḥ" of the popular legend, or myth, and of the "She-Camel of God"[18] of the Qurʾān.

From the versions of the story we do not know whether the Thamūd had specified their request of a miracle to Ṣāliḥ before or after the failure of their idols. The stories vary even in telling us whether the choice of the miracle of the she-camel came from the Thamūd or from Ṣāliḥ.[19]

According to al-Nuwayrī's narration, the Thamūd were precise and demanding in their description of the requested miracle. They specified that the she-camel be truly of blood, flesh, bone, sinew, skin, and coat of hair; that her color be between white and ruddy, i.e., showing the nobility of breed of the camels termed *ʿīs;* that she be slender of belly, but possess udders like the largest of water-jugs, from which pure milk would stream profusely without need to be drawn off, and that the sick who drink of it be cured and the indigent satisfied; furthermore, that she not pasture on their pasture grounds but instead on mountaintops and in the depths of valleys, leaving the pastures to them; and finally, that she have an offspring colt which should follow her and answer her yearning groans.[20]

To all this Ṣāliḥ agreed, with the reciprocal condition that the miraculous she-camel have sole access to Thamūd's only water source on alternate days. So, too, the Thamūd should have their water to themselves on the remaining days, although on the interim days the Thamūd would enjoy the benefit of the unrestricted bounty of that she-camel's milk.[21]

The stage for Ṣāliḥ's miracle was then set: a canopy or dome formed over a huge rock or hillock and a circle of angels hovered over it. Ṣāliḥ approached the rock and struck it with a rod. The rock shook and began rising, extending ever higher, and then once again stood firm in its place. Convulsions as though of a woman in childbirth seized it. Then it burst open, and there emerged the she-camel as though she, too, were a part of the mountain. "This is the She-Camel of God as a sign for you," proclaimed Ṣāliḥ, "so let her graze in God's earth, and let no one do her harm, lest you be afflicted with a painful punishment."[22] And with the she-camel was her offspring.

Events seem to have developed as stipulated in the conditions. Every second day the she-camel drank all the water of the Thamūd, giving them in return her miraculous milk, and every other day the Thamūd had abundant water to drink and to water their herds. Such agreement and harmony, however, would not last, for in the summertime, when the heat was strong, the she-camel took up the high slopes of the valley, frightening away the Thamūd's herds of cattle large and small, and their camels, and driving them into the sultry heat of the valley floor. In the cold of winter, however, the she-camel sought pasturage at the bottom of the valley, causing the Thamūd's herds to flee high up its slopes. Thus, both summer and winter, the herds of the Thamūd were at the mercy of the strange she-camel. In time, this outweighed for the Thamūd their commitment to their covenant with Ṣāliḥ and the bounty they obtained from the she-camel.

In an atmosphere of conspiracy, the Thamūd decided to kill the she-camel without Ṣāliḥ's knowledge. But Ṣāliḥ anticipated their intention and prophesied to them that of the male offspring born to them in a given month, one, who was also to be "a marked one," would be the cause of their destruction. Nine were born and killed in that month, but a tenth infant, by the name of Qudār, was spared by his father and was allowed to grow up to a precocious and arrogant manhood. The stage for the tragedy was further set by the hatred that two women of the Thamūd harbored for Ṣāliḥ. One was named Ṣadūf. She not only was wealthy in herds of cattle and camels, but was also one of the most beautiful women of the Thamūd. The other was named ʿUnayzah. She was equally wealthy, older than Ṣadūf, and the mother of daughters of great beauty. The two women resolved that the She-Camel of Ṣāliḥ that had caused such disruption of the pasturage of their herds had to be killed. In exchange for a promise to carry out her will, Ṣadūf thus offered herself to one of the young warriors of the Thamūd by the name of Miṣdaʿ, "the Eloquent," and as part of the same design the older ʿUnayzah offered one of her beautiful daughters to Qudār, the youth who was also known as the Red One of Blue Eyes. He, Qudār, was thus equally "the marked one" and the one prophesied by Ṣāliḥ to bring about the destruction of the Thamūd. About him especially legends multiply and diverge. His very name, Qudār, has an ominous, foreboding ring in Arabic: one of "enacted" power as well as of predestined occurrence, thus fate—but fate with a flaw, to which there points even the Arabic morphological-semantic mold of *fuʿāl*, into which the name Qudār falls.[23] His characteristics or epithets of being both "red" and "blue" are in the Arabic symbolic association of colors distinctly negative. They point to the liminal "otherness" of an instrument of destiny.

Qudār's redness should take us as far back as the "coded" insistence on the color red in the biblical story of Esau (Gen. 2:23–34). The biblical text tells us with clear emphasis, or, one should say, with charged intentionality, that Esau, the firstborn over his twin brother Jacob, was born "red" *(admonī)*. He grew up to be the stronger of the twins, a skillful hunter, spending his days in the open fields. Jacob, on the other hand, was "a quiet man, dwelling in tents." The archetypal paradox, or the ideology, of the story decrees, however, that Esau, his father's provider, will for a meal of "red pottage" forswear "his birthright" to Jacob. This is stressed "editorially" first by Yahweh, that "the elder shall serve the younger" (Gen. 25:23), and then by Isaac, the father: "Behold, away from the fatness of the earth shall your dwelling be, and away from the dew of heaven on high. By your sword you shall live, and you shall serve your brother . . ." (Gen. 27:39-40). Thus both divine and paternal curses fall upon the *red* Esau, the eponymic ancestor of the "red" Edomites.[24]

The blueness of Qudār's eyes, through folklore (*al-shayṭān al-azraq*, "the blue devil") and legend, points even more directly (in the Arabic context) to a curse and to the fear of hidden evil, or even to a demonic quality. "And there was blueness in his eyes, as though they were two lenses," says al-Nuwayrī in his role as mythographer.[25] Something ominous is sensed here, reminding us of Zarqāʾ al-Yamāmah (the Blue-eyed One of Yamāmah). She, too, has a "glass-like," or "lens-like, glance" *(mithla z-zujājati)*[26] and her ability to see, although she is cursed not to be believed, is only comparable to the Trojan Cassandra's ability to foresee—especially to foresee the doom impending upon Troy—but not be given credence.[27] Like Cassandra in her seer's knowledge of Odysseus's ruse prepared for the credulous Trojans, Zarqāʾ al-Yamāmah had warned in vain her husband's clan, the Jadīs of Yamāmah, of the approaching army of the Ḥimyarites and of their ruse of carrying a screen of bushes before them—a forest advancing, quite like the "great Birnam Wood coming to Dunsinane."[28]

Returning to the conspiracy of the Thamūd, our compounded qurʾāno-narrative mythopoeia tells us that Miṣdaᶜ and Qudār, seduced into action, gather around themselves seven more conspirators and thus become the "nine who spread corruption in the land."[29] Together they set out to "hock" *(ʿaqara)*[30] the she-camel. The prevalent version of the narrative is that it was Qudār who first shot the she-camel with his bow and then, together with Miṣdaᶜ, fell upon her with a sword, killing her.[31] The remaining conspirators then joined them and dismembered her. One version of the story then speaks of the conspirators' pursuit of the she-camel's colt, which, warned by its mother, had fled to the top of a mountain and invoked a curse upon the Thamūd. The conspirators, however, chased it down, slaughtered it, and divided its flesh amongst them.[32] In another version, however, the camel-colt, having witnessed its mother's death, runs off till it comes to an inaccessible mountain called Ḍawʾ (light), or, some say, Qārah (black stones, pitch). Ṣāliḥ, in the meantime, is alerted by some repentant Thamūdeans to the attack upon the she-camel. He reaches her too late, however. He then urges those around him to go out and rescue the colt, for if they can reach it perhaps their punishment may be averted. The Thamūd went out searching for the colt and, when they saw it on the mountain, tried to catch it. But God made the mountain rise up to heaven till not even the birds could reach it. Only Ṣāliḥ came up to the colt, and when it saw him, tears streamed from its eyes and it groaned three times, at which the rock split open and the colt entered the mountain. Only then did Ṣāliḥ pronounce his prophecy of doom.[33]

Then, however, he gave the Thamūd a strange respite of three days, saying to them: "Enjoy yourselves in your abode for three days—this is a promise not to be belied."[34] The Qurʾān, and with it the narrative mythopoeic and exegetic sources, fails to clarify the meaning of this would-be grace period of "enjoyment" *(tamattuʿ)* which is given to the doomed Thamūd. This becomes puzzling. We only know that, as pertains to the qurʾānic text, these enigmatic Thamūd-related occurrences of the motif of "enjoyment" in the context of doom are from that text's "early," still Meccan, period. No self-conscious internal qurʾānic exegesis is in evidence there, although in these Meccan suras we are squarely in the rich thematic area of qurʾānic mythopoeia, which, by its stylistic nature, might have been receptive to expatiation and explanation. When in a later, Medinan, return the Qurʾān (9:68–70) speaks of this motif again, such "enjoyment" (this time in its morphological variant of *istamtaʿa*) seems to have undergone a certain degree of "clarification." There, for the first time, it is linked further—internally exegetically, as it were—to the word meaning "share of happiness" *(khalāq)*. Matters do not become clearer, however. These later Medinan verses indeed explain *tamattuʿ* in its general semantics, but they do not clarify its earlier Meccan Thamūdic context, and with it the rationale of the drama; for in the Medinan sura there is no "drama," no punishment already set in motion for an abomination already committed—as is the case of the Meccan texts. In it we find merely the most unparticularized of admonitions that all good things will have their end—of course a deserved end. As such, the phrasing becomes that of "general wisdom" *(ḥikmah)*, for multiple uses, although its ultimate reference, too, is to "the people of Noah, the ᶜĀd, and the Thamūd . . ." (v. 70). The much stranger, argumentatively unforewarned throwing of *tamattuᶜ* into the midst of the tragedy of the Thamūd is not easily explained in this chronologically "postmeditated" (Medinan), textually *ex post facto*, manner.

In the Thamūd context the "enjoyment" of the condemned may, of course, itself invite an easy and almost flippantly plausible psychological explanation as well—that of the "last wish" principle; or even that of gallows humor. It may also be viewed, as the exegetes view it, as a "respite"—although on what grounds and for what purpose remains unarticulated. These, however, do not seem to me to be proper hermeneutical avenues in the qurʾānic-Thamūdic case of *tamattuᶜ*. Rather, I should introduce an element of broader scriptural intertextuality, namely the extended biblical passage in Exodus 32:5–29.

There we read that, while Moses was "on the mountain" receiving the Tablets, there was a restlessness in the camp of the Israelites, and to assuage that restlessness Aaron fashioned "the golden calf." The Israelites sacrificed to it, and then (v. 6) "they sat down to eat and drink, and rose up to *take their pleasure*" [italics mine].[35] Still up on the mountain (v. 10), Yahweh, cognizant of the goings-on below, announces to Moses that he will punish the Israelites for their abomination, ". . . that my wrath may blaze up against them to consume them" (v. 10). Moses succeeds (in a truly forensic manner)[36] in persuading Yahweh to relent in the punishment (vv. 11–14), but, after himself witnessing the abomination, his own rage prevails. He asks Aaron to summon those in the camp that are "for the Lord." "All the Levites rallied to him" (v. 26), and he ordered them to take their swords and go in the camp from gate to gate: "and *slay your own kinsmen, your friends and neighbors*" [italics mine]. Thus the Levites slew "about three thousand of the people" (v. 28) in an act of their own "consecration" (v. 29).

It is important to note the impact of this account on the further biblical narrative, and mythopoeia, of the Israelites' wandering in the Sinai. For we find events analogous to those narrated in Exodus 32:25–29 very closely rephrased in Numbers 25:1–9. In that latter variant, whose "chronology" is posterior, placing it during the Israelites' sojourn among the Midianites, Moses orders the Judges of Israel to slay those of their men who have joined themselves to Baal; and, as it were, underlining and specifying the abomination, it is Aaron's grandson, the Levite Pinehas, who with his spear transfixes an Israelite and a Midianite woman during their carnal embrace.

The Israelites' abominations were thus twofold: to their *taking other gods* and their idol worship there is added the *immediate* cause of punishment, which is their reveling and indulging in the sin of carnality with Midianite women—the *pleasure* factor.[37]

In a manner that has the effect almost of an editorial intervention and "emendation" that is meant to take, at least in part, the human hand out of a story that ends with the death of 24,000 Israelites—and which can hardly be anything other than a variant of Exodus 32:22-29—verses 8 and 9 of Numbers 25 introduce instead a second, divine executor of punishment in the form of the plague.

In a structural sense, the primary observation to be made here is that in both cases of the Mosaic/Levite blotting out of abomination (Exodus and Numbers), extermination is preceded by *enjoyment*, and the fact and structural placement of that enjoyment are insisted upon most firmly—so much so that even in the much later context of St. Paul's 1 Corinthians 10:1-11, where reference to these biblical texts is made, the warning "not to put the Lord to the test" (v. 9)[38] is connected with the abomination of idolatry. Above all, it brings to the mind of the author of the Epistle the circumstance in which the Israelites had "taken their pleasure" first and then were slain (v. 8).

Even when taking into separate consideration the non-Thamūdic occurrences in the Qur'ān of the word/motif of *tamattu*ʿ, we are able to establish a common denominator there as well. For there *tamattu*ʿ is also invariably preceded by the abomination of turning to "other gods" and is followed by the threat of final punishment—thus in Qur'ān 39:8, 14:30, 16:55, and 30:34 (all of them Meccan). *Tamattu*ʿ and punishment, we find, are thus an indivisible structural whole there too. In the context of the qur'ānic Thamūd story, however, where it occurs at the point of highest dramatic intensity and narrative urgency, and where there is obviously some higher degree of specificity, *tamattu*ʿ must be afforded its broader hermeneutically and literary-critically indispensable intertextuality, which ought to be, ultimately, that of

Exodus and Numbers, in order for that qurʾānic *tamattuᶜ* to be appreciated rather than hesitantly—and invariably with a touch of bemusement—accepted.

And a further problem of affinities, both textual and ideological (albeit extra-Thamūdic): Mild in comparison to the single-minded horror of Levitic "consecration" must appear the profession of loyalty—equally a consecration—of Ḥassān Ibn Thābit, the Prophet Muḥammad's most vocal poet-apologist. He offers the Prophet his property and his life, and "to wage war against all and everyone of the people whom he [the Prophet] regards as enemy—even if it be against the beloved, most sincere friend." In both cases it is the same abstract ideology that prevails even over the traditionally most sacred and cherished ties of blood and custom. Thus we know that, in both cases, a new "covenant" has set in.[39]

Even the qurʾānic retelling of Exodus 32:5–29 and Numbers 25:1–9 in the Sura of al-Baqarah, vv. 54–55 and 57–59, as properly observed by some interpreters—but obviously also apologists[40]—appears mild by comparison with its textual predecessor in the way it presents its Arabic version of the Levitic "consecration" scene and the ultimate harshness that underlies the ideological commitment: "And kill your own selves *[your own kind]!* This will be better for you with [before] your Maker."[41] The slaughter of the scene in Numbers 25:1–9 is also in its entirety "mercifully" given over in the Qurʾān to a "plague," or to "punishment of pollution from the sky/heaven" *(rijzan min as-samāʾi).*[42] Here, too, the accepted (exegetical?) qurʾānic reading (and understanding) of the key word *rijz* as "filth," "pollution," and some nondescript "punishment" comes suspiciously close to implying the abomination of carnality in Numbers 25:6–8; although it should, perhaps, be taken back to the more likely, and stronger, etymology of the root *r-j-z,* which, although phonetically close to *r-j-s* and that root's more nearly proper meaning of "pollution" and "filth," nevertheless possesses in a primary sense the meaning of "[rhythmic] motion," "intermittent roar," and "tremor."[43] We would then have here, once again, a much more characteristic, both stylistically and mythopoeically plausible, punishment with a "tremor" (or an earthquake) in the best qurʾānic tradition relative to the core of the Thamūdic texts.

With the above in mind, we need to consider the now enriched semantics of that particular Hebrew word/term which, *mutatis mutandis*, we propose, corresponds to the Arabic word/term of *tamattuᶜ* in the qurʾānic and exegetic-mythopoetic texts of the Thamūdic legend. For this we shall invoke the hermeneutic efficacy of Numbers 25:1-9 with its clear evidencing of a connection between the two causes of punishment measured out to the Israelites: that of taking other gods and that of falling prey to contaminating carnality expressed in the "pleasure factor." Then, with Numbers 25:1-9 in mind, we shall also turn once more to our primary motival model, Exodus 32:5-29, and specifically to verse six. There we shall take cognizance of the actual terminological Hebrew referent to the "pleasure factor," the word *ẓaḥeq* of *wayyaqemū le ẓaḥeq*, to be understood as "and they rose to take their pleasure," or, as it is more customarily translated (The Revised Standard Version), "and [they] rose up to play"—for, indeed, the verb *ẓaḥeq* means in one sense "to play," while in its main sense, which is also that of the Arabic *ḍaḥika,* it means "to laugh." This the dictionaries of classical Hebrew ascertain fully; but they equally ascertain that, aside from "to laugh," *ẓaḥeq* also means "to fondle (erotically)," as in Genesis 26:8 ("and [Abimelekh] saw Isaac *(Yiẓḥaq)* fondling *(meẓaḥeq)* Rebekah his wife").[44] We thus may not exclude the "pleasure factor" in its fuller semantics from either Numbers 25:1-9 or Exodus 32:6.[45] The strange respite of *tamattuᶜ* of three days, which the prophet of the Thamūd, Ṣāliḥ, gave to his intractable people, was thus an ancient and scripturally-textually diversely extrapolatable respite.

We know further that Ṣāliḥ had warned the Thamūd that on each of the three days of the respite the color of their faces would change: from yellow, to red, to black. And, indeed, on the morning of the first day, the Thamūd woke up and saw that there where the She-Camel had set her pads pools of blood had sprung up, and when they looked at each other, they saw themselves turned yellow. This, however, did not frighten them, but only incensed them in their anger toward Ṣāliḥ. But on the second day their faces turned red, and on the third, black. Now they knew that their fate was sealed. Before sunrise of the fourth day, which fell on a Sunday, they embalmed themselves and prepared themselves for their final hour and for the punishment. When the rays of the sun appeared, there came upon them from the sky a portentous scream, "within which was the sound of every thunderbolt and the voice of everything that had a voice."[46] Then there rose from underground a violent tremor, and all that breathed perished, all motion ceased, voices fell silent, and what was to happen happened. As lifeless corpses the Thamūd remained as though perched in their abodes.[47] And above their abodes there hung a black cloud from which fire rained down upon them for seven days, till all became ashes. On the eighth day the cloud cover broke, and the sun emerged. Then Ṣāliḥ and those of the faithful who had remained with him picked up what they could carry of their possessions and journeyed toward the land of Shām, where they settled in Palestine. There Ṣāliḥ lived until the end of his days.[48]

3

The First Answer to the Puzzle: The Raid on Tabūk

■ This then is the direct, hermeneutically still hardly touched myth that grew out of the downfall of the people of Thamūd, and it is to the apocalyptic closing scenes of this myth that the burial of the golden bough in the grave of Abū Rughāl, or Abū Righāl, belongs. This myth, now with the presentiment of a specific semiotic tenor, must be brought in and allowed to explain to us the meaning of the episode of the golden bough in the events, central as well as circumstantial, of the most ambitious of Muḥammad's military expeditions *(maghāzī),* the Raid on Tabūk.

The plain fact that the route taken by Muḥammad in his campaign against the north-Arabian Byzantine outpost of Tabūk had to lead the expedition past al-Ḥijr, the desolate rock city of the Thamūd, does not tell us anything unusual. For al-Ḥijr marks almost exactly the midpoint between Medina, which was the campaign's point of departure, and Tabūk. What helps us realize that there is a special link between the Tabūk raid and the story of the archaic al-Ḥijr is the peculiar troubled atmosphere that is perceptible in the Muslim camp throughout the phases of the expedition, and that in this it differs from all the other military campaigns undertaken directly or indirectly by Muḥammad and recorded in biographic *(sīrah)* and expeditionary *(maghāzī)* sources. Of the other raids these narrative sources, however extensive, dwell in the main on the presentation of the events as sequences of facts in terms of victories (e.g., Badr) or defeats (e.g., Uḥud). Mythopoeia is reduced to a minimum, even though strong, anthropologically fascinating tribal ritual aspects are not excluded.[1] By contrast, as successful as the raid on Tabūk appears to have been, there is rather an anticlimactic lack of emphasis on that fact. There is instead an overarching insistence, both in Ibn Hishām's *Sīrah*[2] and in al-Wāqidī's account in the *Maghāzī (Expeditions)*,[3] on the apprehension, uncertainty, and doubt in Muḥammad's prophetic entitlement to leadership that were eating away at the Muslim raiders' morale as they considered the hardships that awaited them, or as they responded to the hardships which they actually encountered during the raid.

Undercurrents of resistance to participation in the hazardous enterprise become increasingly foregrounded: at first there was the rather comical excuse of Jadd Ibn Qays that he would not join the raid because he would not be able to resist the temptations to which he would certainly be exposed in the anticipated presence of nubile Byzantine women.[4] Then there were the disaffected among the Medinan contingent who advised against participation in the raid because they disliked the rigor of war and harbored doubts about Muḥammad's truthfulness.[5] So, too, some abstained from joining the campaign for contrived reasons ("although God does not accept their excuse"). And, worse than that, on one occasion during the march itself some of the troops separated themselves from the Prophet's camp and, when the march resumed, stayed behind together with "the hypocrites and doubters," the ones who harbored ill will toward Islam, although they had previously embraced it, and concerning whom it is written in the Qurʾān that "They sought rebellion aforetime and upset things for you."[6] Those hypocrites also spoke ill of ʿAlī, the cousin and son-in-law of Muḥammad, for not taking part in the raid, although Muḥammad himself had made an exception in his case, ordering him to stay behind and look after his family.

It was in this murky and rebellious mood that Muḥammad's troops reached al-Ḥijr and encamped on the outskirts of the ruined town. There was a great need for drinking water in the camp. Nevertheless, Muḥammad forbade the men to drink from the well of al-Ḥijr or to use its water for ablutions. But then, in a manner that is reminiscent of one of the main opening motifs of the pre-Islamic Arabic *qaṣīdah*, Muḥammad warns—not just invites, as did Imruʾ al-Qays with his "Halt, you two, and we will weep" *(qifā nabki)*—those of his men who would enter the ruined city to enter *weeping* for its former inhabitants, for, should they fail to do so, a similar fate would befall them.[7] In al-Ṭabarī's account, at this point, Muḥammad muffles his head in awe and rides away hurriedly till he crosses the valley, which he calls "the valley of abhorrence" *(wādī al-nafar).*[8] Muḥammad's men were furthermore forbidden to venture into the ruined town alone, and one man who failed to heed that warning was indeed found asphyxiated to death.[9] Another man was carried off by a violent wind. Muḥammad, however, prayed for him and brought him miraculously back to life. Also, when the men persisted in their complaints of thirst, "God sent a cloud, and such rain fell that they quenched their thirst and carried away their fill of water."[10] And yet, in spite of the demonstrations of divine and prophetic power and mercy, the "hypocrites" among the men of the raid on Tabūk remained recalcitrant. The saving downpour of rain one of them dismisses as merely, "[Pah], a passing cloud."[11] And there was also Muḥammad's other, contextually (and intertextually) even more significant "miracle of the stray she-camel." For the story goes that, when at one point during the march the Prophet's she-camel had gone astray and could not be found, one of the hypocrites began speaking sarcastically of a prophet who claims to know the things of Heaven but does not know the whereabouts of his own she-camel. To this Muḥammad responded by giving the exact location of the place where his she-camel was to be found, with her halter entangled in the branches of a tree; and indeed, the she-camel was found precisely as detailed by Muḥammad.[12]

These and other incidents of "hypocrisy," recalcitrance, and defiance of Muḥammad's authority thus formed the mood that hung over the Muslim camp before, and during, the Raid on Tabūk; and in a conspicuous if not wholly central way, they are further woven into the narrative of the campaign's passing by and halting at the remains of the Thamūdic al-Ḥijr.[13] As we already noticed, too, these incidents, in their narrative design and function, set the story of the Raid on Tabūk clearly apart from the narrative tone of the other *maghāzī*. It therefore becomes ultimately quite unavoidable that in a close reading of the various retellings of Muḥammad's expedition against Tabūk we recognize certain compelling analogies and strains of intertextuality between the two ostensibly discrete prophetic stories: of Muḥammad on the way to Tabūk and of Ṣāliḥ facing the Thamūd; and that the "situations," predicaments, and much of the symbolic repertory of those two stories' respective protagonists overlap. Most of all, our attention is called to the similarities between the recalcitrance of the disbelieving and plotting Thamūd and that of the "hypocrites" of Muḥammad's expeditionary company. There is even that incident of Muḥammad's stray she-camel which culminates in the "test" of the Prophet's explicitly God-given power that leads to his own, albeit minor, "miracle of the she-camel." And through all of this there runs the thread of injunctions against entering the precinct of the accursed city of the Thamūd, a city which in its name of al-Ḥijr already bears, or rather generates, the sense of the forbidden and ritually taboo. The great classical Arabic scholiast Abū ʿUbaydah (d. 209/824–25) was fully aware of this dimension of the word *ḥijr* ("forbidden") when, in his book on figurative language in the Qurʾān, he explicitly singled out *ḥijr* as a trope *(majāz)* for the forbidden and the ritually impure *(ḥarām),* in the manner in which that term refers itself to food taboos in the Sura of al-Anʿām (6:138).[14] In the story of the Raid on Tabūk, Muḥammad thus replays, as it were, the peripeteia of his "figura," Ṣāliḥ, and the scenario is dictated markedly by the "figural" tragic myth of the Thamūd.[15]

Such an exegesis of the symbolic texture of the story of the Raid on Tabūk should be sufficient in itself, but we must not neglect to integrate into the emerging hermeneutical whole the final, and indeed the most perplexingly original, new mythopoeic element of the double story. For it is from within this "mixed" context that the opening of the grave of the last of the Thamūd, Abū Righāl/Abū Rughāl, and the unearthing of the "golden bough" ought to yield their meaning. It should be recalled, too, that, according to legend, al-Ḥijr, in the autochthonous Arabian sense, is, first of all, the burial place of Hagar and Ismāʿīl.

In the *ghuṣnun min dhahabin* texts we are not told what happens to the unearthed "golden bough" nor who it is that ends up being its new possessor. We only know that the enigmatic object was brought out of the Thamūdic grave in the Prophet's presence and that it was he alone who knew the mystery of that grave. Its mention is otherwise not found directly in the extant versions of the ancient story of the destruction of Thamūd. Narratively it is linked to Muḥammad's Tabūk episode. Unlike the She-Camel of Ṣāliḥ, it thus comes to us unexplained by the Arabian myth. And yet, in this mediated way, it nevertheless has to find for itself a meaning within the original Thamūdic myth and be able to give meaning to the Muḥammadan mythopoeia as well. Or perhaps the Muḥammadan mythopoeia of the "golden bough" incident in its Tabūk context is itself an expression of a hermeneutical stance.

Dwelling on that stance, we shall first assume that it would also have been Muḥammad himself who retained possession of the unearthed "golden bough"—figuratively rather than factually, since we cannot but treat the "incident" as a clear case of mythopoeia. As we already know, it is precisely in the story of the Raid on Tabūk that, through recognizable parallels with the myth of Ṣāliḥ among the Thamūd, Muḥammad finds himself defied by the recalcitrant "hypocrites" and his entitlement to prophethood and leadership insidiously undermined. And, once again, let us recontextualize the artful inference of the miracle of the She-Camel of Ṣāliḥ provided by the incident of Muḥammad's own lost and miraculously recovered she-camel. That incident, or rather the purpose of its inclusion in the story of the march on Tabūk, serves the same surface purpose as the incident of the unearthing of the golden bough—or rather, both incidents have their common, almost vaunting, surface purpose of bearing witness to Muḥammad's more-than-natural insight into the unknown and, ultimately, to his authority. Thus there may even exist a further figurative connection between that "regained" golden bough and Muḥammad's own staff of authority, his *ʿanazah.*[16]

In this respect the brief *ḥadīth*-anecdote in the *Sīrah* of Ibn Hishām, in which Muḥammad gives his own staff to one of his most devoted (and useful) companions, ʿAbd Allāh Ibn Unays, is of distinct semiotic interest. In it, upon the completion of an especially sensitive and dangerous mission in the service of Muḥammad—which was the assassination of the "devilish" enemy Ibn Sufyān Ibn Nubayḥ al-Hudhalī—Ibn Unays is asked to enter Muḥammad's house. There Muḥammad presents him with a staff, along with the solemn words to take this staff and to keep it with him always. When Ibn Unays reappeared with the staff before the people, they asked him: "What is the meaning of this staff?" and he answered that the Prophet gave it to him and ordered him to keep it with him. He knew no more. The people, however, urged him to return to the Prophet and ask him why he did what he did. So he returned to the Prophet and said to him: "O Prophet, why have you given me this staff?" And he answered: "That it be a sign *(āyah)* between me and you on the Day of Last Judgment. Only the fewest shall hold staffs on which to lean that day." ʿAbd Allāh Ibn Unays always bore that staff together with his sword, and when he died it was wrapped by his side in his burial shroud, "and the two were laid in the grave together."[17]

A whole mythopoeia of the destruction of the Thamūd is thus resurrected in the mind by the conjured presence of a "golden bough," which, it is announced, had once been in the possession of the last survivor of the Thamūd. What is more, the golden bough is itself—as object and symbol—a sort of *āyah*, a "sign" and a "proof": its having been buried together with Abū Righāl testifies to its, and Abū Righāl's, Thamūdic provenance and to a somehow overwhelming tragic circumstance. The importance given to the golden bough is here quite clear: "And the *sign* [to be understood within its qurʾānic semantic range] of this is that with him there was buried a golden bough."[18] Only if we give that independent significance to the uncovered golden bough does the argument cease to be circular.

This ought to tell us something about the depth of the perplexity and, indeed, of the anxiety that must have existed not only in the camp of the forces mobilized by Muḥammad to march on Tabūk but even more in the mind and psyche of Muḥammad himself. In this respect, the *maghāzī* narrator's perception of Muḥammad's state of mind during the Raid on Tabūk on the one hand and the impulse to establish an analogy with the story of Ṣāliḥ of the Thamūd on the other may be said to fall into the broader chain of analogies between Muḥammad and the qurʾānic succession of prophets defied by their condemned nations—and ultimately of "the Prophet" defied by the condemned poets—as this is hermeneutically construable from the Sura of the Poets.[19]

4

The Totem and the Taboo

The Multiple Identity of Abū Righāl

We must now return to the mysterious first possessor of the Arabian golden bough, Abū Righāl. The texts that mention the golden bough found in his grave fail to tell us much about the reason for his having been singled out from among the condemned of the Thamūd for possession of the bough—or rather they do not give us a mythically relevant reason for such a distinction. It is true that during the destruction of al-Ḥijr, Abū Righāl is said to have been protected within the sacred precinct *(ḥaram),* which, according to at least one source clearly and to another source somewhat less so, ought to have been a Thamūdic temple-ground at al-Ḥijr itself.[1] While not devoid of further ambiguities, however, in other sources the place where Muḥammad finds the tomb that holds the Thamūdic golden bough is not al-Ḥijr at all but a locale somewhere near al-Ṭā'if, that is, at a fair distance from Mecca in a direction opposite to that of the Thamūdic city. This confusing transmission has its own ultimate hermeneutic merit, however, because it provides a base for the broadening of the semiotics attached to Abū Righāl and his tomb.

Let us, therefore, review the texts, recognizably problematic, although in somewhat tangential ways "necessarily" *ḥadīth*-based, that place Abū Righāl and his tomb in the vicinity of al-Ṭā'if. Here al-Wāqidī is the most narrative as well as the most keen to develop an "airtight" logic of interdependent events. According to his version of the story—which, we are given to understand, comes to us narrated by the Prophet himself in the form of a *ḥadīth*—

when the Thamūd were smitten by the shriek, "all of them perished as far as the sky extended, except one who was spared God's punishment because at that time he was inside the protected, sacred precinct of the *ḥaram*. 'O Prophet of God, who was he?', asked the Prophet's men, and he responded: 'Abū Righāl Abū Thaqīf.' And they said: 'But what was he doing near Mecca?' 'Ṣāliḥ had sent him out to levy the poor-tax *(muṣaddiqan),*' the Prophet answered, 'and he came to a man who had one hundred sheep that gave no milk, but only one milch-ewe, and in whose household there also was a boy whose mother had died the day before. There Abū Righāl announced: 'God's Prophet has sent me to you,' to which the man answered: 'Every welcome be to God's messenger, do take!' But when he took the milch-ewe the man exclaimed: 'But she is as mother to this boy, now that his mother died. Take ten of the other sheep instead!' Abū Righāl refused, and the man said, 'Take twenty, fifty, take them all, except this one ewe!' But Abū Righāl said no, at which the man exclaimed: 'If you like milk so much, then so do I.' He reached for the arrows in his quiver and, calling out 'God be my witness!' readied an arrow and killed him. This done, he said: 'Let no one bear this news to the Prophet before me!' He then went to Ṣāliḥ and informed him of what he had done, and Ṣāliḥ, raising his hands toward heaven, thrice exclaimed: 'O God, curse Abū Righāl!'"[2]

The author of the lexicon *Lisān al-ʿArab,* Ibn Manẓūr (d. 711/1311-12), has as many as three divergent identifications of Abū Righāl and his grave. In one we are told that Abū Righāl "was a tyrannical tithe-gatherer *(ʿashshār)* in ancient times, and that his grave, which lies between Mecca and al-Ṭāʾif, is stoned till this day."[3] But he also tells us that Abū Righāl was a slave of the Prophet Shuʿayb. Thus quite a different prophet, not of the Thamūd but of the Midianites, is here the master of Abū Righāl.

Ibn Manẓūr's second version introduces an even more discrepant Abū Righāl, or rather a summary of the story in Ibn Hishām's *Sīrah* in which a man by that name is said to have served as the interpreter and guide for the Abyssinian invader Abraha in his march on Mecca. This treacherous, or merely coerced, Abū Righāl dies during the march before reaching Mecca and is buried in the lands of the Banū Thaqīf, in al-Mughammas, that is, between Mecca and al-Ṭāʾif. "There people stoned his grave."[4] The legend of this second ill-fated Abū Righāl thus takes us out of the "mythical antiquity" of the Thamūd into the "historicity" of the second half of the sixth century A.D., or, even more precisely, into the year of Muḥammad's own birth (ca. 570), which, according to Islamic tradition, is the Year of the Elephant.[5]

Only Ibn Manẓūr's third version, which resembles closely that of al-Wāqidī, returns Abū Righāl to his Thamūdic context. For being a callous tax collector, he is, in one possible denouement, killed by the irate protector of the sole milch-ewe, or, in another, he dies struck by a heaven-sent calamity. In both cases, Ṣāliḥ curses him; and his grave, placed here, too, between Mecca and al-Ṭā'if, is an object of stoning.[6]

Of our other narrative sources only al-Ṭabarī, Ibn Kathīr, and al-Thaʿlabī mention the episode with the grave of Abū Righāl. Al-Nuwayrī does not. Furthermore, only al-Ṭabarī and al-Thaʿlabī place the episode within the anecdotal *ḥadīth* material that bears on Muḥammad's raid against Tabūk. On that point Ibn Kathīr is, to say the least, ambiguous. For, even though the larger context of his narration in *Al-Bidāyah wa al-Nihāyah* is still that of the Raid on Tabūk, his interest in the story lies, first of all, in that it is a *ḥadīth* replete with strangeness: of a man by the name of Abū Righāl, insistently also referred to (it would appear incongruously) as Abū Thaqīf, who, as a lonely Thamūdean, lies buried at an unreasonable distance from his unfortunate city, somewhere along the trail between Mecca and al-Ṭā'if.[7] Ibn Kathīr is not retelling the myth of Thamūd. Here a paratactic "leap" is necessary to ensure understanding.[8]

Our oldest text to actually name Abū Righāl—that is, if we accept that text's authenticity, inasmuch as it may just as well reflect the anti-Thaqafī bias that had surged in the Umayyad period—is the opening verse in a short poem of invective *(hijā')* directed against the Banū Thaqīf (of Ṭā'if) by the poet closest to Muḥammad, Ḥassān Ibn Thābit (d. ca. 40/661):

> Tell the Thaqafite who vies with you in glory
> "Reckon how Abū Righāl has fared!"[9]

Being the oldest, it is not the clearest text, however, for its insistence—sustained further in that poem's verses four and five—on the identification of Abū Righāl as a man of the Thaqīf, that is, a Thaqafī, seems to blend the two personae, the treacherous guide of the Abyssinian host in their march on Mecca and the last survivor of the Thamūd, into one construct of no longer necessarily distinguishable mythic provenance. Only the commenting scholiast seems to have had the certainty that the intended Abū Righāl was the anecdotal tax collector of Ṣāliḥ.[10]

At that same early date, too, Umayyah Ibn Abī al-Ṣalt (d. ca. 9/631), a poet imbued with a chaotic bounty of pre-qurʾānic religious and legendary traditions, and one who was even reputed to have had an independent claim to prophecy, blends the two Abū Righāl traditions into one in a highly oblique but no less revealing way. In one of his poems he thus speaks of the site called al-Mughammas, near al-Ṭāʾif (of the Thaqafites), which, as one variant of the Abū Righāl mythopoeia has told us, is the forever-stoned burial place of that heartless Thamūdic tax collector. Ibn Abī al-Ṣalt's theme, however, is not that of ancient Thamūdic lore. Instead, it is meant to be that of the Abyssinian campaign "of the Elephant" against Mecca of ca. A.D. 570, that campaign whose outcome, according to legend and qurʾānic exegesis, was the miraculous defeat of the Abyssinian army together with their awe-inspiring elephant. All this occurs at al-Mughammas, the place of the double association with Abū Righāl. But, more importantly, the death of the "elephant" and the death of the Thamūdic she-camel, the one that brought destruction upon the Thamūd, must here be thought of together as well. Both die "hocked," or "hamstrung" *(maʿqūr):* one plays out the fate of the other in a place where two Abū Righāls share a forever-stoned grave. This poet thus achieves his implicit "conflation" of the persona of Abū Righāl not merely by "contextualizing" al-Mughammas but, more so, by employing in that context the unequivocally charged term *maʿqūr* for the felled Abyssinian elephant, a term necessarily reminiscent of the "hamstrung" she-camel of the Thamūdic Ṣāliḥ. In Umayyah Ibn Abī al-Ṣalt's poem the Abyssinian elephant is thus hamstrung—as once the Thamūdic she-camel was—at al-Mughammas, there where the traitor Abū Righāl died and was buried. *"Maʿqūr"* and al-Mughammas should not stand together—unless the sub-contextualized reference is thus intended:[11]

> At al-Mughammas the elephant was thwarted till
> It dragged itself as though *hamstrung.*[12]

It is thus proper to follow the legend and accept that Abū Righāl is said to have been at first protected within the sacred precinct *(ḥaram)* that was supposedly a Thamūdic temple—and, if we remain in our mythic/legendary chronology, there could hardly have been any other temple there. But even Abū Righāl's finding himself in that place at that crucial time when retribution descended upon the Thamūd is not given its integral textual validation. Aside from his name, or rather the byname of Abū Righāl, the man is left unidentified, the event either left unexplained, in almost perfunctory suspension, or else outrightly confabulated (Abū Righāl the callous tax collector, the milch-ewe, and the orphaned child). Furthermore, his second byname, Abū Thaqīf, leads us astray into areas *prima facie* unrelatable to Muḥammad's campaign against Tabūk, pointing instead in the direction of a different legend and a different abomination with their own myth and mythopoeia, spun around the Sura of the Elephant.[13] What is left for us is merely to accept that the *ḥaram,* being a sanctuary or temple, had exercised its "efficacy," saving for a time, quite accidentally, an accidental Thamūdean. With such an explanation, however, we obtain at best a myth-denuded "generic" symbolic validation of an extrapolated or abstracted place of sanctuary or taboo. It was not the golden bough that had given Abū Righāl safeguard in the *ḥaram*. So, too, neither the *ḥaram* nor the golden bough had exempted him from subsequently sharing the fate of the condemned Thamūd—that is, unless that golden bough had to do with a somehow special identity of Abū Righāl and with the symbolic fabric of the Thamūd myth, thus contributing further to the significance of the discovery of the grave and the recovery of the golden bough itself.

Of the likelihood of the latter case we are indeed given an indication in a further, *ḥadīth*-based Abū Righāl text found in al-Qalqashandī's (d. 821/1418) *Ṣubḥ al-Aʿshā,* where, without reference to the golden bough, Abū Righāl's grave is nevertheless identified as that of *ʿāqir al-nāqah,* the one who slew, or "hocked," the fateful she-camel.[14] Abū Righāl is, therefore, not a stray tax collector but none other than the tragic, fated executor of the Thamūdic abomination, Qudār. Concerning Qudār's bearing the byname *(kunyah)* Abū Righāl, *Ṣubḥ al-Aʿshā* explains further—with a clear hermeneutical intent that is relevant to us—that, whenever a *fitnah,* that is, a "dissention," or "source of dissention," as well as "a trial" and "an affliction by which one is tried," was feared if a person were named by his primary name, a *kunyah,* that is, an "oblique," or "masked," byname was used;

just as, according to a *ḥadīth,* if a person was named directly, without a *kunyah,* that in itself would indicate that no *fitnah* was feared from mentioning that person in such a way.[15] It is of note here that this fear of the *fitnah,* as amounting almost to the fear of a curse, is already present in the qurʾānic announcement that the tragic she-camel shall be sent to the Thamūd as a *fitnah:* "We shall send the she-camel as a[n inauspicious] *trial* for you."[16] The threat of some impending evil implicitly present in Abū Righāl's byname is thus the same as the explicitly ominous "test," and threat, boded by the qurʾānic verse.

The Ambiguities of Stoning

Broadening the mythopoeic circle, we recall[17] that the byname of Abū Righāl also possesses its own tragic currency outside of the Thamūdic story. Thus in Ibn Hishām's *Biography of the Prophet (Al-Sīrah al-Nabawīyah)* the first mention of that name occurs in connection with the narration of the failed Abyssinian campaign against Mecca that had as its goal the destruction of the Kaᶜbah. This campaign, too, has entered into pre-Islamic Arabic mythopoeia, and is referred to in the Qurʾān as the Campaign of the Owners, or Men, of the Elephant.[18] In Ibn Hishām, as well as in al-Masᶜūdī's *Meadows of Gold (Murūj al-Dhahab),*[19] which falls into the broad mediaeval category of historical narrative, legend, *mirabilia,* and even arcana, we read that when Abraha, the commander of the invading Abyssinians, entered "the Arab country," he found himself in need of guides. It was after the surrender of al-Ṭāʾif, with its temple dedicated to the goddess al-Lāt—which was spared by the Abyssinians—that Abraha was offered by the surrendering Thaqīf (of al-Ṭāʾif) a certain Abū Righāl as his guide to show him the easiest way to Mecca. This Abū Righāl brought the invading army as far as al-Mughammas, halfway between Ṭāʾif and Mecca. But there he died and was buried. For the abomination of having served Abraha, his grave was then stoned by the Arabs whenever they passed by it. In this manner the practice continued into the days of Ibn Hishām.[20] Here we may thus begin to understand, or suspect, something of the provenance of the byname Abū Thaqīf borne (inauspiciously) by the Abū Righāl of the Tabūk/Thamūd *ḥadīths*. The custom, or topos, of stoning the grave of Abū Righāl was given further currency in Arabian folklore.[21] It is also found in verse, as when the Umayyad poet Jarīr (d. 110/728–29) builds it into one of his lampoons against al-Farazdaq (d. 110/728 or 112/730):

> When al-Farazdaq dies, stone him
> Just as you pelt the grave of Abū Rughāl![22]

So, too, with very similar phrasing and in the same meter *(al-wāfir)* does al-Farazdaq's contemporary and antagonist, Miskīn al-Dārimī:

> I stone his grave year after year,
> As people stone Abū Rughāl's grave.[23]

And, once again in the same meter, ʿAmr Ibn Darrāk al-ʿAbdī exclaims that should he break his covenants he would be

> Of greater foulness than Abū Rughāl,
> More wrongful in dispensing justice than Sodom.[24]

Thus under the byname of Abū Righāl/Rughāl, Qudār, the slayer of the She-Camel of Ṣāliḥ, goes down as "the eternally accursed one" of Arabian myth and legend and, as it were, as the one condemned to be stoned in his grave for all eternity; and it is in those mythic terms that his grave is not wholly different in kind from the enigmatic herms of Minā, anathematized in the "stoning" *(rajm)* of the Islamic rites of the pilgrimage *(ḥajj).*

Knowing as little as we do—chiefly through Islamic pietistic folklore and through highly restrictive exegetic channels—of those truncated hermlike pillars of Minā and of the origin of the custom of "stoning" them, or merely of accumulating pebbles around them, a practice that contributed to their appellation as *rujam* (sing. *rujmah*), one is prevailed upon by one's own curiosity to open them to further interpretation. Thus the broader semantics of the word *rujmah,* by implying an act of "stoning," produces a coalescence of terms such as "heap of stones" as well as "tombstone," or the "tomb"/"grave" itself—but also as that which is produced by, or results from, "casting stones." Of these stoned herms the Islamic popular belief tells us that they are representations of the *shayṭān* (Satan) and that as such, implicitly, and ultimately ritually, they demand stoning.

On the other hand, however, we know that in pre-Islamic times there existed the ritual of stoning those very same marked sites of Minā, already there and then known as *rujam*. Furthermore, as we know on the authority of Ibn Isḥāq,[25] the ritual of this pre-Islamic stoning was performed only at sundown of the day of departure, after the performance of the pilgrimage. There is thus little doubt that the obligatory stoning had in this case everything to do with the act of separation, or departure, from the precinct of the places of pilgrimage, and thus with the crossing of a border or boundary, and that the casting of stones—and the resultant formation of herms amidst heaps of pebbles—was part of a rite of crossing the border that separated two ritually distinct realms. Only in such a way may we, to my mind, properly understand the existence of such herms at Minā and the ritual roots of their present (Islamic) stoning. For the herm is in its archaic sense a border-stone, or the stone of some significant demarcation. It points *outward* apotropaically to the liminal and alien sphere, as well as *inward* to the inviolable, or sacred, sphere. It separates the space of the *ḥaram,* that is, the interdicted domain, or sanctuary, from hostile space. Indeed, this binarism of "sacred space"/"interdiction," "excommunication," "anathema" exists already in the two-tiered semantics and semiotics of *ḥaram/ḥarām* and, one should insist, in the core etymology of that root.[26]

In one of its earliest and clearest forms, the "liminal" herm comes to us from the book of Genesis (31:44-52), where the Aramaean Laban confirms a pact, or covenant, with his son-in-law, Jacob, over such an erected stone surrounded by a pile of rocks. Thus we read that, as a testimony to that covenant, "Jacob took a stone and set it up as a pillar" (Genesis 31:45). Then Jacob asked his kinsmen to pick up stones and make of them a heap, and there they ate (v. 46). To Laban this herm was *yegar shahadūtā,* "the mound of testimony," and to Jacob *galʿed,* the "reminder of contract" (v. 47). Then Laban qualified the meaning of the constructed herm further, for he said to Jacob: "See this heap *(haggal)* and the pillar *(hammaẓẓebah),* which I have set *between* you and me" [italics mine] (v. 51). "This heap is a witness, and the pillar is a witness, that *I will not pass* over this heap to you, and *you will not pass* over this heap and this pillar to me, for harm" [italics mine] (v. 52).

In interpreting this covenant scene between Laban and Jacob we must go further than the explanation given by Robertson

Smith, according to whom, we would have in it merely an example of the "original altar among the northern Semites, as well as among the Arabs," and that the purpose of erecting a pillar with its cairn may not have been other than the setting up of an altar at which a communal meal, implicitly sacrificial, was to be consumed.[27] For the Genesis text itself goes explicitly further: it identifies first of all a herm that is a border-stone: it is placed *between* two defined "spaces," and neither one of the contractual sides must cross "for harm" the border thus established. In this manner, as herm, it therefore institutes a taboo. This function of the archaic pillar and cairn is clear to Robertson Smith in another, nonbiblical context, namely when he speaks of the Arabian institution of the *ḥimā* ("preserve"—as privileged, or tabooed, pasturage; and "consecrated domain"). There he is unambiguous: "In Arabia. . . . the *ḥimā* sometimes enclosed a great tract of pasture land roughly marked off by pillars and cairns, and the *ḥaram* or sacred territory of Mecca extends for some hours' journey on almost every side of the city."[28]

The *jamarāt* (cairns, or herms, with heaps of pebbles) of Minā are precisely such "pillars and cairns"; that is, in their function they are quite like the herm that came to separate the domain of Laban from that of Jacob. They marked the border of the tabooed precinct *(ḥaram)* devoted to the pre-Islamic, and then Islamic, rites of Arabian pilgrimage.

But there is also clear evidence that brings the ritual function of the Arabian herm closer to the "witnessing" and "contractual" aspects of the herm of Laban and Jacob (Gen. 31:44–52) to which Robertson Smith limited himself. Thus, concerning the cairn/herm of ᶜAqabah (Jamrat al-ᶜAqabah) we are told that "over" it seventy men and one woman had publicly *(jahran)* entered into the covenant of acceptance of the prophethood of Muḥammad *(bāyaᶜū rasūla l-Lāhi).*[29] At the same time, however, it also appears that those entering into such a "contract" or "pledge" over the herm of al-ᶜAqabah at Minā were, in the archaic sense, with full ritual awareness of the process, gaining entry into the *ḥimā* precinct of Mecca. Thus the Jamrat al-ᶜAqabah serves here the twofold ritual function: as liminal herm and as an altar of covenant.[30] That the Jamrat al-ᶜAqabah was of special significance as the place for Muḥammad's still secretive, early proselytizing becomes clear from Ibn Hishām's *Sīrah,*[31] which tells us that there the new converts were met outside the inhabited space. Indeed, they were met in an eminently ritually defined "liminal" place which, as we know, was in pre-Islamic days "stoned" by pilgrims as a sign of their imminent departure from Minā. From that period, however, we as yet know nothing of a "pelted *shayṭān.*" What the preexisting connection between the Jamrat al-ʿAqabah and the "pledges of faith" leaves thus unanswered is the subsequent Islamic connection between that function and the ritual of the stoning of the Shayṭān.

This connection, however, ought to be weighed in the mind, because more than a hint at a properly Arabian avenue that leads from the stoned herm to the stoned Shayṭān (or "a" *shayṭān*) comes to us from the Arabic word *wathan* with its meaning of a "[set up] idol." From it the Arabic language then obtained its term for "pagan" *(wathanī)* as a worshiper of idols—for purposes quite distinct from those of the meaning of *jāhilī* with its cultural-historical, including ideological, specificity.

We would not be able to arrive at the full semantics and semiotics of the word *wathan,* however, if we did not broaden its etymology, or rather its semantic range, to its Sabaic meanings of "stela" ("boundary mark") and "frontier"[32]—so that it includes "herm" in its archaic sense of cairn, that is, *rujmah.* For it is the Sabaic scope of the meaning of *wathan* which reveals its function as a "boundary mark" and as such as a place or object of ritual or even of cult. The archaic *wathan* is thus, in a sense, functionally equivalent to the herm and nearly synonymous with both the pre-Islamic as well as the Islamic *jamrah:* the demonlike object of apotropaic stoning. Furthermore, even the word herm itself, through its own etymology as *erma,* that is, as the demon that haunts, or occupies, a heap of stones set up by the roadside, will help us understand that the difference between the stoned demon of the archaic herm and the stoned *shayṭān* of the Islamicized *jamarāt* is one of change in the understanding of the concept of demon/*shayṭān*, and that only they, the "indwelling" demon and the Shayṭān, have *changed*. The herm and the *jamrah* have retained their form and their place by the roadside—and elsewhere—wherever archaic apotropaic taboos, rituals, theogonies, and folk-religiosity have ever placed them first or encountered them later.[33] Only when the limit of the *ḥimā* is no longer ritually remembered as the site of the reception of the covenant of conversion does the archaic sense of danger that was dormant in the herms of Minā reassert itself—this time in the new guise of the Shayṭān.

That the herms of Minā, three in number, are called *jamarāt* (the First Jamrah, the Middle Jamrah, and the Jamrah of the Steep Track, thus forming the *al-jamarāt al-thalāth*) is due in the first place to *jamarāt*'s being a metathesis of *rajmah,* that is, to their being herms. For, by itself, *jamrah* should mean "live coal" or "ember." As *al-jamarāt al-thalāth,* these are then the "three live coals" of the astronomy-related "three degrees of heat" in air, dust, and water;[34] but they are also the "three *jamarāt* of the Arabs," of the ill-boding dream of a woman who dreamt of having given birth to ᶜAbs, al-Ḥārith, and Ḍabbah as three live coals.[35] One needs to go further, however, and justify the intersection of meaning that led to the metathesis as having been facilitated, if not altogether triggered, by the broader etymological middle ground of *j-m-r/j-m-l,* denoting "gathering" and "accumulation," together with its nearly synonymous variant *r-j-m/r-k-m,* both sharing the meaning of "heaping up." The figurative and semiotically decisive amalgamation of referentiality which results from this confluence and permutation of roots is then that of "throwing of stones," "erecting of pillars," and "heaping up of things (into mounds)." Thus, too, is formed a semantic and ritual whole, to which, on the farther side, there is then added the connotative burden of *al-jamarāt al-thalāth,* which evoke the still obligatory association with the number three of the *jamarāt* of the fire-blackened, tripod-like fireplaces, *al-athāfī,* "the three fire-blackened stones" of the abandoned Bedouin fireplace. These, in turn, constitute one of the chief elegiac topoi in the opening section of the classical Arabic ode.[36]

Having thus far taken notice only of the way the Arabian *rujam* and *jamarāt* as cultic sites and liminal apotropaic markers fall into the archaic semiotic circle of the herm/cairn of the Aramaean Laban and the Hebrew Jacob, the circle of analogies and associations of our Arabian herm must at this point, for the sake of symbolic comprehensiveness and clarity, be widened further before it is again allowed to close in properly upon its own Arabian significance, or significances.

Turning first to the broader question of terminology, we see that already in the Laban/Jacob case there existed the clear intent to go beyond the descriptive semantics of cairn-and-pillar and an insistence on respective Aramaic and Hebrew concrete names, if not altogether "terms" (Gen. 31:47): *yegar shahadūtā/galᶜed* ("heap of stones of witnessing"/"mound of testimony"). Then, in the Book of Joshua (7:25–26) we meet with another aspect of the archaic symbolic function of the cairn—one that is equally directly present in our Arabian web of the mythopoeia of the stoned burial of the once Thamūdic, and then Thaqafite, Abū Righāl. In the Hebrew legend, it is ʿAkhan, the perpetrator of the abomination of concealing a portion of Jericho's tabooed booty. For this he is stoned to death and a great heap of stones is raised over him, and as such "it remains to this day" (v. 26). It is to be noted further that the Hebrew verb for "stoning," *ragam,* corresponds in its entire denotational and connotational scope to the Arabic verb *rajama,* and that, furthermore, the Hebrew substantive *rigmah* ("heap of stones") is morphologically and semantically the Arabic cultic *rujmah* of the hermlike cairn-and-pillar of the pilgrimage station of Minā.

Most of our cognate anthropology as regards the manifold functionality, as well as the specific shape, of the Arabian *rujmah/jamrah,* however, will take us to the Greek anthropological model and its terminology—itself reflective of myth. The model hardly differs from the Arabian one—except in its subtler ramification and attention to functional, or call it mythopoeic, detail as regards recorded text and evidenced artifact. Walter Burkert sums up its philology, which carries with it also its progression through Greek cultural time, as the power encountered in the cairn that is personified as *Herma-as* or *Herma-on,* which "in Mycenaean is written as *e-ma-a,* in Dorian as Herman and in Ionian-Attic as Hermes."[37] If compared with the Arabian *rujmah/jamrah,* the distinguishing characteristic of the Greek "heap of stones" is thus primarily its personification, that is, its being not merely equated with but actually embodied in and symbolically articulated through the many-faceted persona of a mythical Hermes. The Greek embodiment is thus a form of allegorization, of monument-encased, potential enactment, that is, kinesis—which is missing in the Arabian model. Not even the Islamicized implicit presence of the somewhat less than distinct *shayṭān* of Minā comes close to being the complex, energized persona of Hermes. But the similarities, once the herm/Hermes becomes depersonalized, that is, abstracted, are nonetheless approaching full archetypal identity.

Thus the Greek pillared cairns, too, were first of territorial demarcation, separating properties, fields, and lands. They were found by roadsides, where all who passed by threw a stone, adding to the heap. As such they were also apotropaic;[38] and, according to Strabo

(VIII 343. XVII 818), they were meant to serve as road markers. In a fashion where one looks not for a beginning but rather a process, Hermes has thus become the herm itself, and the herm has turned into Hermes. Its properties have become his, and much of his mythological persona and cultic circumstance redounded to it. A symbiotic circle of meaning and of symbolic and ritual praxis resulted. And, having been as much archaic-regional as set at the core of a specifically Greek acculturation, both herm and Hermes also expand prodigiously, regionally and temporally, ultimately saturating with their archaizing custom, myth, and mythopoeia the entire span of the Hellenistic and Imperial Roman world. This phenomenon must enter into consideration as we construct, and reconstruct, our Arabian textual, philological, legendary, and "monumental" evidence that connects us to the overarching phenomenon of herm/Hermes. For somewhere within it there lies not only the *shayṭān*[39] of the *jamarāt* of Minā, but the grave of Abū Righāl/Qudār as well. The space and time of pre-Islamic Arabia may thus not be excluded offhand from the context of Hermes, although, as we already know, the archetypal herm rather than the more "sculptured" Hermes-pillar must be the means of comparison. Further contributing to our contextualization is the characteristic square shape of the herm/Hermes-pillar, which is also, equally characteristically, the culticly perpetuated shape of the Arabian herm: it is necessarily square.[40] Such are, thus, the "Islamic" herms of the *jamarāt* of Minā. So, too, the Greek cathartic meaning of stoning the herm/Hermes when it represents an *accursed* burial place[41] appears to be equally that of the Arabian stoning of the grave of Abū Righāl.

With this wide-ranging exegesis of the meanings that crowd the grave of Qudār/Abū Righāl and the complexity of the questions suggested by an anthropology of Arabian liminal markers, the vestigial altars of covenants, a philology of metathesis that speaks of symbolic transmutations of stones of anathema into live embers that are as much cosmological figurations as they are incubi and presages of tragic fate—with all of this as backdrop, we should be able to return to the admittedly all-too-parsimonious text of the Thamūdic "golden bough" with an enhanced degree of faith in the symbol. It is simply not possible that in our Arabian occurrence of the "golden bough" we should have merely a decontextualized, "migrant" textual accident.

5

Poeticizing the Thamūd

To take a further step toward measuring the importance in Arabic legend and mythopoeia of Qudār and the tomb of Qudār, and with them of the Thamūdic "golden bough," we shall turn once again to the radical core of the Arabic mythopoeia of the fall of Thamūd—this time as it is reflected in Arabic poetic lore. In keeping with the nature of the treatment of residual mythical ideas in Arabic poetry, the Thamūdic myth, too, is almost always only alluded to with the greatest economy of expression, or else used in further metaphorizations for more personal and specific poetic purposes. As such, however, it not only shows a greater diversity of focus than do the narrative sources, but it also goes more to the core of its own symbolic dimension.

Thus one of the Mukhaḍramūn (those poets who span the pre-Islamic and Islamic periods), the Prophet Muḥammad's most militant defender, Ḥassān Ibn Thābit (d. before 40/659), alludes to Qudār by the epithet "the most wretched of the Thamūd" *(ashqā Thamūda),* who, to his perdition, took it upon himself to commit the monstrous crime of killing the "mother of the camel-calf, with the camel-calf present."[1] In such a reference we notice above all two things: the clear sense of the taboo connected to the she-camel, especially as she is also "the mother of the camel-calf," and, furthermore, an opening of that archaic taboo, and of Qudār as the perpetrator against it of the ultimate abomination, to subsequent assimilation into the Islamic hagiographic tradition, where Qudār, together with the killer of ʿAlī, the fourth caliph and Muḥammad's son-in-law, figures as the most wretched man of all mankind.[2]

Umayyah Ibn Abī al-Ṣalt, equally Mukhaḍram, is the only early poet to give, or to have ascribed to him, something approaching an anthology of the qurʾānic (as well as narrative) Thamūd-related themes in versified paraphrase. Once again, Qudār is the killer of "the mother of a camel-calf," and it is the groan of that calf that from the sky sends destruction upon the Thamūd.[3]

This exegetically established meaning of the myth becomes in later Arabic poetry a handily reusable metaphor of aberration or of breach of loyalty. Thus, the Abbasid poet Abū Tammām uses it in speaking of the self-destructive treachery of the Caliph al-Muᶜtaṣim's general al-Afshīn, and there his voice seems to ring as much with pity for the slain she-camel as for the fallen general:

Wa Thamūdu law lam yudhinū fī rabbihim
lam tadma nāqatuhū bi sayfi Qudāri[4]

Had the Thamūd not sought to gull their Lord,
His she-camel would not have bled
  by the sword of Qudār.

Much closer to the qurʾānic phrasing and to its exegesis is Saladin's courtier's, al-Qāḍī al-Fāḍil's, defense of his entitlements, over against his rivals, to a share in princely favors. This vein of the myth's power has by now obviously been exhausted, although it remained dialectically and rhetorically pliable: the poet sees only greed—both in the distant Thamūd and in his rivals:

Wa inna Thamūdan taddaᶜī l-māʾa kullahu
fa qul li Qudārin: waylahū qad raghā s-saqbu
Wa ᶜiẓhum bi anna l-māʾa bi l-ᶜadli qismatun
fa lī shirbu yawmin baᶜdahum wa lahum shirbu[5]

The Thamūd claim all of the water.
Say to Qudār, however, woe upon him,
  the camel-colt has groaned!
What weighs upon them grievously
  is the water's fair division:
After them a day for me to drink,
  and then for them a turn.

Altogether, however, already in the earliest Arabic poetic texts, the *nāqah* and Qudār myth falls at some distance from the qurʾānic exegetical tenor and subsequent imprint—either for being pre-Islamic and thus unaware of it, or else for marching to the beat of a different drummer even in subsequent, firmly Islamic historical periods.

Thus in a battle scene of Bedouin tribal praise, the pre-Islamic bard ᶜAlqamah sees his champion as the heroic executor of the curse of the camel-calf and his foe as the crushed Thamūd. The scene itself is primarily a heroic icon, but for the infusion of the darker coloration of broken taboo:

Ka anna rijāla l-Awsi taḥta labānihi
wa mā jamaᶜat Jallun maᶜan wa ᶜAtību
Raghā fawqahum saqbu s-samāʾi fa dāḥiḍun
bi shikkatihī lam yustalab wa salību
Ka annahumū ṣābat ᶜalayhim saḥābatun
ṣawāᶜiquhā li ṭayrihinna dabību[6]

As though the men of Aws were under
his charger's breast,
And equally Jall and ᶜAtīb.
There groaned over them
the camel-calf of heaven,
As one fell, slipping in his full array,
not yet despoiled, already stripped the other.
As if a cloud had poured upon them thunderbolts,
that left the vultures creeping on the ground.

Nothing remains of the Thamūd (and of Iram/ᶜĀd) but the archaic memory of the fierceness of their destruction in the verses of Imruʾ al-Qays. There is no room for later, exegetical readings. If there is blame, it is the false blame that is rejected by Imruʾ al-Qays. Unless we read into his poem a mythical subject, Qudār is nowhere. There is only the heroic reverberation of a mythical devastation:

Annā ᶜalayya -statabba lawmukumā
wa lam talūmā Ḥujran wa lā ᶜUṣumā
Kallā yamīna l-Ilāhi yajmaᶜunā
shayʾun wa akhwālunā Banū Jushamā
Ḥattā tazūra ḍ-ḍibāᶜu malḥamatan
ka annahā min Thamūda aw Iramā[7]

Why has your blame set upon me so fast,
When you blame neither Ḥujr nor ᶜUṣum?
No, I swear by God, nothing will join us
To Banū Jusham, our maternal clan,
Till the hyenas visit a field of death
Like that of the Thamūd or of Iram!

A similar heroic self-assurance is reflected in an early, still pre-Islamic verse by another Mukhaḍram, ᶜAbd Allāh Ibn Rawāḥah, a poet who later became one of the closest followers of the Prophet Muḥammad:

Wa rahṭa Abī Umayyata qad abaḥnā
wa Awsa l-Lāhi atbaʿnā Thamūdā[8]

Of the kin of Abū Umayyah we had made free prey,
And the Aws of God we sent where
the Thamūd had gone!

Here we must ask ourselves who were, to Ibn Rawāḥah, the hostile tribe Aws. Who were the Aws of God? Were they the "Gift of God," for the word *aws* also means "gift," or were they a totemic Dog of God, which may be another meaning of the same *aws?* Either one or the other, or both, would point to the "She-Camel of God" of the Qurʾān, and to Ṣāliḥ, as the prophet-shaman's totem of, and gift to, the Thamūd. Poetically, however, we have here primarily a heroic poet's heroic stance.

Equally part of the heroic stance, although at the same time contemplatively elegiac rather than boastfully aggressive, is the evocation of the fallen race of Thamūd in a verse by the pre-Islamic Christian poet Abū Zubayd al-Ṭāʾī:

Min rijālin kānū jamālan nujūman
fa humū l-yawma ṣaḥbu āli Thamūdi[9]

Men that were stars in beauty
Are now the company of the race of Thamūd.

The elegiac motif of the topos of *ubi sunt* envelops here the "race of the Thamūd" as well—indeed, it is built on the melancholy air which the Thamūd are capable of generating at this ideologically still unaffected pre-Islamic point in time.

Such an elegiac air also envelops the verse of the already Mukhaḍram poet Mutammim Ibn Nuwayrah:

Suqū bi l-ʿuqāri ṣ-ṣirfi ḥattā tatābaʿū
ka daʾbi Thamūdin idh raghā saqbuhum ḍuḥā[10]

Alas, they were served unmixed wine of good effect
till, one upon another, they followed
The way of the Thamūd when, in mid-morning,
their camel-calf groaned.

A fiercer, more accusatory perspective nevertheless predominates in the myth-related references in Arabic poetry to the role of Qudār and the symbolic nature of the Thamūdic she-camel. To the pre-Islamic Zuhayr Ibn Abī Sulmā, one of the poets of the *Muʿallaqāt,* intertribal war calls up symbolically the discord-bearing she-camel that is killed by Qudār, the Red One:

Fa tuntij lakum ghilmāna ashʾama kulluhum
ka aḥmari ʿĀdin turḍiʿ fa tafṭimi[11]

It [the war] will bear you sons,
all of them of ill fortune,
Like the redhead of ʿĀd—then it will
suckle and wean them.

This she-camel is the intertribal *fitnah,* later to become the qurʾānic *fitnah* as the exegetically tinted "trial." It is war itself to Zuhayr Ibn Abī Sulmā. It is then with reference to this verse specifically that the Egyptian critic Muṣṭafā Nāṣif remarks that "the she-camel became a mythical animal to which poets resort in speaking of the dark powers of evil that have mastery over man—or of the powers of death itself."[12] This is myth without a trace of the exegetical intent.

Other early poets are even more direct. To ʿUrwah Ibn al-Ward's female blaming voice *(ʿādhilah),* that brigand poet's restlessness is like the curse of the mythical "ill-tempered she-camel that bears male offspring" *(innanī arāka ʿalā aqtādi ṣarmāʾa mudhkirī).* She is

Fajūʿin li ahli ṣ-ṣāliḥīna mazallatin
makhūfin radāhā an tuṣībaka fa -ḥdhari[13]

A bearer of sudden death to the righteous ones *[aṣ-ṣāliḥīna]*
among the people, a source of error,
Her perishing a threat to afflict you:
so beware!

Together with the sense of autochthony and pride in the remote lineage of the Thamūd that emerges from early Arabic poetry there is in that poetry also a thematic strain of accusation against the slain She-Camel of Ṣāliḥ and thus, as it were, of ambiguity about Qudār himself. These symbolic "deductions," or products of a freer interpretation of the Thamūdic myth, are in evidence particularly in the poetry of the Abbasid period. Thus to Abū Tammām, in an entirely free play of referentiality, the ancient she-camel is a dramatic "camel of iniquity" *(baʿīr al-ẓulm).* She is not the animal that could have been beneficial to the people but rather one that had to be appeased, "kept sleeping," not "stirred up," for arousing it from its placidity meant perdition. Vis-à-vis the exegetical tradition there is thus this symbolically (and mythically-hermeneutically) clearly intended ambiguity concerning the She-Camel of Ṣāliḥ: if in such an expression of the poetic tradition she was perceivable as "the she-camel of iniquity," where, then, does the qurʾānic image of an instrument in the hands of Ṣāliḥ-as-prophet fit in hermeneutically? Thus Abū Tammām:

Kulū ṣ-ṣabra ghaḍḍan wa -shrabūhū fa innakum
athartum baʿīra ẓ-ẓulmi wa ẓ-ẓulmu bāriku[14]

Eat the bitterness of patience fresh,
 and drink it,
For you have stirred up the she-camel of iniquity,
 while iniquity was at rest!

To go further, the Syrian poet Usāmah Ibn Munqidh (d. 584/1188) extends the condemnation of the She-Camel of Ṣāliḥ, subsuming it within the complaint already present in the Bedouin symbolic understanding of the she-camel: as the animal that in a radical sense is the executor of separation and of loss—as this is first given to him, in a rather formulaic manner, by the Umayyad poet Dhū al-Rummah:

Qawāṭiʿu aqrāni ṣ-ṣabābati wa l-hawā
min-al-ḥayyi illā mā tujinnu ḍ-ḍamāʾiru[15]

O you breakers of affection's and of passion's links
Among kin and kindred, but for what hides
 deepest in the heart!

But to Ibn Munqidh the she-camel is more: She is the root of all evil. She is the one who commits the crime of separation, and it is upon her that the blood of vengeance falls; and, symbolically, she is none other than the She-Camel of Ṣāliḥ. Thus the ancient mythical She-Camel of Ṣāliḥ and the poet's own mount become identified with each other as tragic instruments:

Layta l-maṭāyā mā khuliqna fa kam damin
safakathu yuthqilu ghayrahā awzāruhu
Mā māta ṣabbun ithra ilfin nāziḥin
wajdan bihī illā ladayhā thāruhu
Fa law-istaṭaᶜtu abaḥtu sayfī sūqahā
ḥattā yaᶜāfa dimāʾahunna ghirāruhu
Law anna kulla l-ᶜīsi nāqatu Ṣāliḥin
mā sāʾanī annī l-ghadāta Qudāruhu
Mā ḥatfu anfusinā siwāhā innahā
la hiya l-ḥimāmu utīḥa aw indhāruhu[16]

O, had camels never been created,
    for how much blood
They spilled and left their burden upon others!
No ardent lover ever died of passion
    for a far-off love
But that upon them fell his debt of vengeance.
And were it in my might, I would allow my sword
    to strike them down
Till it were sickened of their blood.
Were every amber-colored camel
    the She-Camel of Ṣāliḥ,
It would not pain me that, on this morning,
    I were her Qudār.
None but they are our souls' death.
They are the foreordained death itself,
    or its harbinger.

Does the She-Camel of Ṣāliḥ, then, really have the potential of being the force of evil? Already the pre-Islamic poet ᶜAdī Ibn Zayd al-ᶜIbādī in his curious "Creation" poem likens the primeval serpent to the she-camel:

Fa kānat il-ḥayyatu r-raqshāʾu idh khuliqat
kamā tarā nāqatan fī l-khalqi aw jamalā[17]

The spotted serpent, when it was created,
Was among creatures quite as you see
    a she-camel, or a male.

Then al-Kisāʾī's *Tales of the Prophets* and al-Nuwayrī's encyclopaedic compilation *Ultimate Aspiration* seem to want to answer that question. There we read that the snake of Paradise had originally the form of a camel, and that in that form it was accompanying Adam and Eve in their walks through Paradise, acquainting them with the trees—the implication being that one of the trees was the tree of their misfortune.[18] In this story, too, al-Nuwayrī only marginally departs from this snake-camel lore's much earlier encyclopaedic summation in Ibn Qutaybah's *Things to Know,* in which we are told (or rather reminded) that the camel-legged serpent of Paradise, having been "God's finest creation" *(wa kānat aḥsana khalqi Allāhi),* was made by God to serve Adam. But then it was also the camel which carried Iblīs into Paradise.[19] And even the sober collector of zoological information, al-Jāḥiẓ, although stopping surprisingly briefly over the entry on camels in his animal encyclopaedia, nevertheless finds time to record some striking "folkloric" curiosities *(aqāwīl ʿajībah),* according to which some Bedouins claim that in camels there is a demonlike strain inbred from their having mated with the jinn. Those Bedouins even recoiled from praying at water holes where camels drank, because camels remained indwelt by characteristics that derived from demons *(al-shayāṭīn).*[20]

6

Demythologizing the Thamūd

The two key accounts of the miracle of the she-camel, those of al-Ṭabarī's *Commentary* and al-Thaʿlabī's *The Stories of the Prophets,* dwell in a special way on the effect which that extraordinary animal had on the seasonal pasturage conditions of the Thamūd. The Thamūd represented here are not nomadic or transhumant, but sedentary, with their city *(madīnah)* of al-Ḥijr as the center of habitation. They possessed herds of both small and large livestock. To this has to be added that they were the providers of the vast numbers of caravan camels needed for their own, and their suzerain Nabataeans', overland trade. The seasonal cycle determined the grazing habits of these herds: in the surrounding uplands during the months of greatest summer heat, and in the lowlands and valleys during the cold winter months. Into this cycle entered the miraculous she-camel—and here arise the contradictions between the stark, minimalistic myth of the qurʾānic version and the more extensive narratives of the commentaries and the prophetic lore.

We cannot but sense that a restive tension has been introduced between the qurʾānic *exemplum* of the "She-Camel of God" and the narrative expatiation of the *exemplum*, in which the Qurʾān-generated exegetical intent appears to have lost its direction, thus allowing the story its own rationale and, it is to be assumed, its actual reemergence.[1] Furthermore, in its enlarged form, the story of the downfall of the Thamūd seems to have acquired a degree of interpretive historicity, aside from its mythic, atemporal teleology and "figural" quality.

In the story that thus comes together we are confronted with three main objectifying factors: the appearance of the alien she-camel, the primary right to the source of water, and the right to the seasonal pasture grounds. We are also encouraged to approach the story from two opposing points of view: that of the intruding she-camel and of him whom she represents, and that of the owners of the herds of the Thamūd, or, in broader terms, the polity of the Thamūd. Then we must establish who is the final narrator, or redactor, of the myth/legend/story/tradition: i.e., whose point of view is thus represented.

Beginning with the question of the narration, we observe that "the final word"—certainly from a point of view still linked to the qur'ānic intent and to its claim to the wholeness of the chain of prophecy and prophethood—belongs to the side that remained beyond the destruction "to tell the story." In this respect, therefore, the account is to be taken ideologically, and perhaps also more particularly politically, as the account of the "victor." But here, too, just as in the Homeric story of the destruction of Troy, there lingered an after-story. There it engendered the Vergilian counter-myth; here it sowed the seeds of a different sort of legendary historicity—one that invites a reversal of perspectives. That is, the expanded story of the non-qur'ānic Thamūd texts does not necessarily address itself at every step to the ideological wholeness of the Qur'ān-established mythical tradition; even in its constructionist hermeneutics it still reveals an awareness of the possibility that the subject matter it deals with may have been a much darker myth that arose out of a clash of forces that fall outside the qur'ānic exegetic purview and that, ultimately, the power of this myth derives from the repressed way in which it speaks of an overwhelming tragedy that must have touched the very heart of the Arabian ethnos. Ultimately, too, as is the nature of tragedy, the very violence and uncompromising consummation of fate outweigh the apparent, exegetically tailored verdict of the mythos as to which side in the clash of destinies was right and which was wrong. In such tragedy there is, therefore, not even a "winner." This, then, seems to be the corrective point of view—one that is always intrusive and at all times insidious—in the narrative legacy of the downfall of the Thamūd.

In a manner that defies the main exegetic logic of his *Commentary,* al-Ṭabarī thus implies that there was a strong Thamūdic cause for complaint against the miraculous *nāqah*'s invasion of the seasonal pasture grounds, and that "this became too much for them to bear. Recalcitrant, they turned against their Lord's command and unanimously resolved to slay the she-camel."[2] The reader of this narrative notes further the starkness of the narrator's dwelling on the fact that (on her assigned days) the she-camel was drinking the Thamūdic well dry to the last drop, till there was no water left in the valley.[3] He is also made to remember the great wealth in herds of the Thamūdic woman Ṣadūf, who was Ṣāliḥ's most bitter foe precisely because of his (or God's) she-camel's bothersome presence;[4] and that Ṣāliḥ's other bitter foe's (also a woman) byname was none other than Umm al-Ghanam (Mother of Flocks)[5]—in itself distinctly pointing to its bearer's economic station and interests. Then, too, there is brought up the Thamūdic argument that to them water was more valuable than the milk Ṣāliḥ's she-camel was giving them in exchange.[6]

In his retelling of the story of the Thamūd and of the She-Camel of Ṣāliḥ, the mythopoeically inclined historian al-Masᶜūdī (d. 345/956), too, speaks of the ruins of al-Ḥijr with the noticeable stylistic intention of reproducing the elegiac tone of the poets of the Jāhilīyah as those poets had halted and mused over their "ruined abodes" *(aṭlāl).* And he also states quite clearly that, in spite of the fact that the She-Camel of Ṣāliḥ was supplying the Thamūd with abundant milk, "she vexed them in what concerned pasture and water."[7]

Together with repeating many of al-Ṭabarī's ambiguities of the story, the author of *The Stories of the Prophets,* al-Thaᶜlabī, mentions further how gargantuan the belly of the she-camel became after she had drunk all of Thamūd's water.[8] Here one senses almost a folkloric narrator's delight in grotesque details and in imputing gluttony to the sacred animal *(nāqatu l-Lāhi).*

Al-Nuwayrī, too, stresses the Thamūdeans' dependence on "one sole well," adding that those among the Thamūd who were unfaithful and had drunk the she-camel's milk were afflicted with scabies on their bodies, for which there was no cure. For this they assembled and pronounced: "'Nothing good comes to us from this one.' And they agreed to kill her."[9]

Even Ibn Kathīr, who shows little concern for exegetical argumentation (other than restating the case according to the qurʾānic tradition), nevertheless in the end displaces the blame for the contumacy of the Thamūd by stressing that it was the Shayṭān who implanted in the Thamūdean minds discontent with the she-camel's presence among them, as well as their preference for water over milk.[10]

At this point it ought to be quite clear that the complexity of the Thamūdic myth goes far beyond what the Qur'ān tells us and what the canonical levels of its exegesis intend us to understand. For not only is the Qur'ān and its exegesis difficult to bring to full agreement with the way the she-camel myth is reflected in the classical Arabic poetic lore,[11] but, indeed, there lies dormant in the Qur'ān itself a perhaps even more serious impediment to bringing exegetically into agreement the divinely tabooed She-Camel of the Thamūd *(nāqatu l-Lāhi)* with the other qur'ānic reference to tabooed she-camels of pre-Islamic Bedouin Arabian custom, namely the *baḥīrah* and the *sā'ibah.*

From the merely philological point of view, the classical Arabic lexicons tell us that the *baḥīrah* is a she-camel of which the mother, a *sā'ibah,* had given birth to ten, or five, females consecutively; the *baḥīrah's* "ear was slit" as a sign *(mark),* distinguishing her in her state of taboo. No use was to be made of her milk, nor could she be ridden, but she was entitled to pasture freely and to drink from any water to which she came. Above all, the *baḥīrah* was protected from being slaughtered.

The *sā'ibah* of pre-Islamic Bedouin custom was in most respects as tabooed as the *baḥīrah.* As a she-camel whose offspring have themselves produced offspring, she too was not to be ridden or submitted to transport burden, and was left to pasture freely without a herdsman. Her name *(sā'ibah),* pointing etymologically to the root meaning of "to run, or flow, unchecked," is furthermore, aside from being a separate technical term, equally an epithet of the *baḥīrah.*[12]

It is, however, this special and, in the pre-Islamic Bedouin understanding, distinctly "meritorious" rank of a she-camel as *baḥīrah* or as *sā'ibah* that is castigated in the Qur'ān with a special anathematizing dictum: "It was not God who instituted a *baḥīrah,* or a *sā'ibah,* or a *waṣīlah* ['one bearing females in seven consecutive years'], or a *ḥāmī* ['stallion-camel freed from work'], but the unbelievers were those that forged lies against God."[13] The essential identity of the "non-divine" taboo of the *baḥīrah* and the *sā'ibah* to the "divine" taboo of the *nāqatu l-Lāhi* is thus both the paradox and the rationale of the condemnation. Played out in it there is a deeper-seated rivalry of two almost identical and equally autochthonous and archaic taboos that carries over into other qur'ānic binary and dialectical confrontations and paradoxes of analogy and incompatibility.[14] Only these factors allow us to understand, and justify, the strength (and ultimate tragic efficacy) of one taboo by the grim fervor of the condemnation of the other. Of great interpretive assistance toward a fuller understanding of this qurʾānic anathema cast on the "rival" taboo of the *baḥīrah/sāʾibah* is its translation in the form of a gloss into the no less than Dantesque eschatological punishment of a certain ʿAmr Ibn Luḥayy, the purported originator of the custom of consecrating the *sawāʾib* (plural form of *sāʾibah*). Thus we read that "It is said in a tradition, 'I saw ʿAmr Ibn Luḥayy dragging his intestines in the fire [of Hell]': and he was the first who set at liberty *sawāʾib*, which is forbidden in the Qurʾān."[15]

The noncanonical bases of the "memory" of the Thamūdic tragedy, however, demand more far-reaching consideration, and this consideration may, in part at least, be quite starkly euhemeristic and demythologizing—something that should be unavoidable whenever myth is deconstructed into history: whenever one radical sense of time has to cede before another.

According to Mikhail B. Piotrovskyj, the downfall of the sedentary Thamūd and of their city of al-Ḥijr was the outcome of the period of "bedouinization" that took place in northern Ḥijāz between the second and fifth centuries A.D. In his view it was those encroaching Bedouins, the representatives of a camel-breeding culture, who were the decisive force that destroyed the Thamūd. It is also in this context that Piotrovskyj sees "the she-camel becoming, as it were, the symbol of the relationship between the sedentary Thamūd and the encroaching nomad camel-breeders."[16] The Thamūd killed the she-camel because they did not wish to share (their) water with her, but in the she-camel they slew "live" milk. "From the point of view of a nomadic camel-breeder this was an abomination,"[17] especially within the Arabian tradition of the consecration of animals within the *ḥimā*.[18]

This basic drawing of lines in the interpretive symbolization of the fall of the Thamūd should be quite convincing. It is, however, too neatly integrated into the decline and fall of sedentarism and the growth of nomadism in Arabia. What I mean is that such schematization does not answer more detailed questions of symbolism, mythogenesis, and mythopoeia. Neither does it address itself to textually scattered, but cumulative, literary questions of implicit hermeneutical value. Above all, Piotrovskyj adopts, without alerting us to it, the all-too-convenient qurʾānic point of view, which is that of the historical "victor," that is, the view of scriptural narratological legality.

Undoubtedly there existed an accelerated bedouinizing trend in the middle and northern Ḥijāz after the fall of the Nabataean "caravan empire" to Rome. On the other hand, however, the Thamūd had been affiliates of that empire not only as sedentary dwellers of the mercantile outpost of al-Ḥijr but also as the camel-breeders and providers to the caravan needs of the Nabataeans. The interests of the Bedouin camel-breeding economy were thus also the interests of the Thamūdic al-Ḥijr, and the camel-centered totemism of the Bedouins was also their, the Thamūdic, symbolism and totemism. Only in this way can we bring in the She-Camel of Ṣāliḥ as a valid, unifying totemic presence.[19] We may infer this much even from the *nāqat Ṣāliḥ* narratives that single out the role of the two Thamūdic women, ʿUnayzah and Ṣadūf, who, as we know from our extra-qurʾānic narrative texts, represent the camel-breeding economy of al-Ḥijr at the point at which that economy is being threatened by the monstrous—in bulk and in water consumption—She-Camel of Ṣāliḥ. If, with this in mind, we return to Piotrovskyj's understanding of the symbolism of the She-Camel of Ṣāliḥ, it becomes necessary to infer that the she-camel must have been a totemic animal and an object of taboo to both varieties of camel-breeders, the settled Thamūd as well as the "encroaching" nomads. Was there merely a difference of intensity in the sense of the totem and the taboo that in this respect stood between the sedentary "exploiter" of the camel economy, the Thamūd of al-Ḥijr, and the "organic" economy of total dependence on the camel of the Bedouin?

To further our understanding of the myth of the She-Camel of Ṣāliḥ as a Thamūdic totemic animal, we ought to consider the possibility, or rather outright evidence, of an archetypal relationship between this myth and that of the Trojan Horse. Both myths speak essentially of a city or polity. The she-camel and the horse were, each one in its own way, "gifts," although pregnant with warnings *(timeo Danaos et dona ferentes)*.[20] Both were meant to contain the promise of redemption and peace, and of perpetual fulfillment and abundance; but inside it one had brought the male camel-colt *(saqb)* of ultimate doom to the Thamūd, while the other carried within it the Greeks that were to burn down Troy. Both, too, were of singularly enormous size, and above all both were, respectively, a broken taboo and a fraudulently used totem.

If it has been part of our method to bring to light the hermeneutical and narratologically complimentary, although not necessarily chronologically posterior, place of the narrative mythopoeia of the Thamūd vis-à-vis the qurʾānic Thamūd fragments of the She-Camel of Ṣāliḥ, we also find that nowhere in Vergil's *Aeneid* (2: 13-267) is that work's hermeneutical role vis-à-vis the *Odyssey* clearer than in the expanded story of the Trojan Horse. For in the *Odyssey* (4: 242-50, 266-79, 500-01; 8: 493-95, 499-515) the sketchiness of the Trojan Horse references would be almost disappointing as narrative were it not that in that sketchiness there is actually reflected an almost cinematographic diversity of angles of vision, which, too, makes us aware of the multiplicity of the *Odyssey*'s underlying narrative source strata. Even the *Aeneid*, however, in spite of the more consolidated narrative line of its Trojan Horse segment—which thus carries much of its hermeneutical vigor vis-à-vis the *Odyssey*—is no less dependent on a multiplicity of pre-Vergilian, and eventually even pre-Homeric, sources.[21]

In his discussion of the use of epithets in the *Iliad*, C. M. Bowra speaks at some length of the special status of the horse among the Trojans.

> They are also called "trainers of horses" 21 times, while the same epithet is given to their commander Hector. This is founded on fact. The cities VI and VII at Hisarlik, which correspond to the Homeric Troy, are rich in horses' bones, and there is no doubt that the Trojans bred horses on their rich plain, which was in the first years of this century the breeding-ground for the stud-farm of Sultan Abdul Hamid II. This epithet is as true to the Trojans as "well-greaved" is for the Achaeans. Both must go back to a very early date, when they were deserved by their distinguishing correctness.[22]

Also, as stressed by Gilbert Murray, "The Trojans in the *Iliad* . . . have almost a monopoly of names compounded with *-ippos*."[23]

It was thus not at all accidental that Odysseus "suggested" that a horse be used for the Greeks' fateful ruse; and—from the point of view of the Homeric, and Vergilian, narrative—it appears clear that the reason the Trojans broke the walls and brought the huge "form" of the animal into their city was that it represented their totemic animal. Similarly, it is not accidental that in our Arabian myth the tabooed animal, the she-camel, was chosen by the Thamūd *themselves* (according to some versions of the mythopoeia) to become their fateful "sign" of discord and trial *(fitnah)*.

The implicit danger in a totem as defended, but also threatened, by its taboo is thus in evidence in both the Trojan and the Thamūdic cases.[24]

The further question is: What are the place and the role of the man/prophet Ṣāliḥ as he enters—with "his" she-camel—the complexities of the Thamūdic camel economy? To begin with, who is he? First we must notice the manifest peculiarity of his name among all the other names of the prophets that figure in the Islamic prophetic register, those of biblical provenance as well as those that may be considered Arabian autochthons. Ṣāliḥ, the "righteous," "virtuous," "incorrupt one," figuring firmly, as far as the qur'ānic parceling is concerned, among the autochthons, bears the sole directly qualitative epithetic name of all the prophets recognized by Islam before Muḥammad.[25] The name is neither theophoric nor an archaic, etymologically unrecognizable linguistic borrowing, as were the names of the prophets co-opted from the Hebrew Bible. As a free-floating, distinctly positive potential epithet, it was ideally suited to become attached to a prophet-reformer. In the Qur'ān it also provides for the clearest antonym of, and rhetorical counter to, "corruption" *(ifsād)*,[26] becoming in that text an integral concept critically important for the understanding of the cyclical structure of Islamic mytho-history with its pervasive confrontational binarisms of "righteousness"-"abomination"/"prophet"-"antiprophet." Above all, understood as *ṣāliḥ* the epithet, it contributed to Muḥammad's strongly osmotic viewing of Ṣāliḥ the prophet as his own "figura," or rather, it allowed him to project his own prophetic and organizational difficulties, and even agonies, back upon his mythical predecessor—thus constructing his own "persona" to the extent that he constructed the "figura" of Ṣāliḥ.[27]

Outside the qur'ānic exegesis, however, is Ṣāliḥ still a Thamūdean or, as Piotrovskyj would have it, a representative of the (hostile?) Bedouin periphery? The legend establishes him as wholly a Thamūdic autochthon. In his ancestral line he is Ṣāliḥ Ibn Asif Ibn Māsikh Ibn ʿAbīd Ibn Khādir Ibn Thamūd Ibn Jāthir Ibn Iram Ibn Sām Ibn Nūḥ.[28] His "otherness" as prophet within the Thamūd is purely a qur'ānic hermeneutic product. At the present point we can no longer work with such an extrapolation of Ṣāliḥ. If, then, the prophecy-myth fails to apply, Ṣāliḥ and his she-camel become merely another "economic" force within the

Thamūd: the most powerful and the most threatening rival of the economic "establishment" behind which stand ʿUnayzah and Ṣadūf, and with them, Qudār. All these are representative forces.

Although very much in passing—so much so that the matter remained practically unnoticed by all the principal classical Qurʾān exegetes, including the "modern" Muḥammad ʿAbduh—the Qurʾān may indeed be suggesting the possibility of a social and economic clash between the Thamūd and Ṣāliḥ. But there, as in Sūrat al-Aʿrāf, vv. 75-76, the powerful and "arrogant" ones are the Thamūd—ʿUnayzah and Ṣadūf, we may supplement—and the "weak" ones are the believers around Ṣāliḥ. It is to such a reading that the English translator and otherwise strongly socially oriented exegete Abdullah Yusuf Ali is most inclined: "The Thamūd were addicted to class arrogance. They oppressed the poor. The prophet Ṣāliḥ reproached them, and put forward a wonderful she-camel *as symbol of the rights of the poor*, but they hamstrung her" [italics mine].[29] The problem with this exegete's not at all dull reading is that the sword of dialectical interpretation and of terminology of recognizable socio-ideological provenance must be allowed to cut both ways.

It is at this point that the factor of *water* comes in. The fact that water was the essential clause in the contract between Ṣāliḥ, the owner of the she-camel, and the Thamūdic owners of camel herds emerges from every version of the mythopoeic narrative as well as from the qurʾānic texts: access to water has to be rigorously divided, but the seeming initial equity of that division becomes ultimately quite clearly disadvantageous to the general camel and herding economy of the Thamūd;[30] and Ṣāliḥ, having divided the water "equitably," nevertheless emerges as the sole possessor of the advantageous seasonal grazing grounds of the Thamūd.

A further interpretive step, quite logical in its context, should also be the translation of the exorbitant size of Ṣāliḥ's she-camel—and her ability to empty the well of the Thamūd to its last drop—into an equally exorbitant size of the rival camel herds of Ṣāliḥ. We should thus obtain a picture of a clash of grazing and water interests together with the suggestion of limited water resources and their overuse. Thus the regimentation of the use of water may have had another purpose as well, that of economizing it. This the Thamūd failed to do. The ensuing drying up of their wells led to what the Qurʾān refers to *(ad sensum)* as *biʾr muʿaṭṭalah* (an idle and neglected well).[31] From within the Arabic linguistic sensibility it is thus especially at this point hermeneutically appropriate not to shy away from the unavoidable etymological, or merely phonetic, association made in the mythopoeically active mind—the Arabic mind not excluded—between the name of Thamūd, inasmuch as that name's entire tragic complexity turns around the symbols of water, and the meanings of *thamada; thamad; thimād* ("to exhaust a well by drawing water," "to exhaust [the she-camel] by milking"; "water that is little in quantity, that has no continual increase"; "a little water remaining in a tract of hard ground"; "water that appears in winter and goes away in summer").[32]

To give matters their demythologizing balance, there is to be taken into account—as a belated backdrop to all that preceded—albeit outside both the qurʾānic and the narrative mythopoeic texts, the objectively verifiable course of basic historical events which determined (at least by accelerating it) the fate of the Nabataean metropolis of Petra and, consequently, also the fate of the southern outpost of that metropolis, the Thamūdic al-Ḥijr. It was in the process of the Romanization of Arabia, with the fall of Petra to the legions of Trajan (A.D. 106), that the centers of Arabian caravan commerce were displaced northward, to Bostra and to Roman Syria. With that displacement the economic base of the Thamūd, their camel husbandry in the service of the caravan trade, was dealt a severe, and ultimately wholly destructive, blow. Thus, too, nothing mythical needed to have happened to the Thamūd: merely the course of history.[33] And in the course of history there seems not to have been much room for pathos or for mythopoeia, especially not in the power-divested—and increasingly identity-divested—periphery of the new hegemony of Rome. From that point on, in documents and inscriptions that extend well into the fourth century, the Thamūd figure chiefly as militarily attached to, and ultimately integrated into, Roman garrison units. Thus we know that in the later 160s, on behalf of Marcus Aurelius and Lucius Verus, a Thamūdic tribal group, or garrison, had built a temple provided with dedicatory inscriptions in Ruwwāfa, some 200 km northwest of Madāʾin Ṣāliḥ. The temple's Greek inscription refers to the builders as "the *ethnos* of the Thamudénoi," while in the Nabataean one they figure as the "SRKT TMWDW."[34]

Out of that period, too, notice comes to us of a group patronymically referred to as Banū Ṣāliḥ, who, as suggested by Irfan

Shahīd, "could have belonged to the group of the Prophet Ṣāliḥ, namely, Thamūd."[35] According to the tenth-century author Saʿīd Ibn al-Biṭrīq (Eutachius), those Banū Ṣāliḥ were the remnants of the community brought to Mt. Sinai from Egypt by Justinian in the sixth century. According to Shahīd, however, "they were certainly in Oriens in the fourth century, but how and when they separated from the main tribe and wandered into Sinai is not clear."[36] These Banū Ṣāliḥ of Mt. Sinai were, supposedly, entrusted with the protection of the monastery, and even in the nineteenth century they remained there as the mountain's protectors, carrying the plural patronymic of Ṣawāliḥah.[37] Shahīd notes further that till today "There is a site twenty-five miles northwest of Mt. Sinai called Nabī Ṣāliḥ," and he goes as far as to call the Banū Ṣāliḥ, in what to us is no doubt an interesting and suggestive way, the "custodians of the Holy Mountain."[38]

This, however, was not the way in which, generations after the downfall of the Thamūd—indeed, several centuries thereafter—those that had survived the acts of history would yet "remember" them. Their memory, although pregnant with a sense of loss and sorrow more gnawing and cumulative than singularly cataclysmic—or precisely because it was pregnant with a sense of loss and sorrow that was ill-encompassed in its enormousness—was quite likely to blot out the concreteness of historical events and allow myth to replace them. The civic polities of Petra and al-Ḥijr had fallen, and the surviving—not necessarily conquering—Bedouinity of the "encroaching nomadization" would not find in the Roman legions the mythogenic force needed to speak of their past. This would not have required a particularly regional (in the cultural-historical sense) disposition to mythopoeia versus historicity. The Germanic and Celtic legendary and mythical imagination, too, had worked from within the self-awareness and self-absorption of the ethnos, unmindful, or almost, of external formative historical forces. The fact remains that in the Thamūdic and subsequently, by legacy, in the Arabic-Islamic case we have a history of dénouement which fails to metamorphose into myth and a myth that does not account for history.

One further aspect of the Thamūdic irreality of historicity and its strong reality of myth remains, however: that of the reality or irreality, or rather of the adequacy or inadequacy of a division of roles into victim of the abomination, that is, the she-camel whose slaying broke the taboo, and into that abomination's perpetrator: the Thamūd collectively and Qudār singularly. Furthermore, we have thus far been using the names of the actors or perpetrators of the abomination quite unreservedly and self-assuredly in conjunction, merely in the form in which they are brought together and interrelated by the tragic story itself—that is, with Thamūd being the collectivity and Qudār that collectivity's individuation. Their "reality" as regards their mythical, or legendary, juxtaposition precisely in those roles, or their narrative contingency, ought, however, to beg for elucidation or at least for some form of annotative questioning.

First we will consider Qudār. We already know something about the surface etymology of that name within the Arabic morphological derivational scheme and the degree to which that scheme even determines its unpropitious connotational semantics within the Thamūdic tragic story as a whole.[39] What we must add to that knowledge, however, is the strong notion that not only is there more to the etymology of the name Qudār, but that above all there is in it a further history all its own and even an intertextuality that deposits us, no doubt with initial tentativeness, in the nebulous territory of archaic regional eponymy and an independent (at least linguistically and chronologically) body of literature. This way we shall also enter a realm of intriguing further possibilities of exploration that remain overlooked in the familiar Thamūd sources of *ḥadīth* and narrative mythopoeia—as those sources speak of Qudār explicitly or, as does the Qur'ān, merely imply his contextual presence.

Thus, that which calls our attention to begin with is Qudār's striking genealogical patronymic, Ibn Sālif.[40] Meaning here Son of the Ancient One (or of the Forefather), such a patronymic necessarily suggests that its bearer is not merely someone named according to an ill-defined, broadly current custom but that rather, in the genealogical sense, the patronymic contains a reference to some point of origin in the formation of its bearer's clan, tribe, or people—and that that clan's, tribe's, or people's name ought itself to have been Qudār, or a still traceable (in spite of the undeniably corrosive process of Max Müllerean "disease of language") phonetic variant thereof. The likelihood of dealing here with an eponym presents itself therefore in an almost classic fashion. Initially, however, in order to pursue the eponymic avenue, we have to step outside the Thamūdic myth as we know it and turn to the external, and not-so-external, textual source, the Hebrew Bible, which, in its own mythogeny and mythopoeia, is itself eminently dependent on eponymy.

First we shall note how much the modern Iraqi historian Jawād ʿAlī almost prods us to proceed in that direction. Thus, after discussing in the opening chapters of his voluminous history of the Arabs before Islam, *Al-Mufaṣṣal*,[41] the legendary pre-autochthons, *al-ʿArab al-bāʾidah* ("the perished Arabs"), amongst whom figure the Thamūd, and with them Qudār, Jawād ʿAlī proceeds to the discussion of the two "surviving" Arabs, the *al-ʿArab al-ʿāribah* ("the autochthonous Arabs") and the *al-ʿArab al-mustaʿribah* ("the naturalized, or assimilated, Arabs"). The autochthonous *al-ʿāribah* are the eponymic descendants of Qaḥṭān, himself no other than the biblical Yoqṭān, son of ʿEber;[42] while the naturalized *al-mustaʿribah* have as their eponymous founder ʿAdnān, a descendant of Ismāʿīl, son of Abraham, and his wife Raʿlah Bint Muḍāḍ of the supposedly autochthonous line of al-Jurhum. Thus, within the Arab tradition, ʿAdnān is an Ishmaelite, just as Qaḥṭān is of the postdiluvian line of Noah. By being an Ishmaelite, ʿAdnān, therefore, also belongs to the line of descent of Nābit/Nebayot and Qedar/Qêdar, the two first-born sons of Ismāʿīl—from among his twelve male offspring—with whom, according to a somewhat nebulous and paradoxical tradition *(khabar)*, the Arab ethnos proper begins.[43]

As part of this genealogical web, Jawād ʿAlī brings us the Hebrew Bible's own story of the Ishmaelites, and within that story he dwells on the recurrence of the name Qedar in a rather significant number of biblical texts—while acknowledging the name's Arabic phonetic variants, such as Qīdar/Qaydar/Qaydār/Qaydhar. This done, the Iraqi historian does not draw explicit conclusions but, by placing his discussion of the Ishmaelite Qedar in a philological and logical succession to the discussion of the Qudār of the Thamūd of the qurʾāno-mythopoeic story, he nevertheless reveals his train of thought.

The biblical Qedar texts begin with Genesis 25:13 and 1 Chronicles 1:29 with the enumeration, in the order of their birth, of the twelve sons of Ishmael—the two eldest being Nebayot and Qedar. It is only the prophetic and poetic texts, however, which give us more than merely genealogical information. These texts are Isaiah, Jeremiah, Ezekiel, Psalms, and Song of Songs.[44]

In Isaiah (21:13–17) "the sons of Qedar" fall within clearly knowable geographical points of reference, Dedan and Têmā/ Taymāʾ:

> 13. The oracle concerning Arabia.
> In the thickets of Arabia you will lodge,
> O caravans of Dedanites.
> 14. To the thirsty bring water,
> meet the fugitive with bread,
> O inhabitants of the land of Têmā.
> 15. For they have fled from the swords,
> from the drawn sword, from the bent bow,
> and from the press of battle.
> 16. For thus the Lord [Adonay] said to me:
> "Within a year, according to the years of a hireling,
> all the glory of Qedar will come to an end;
> 17. and the remainder of the archers of the mighty men
> of the sons of Qedar will be few; for the Lord [Yahweh],
> the God of Israel, has spoken."

In this "oracle concerning Arabia" Qedar is thus placed in the vicinity of Dedan, the present al-ʿUlā, which is adjacent to the Thamūdic al-Ḥijr, and northeast of which is to be found Têmā, the Taymāʾ of pre-Islamic Arabia. We are, therefore, in a very clearly delineated space: northern and northeastern Ḥijāz. Further on in Isaiah (42:11), Qedar is mentioned as inhabiting villages *(ḥaẓerīm)*, and, although the immediate context does not appear to be one of condemnation or the usual "prophetic" anathema, the subsequent verses, especially verse 14, speak of devastation. And again, in 60:7, Isaiah makes a pledge to Israel: "All the flocks of Qedar shall be gathered to you, the rams of Nebayot[45] shall minister to you."

In Jeremiah there are two separate references to Qedar. In 2:10 (with v. 11 as its extended context) Qedar is given as an example of how even an unconsecrated people *(goy)*, whose gods "are no gods," is yet unwilling to change them. It is, however in 49:28–33 that we find Jeremiah's main Qedar text:

> 28. Concerning Qedar and the kingdoms of Ḥaẓōr which
> Nebūkhadreẓẓār king of Babylon smote:
> "Rise up, advance against Qedar,
> and destroy the people of the east!"
> —Thus says Yahweh—

> 29. "Their tents and their flocks shall be taken,
> their curtains and all their goods;
> their camels shall be borne away from them,
> and men shall cry to them: 'Terror on every side!'"

Without stepping out of the Qedar context, Jeremiah continues by directly anathematizing "the kingdoms of Ḥaẓōr" in behalf of Nabūkhadreẓẓār (v. 30), thus justifying and championing, as it were, the Babylonian cause.[46] Here, too, the anathema is declared, albeit through the prophet, as being the word of Yahweh (v. 31):

> 32. "Their camels shall become booty,
> their herds of cattle a spoil.
> I will scatter to every wind
> those who cut the corners of their hair,
> and I will bring their calamity
> from every side of them," says Yahweh.
> 33. "Ḥaẓōr shall become a haunt of jackals,
> an everlasting waste;
> no man shall dwell there,
> no man shall sojourn in her."

Ezekiel (27:21), however, does not speak of the woes of Qedar. His god's admonitory punishment descends on Tyre instead. Arabia and Qedar, and once again Dedan (v. 20), although bearing the semiotic burden of the context, belong to the time before the fall of rich and imperious Tyre. In this secondary context our knowledge of Qedar's economy is nevertheless furthered:

> 21. Arabia and all the princes of Qedar
> were your favored dealers in lambs, rams, and goats;
> in these they trafficked with you.

The reference to Qedar in Psalm 120 is, on the other hand, direct and unmediated in its accusatory tone:

> 5. Woe is me, that I sojourn in Mesekh,
> that I dwell among the tents of Qedar!
> 6. Too long have I had my dwelling
> among those who hate peace.
> 7. I am for peace;
> but when I speak,
> they are for war!

Only in Song of Songs 1:5 does Qedar appear in a context of crystalline lyricism and in images of beauty that are unscathed by any underlying discrepancy of intent or purpose so characteristic of the other biblical occurrences of Qedar:

> 5. I am very dark, but comely,
> O daughters of Jerusalem,
> like the tents of Qedar,
> like the curtains of Solomon [Shalmā (?)].[47]

And further on (2:1), this mysterious maiden, "dark like the tents of Qedar," of the biblical "eclogue," also sees herself as "a rose of Sharon, a lily of the valleys." This is a totally different image of Qedar. It belongs not only to a different sensibility, but also to a contrastive ideology in which the tents of Qedar as the "black tents" of the Bedouin are no longer hostile.

In connection with this "otherness" of Song of Songs 1:5 we note further that there exists a related image, indeed a firm topos, in pre-Islamic Arabic/Bedouin *nasīb* lyricism that shares even its common philology with the first stanza of the Song. Especially noteworthy here is the *Muʿallaqah* of Imruʾ al-Qays which demands to be introduced into that separate contextuality of the Song, side by side with the motif of the "dark but beautiful" maiden who is like the "black tents of Qedār" and like the "curtains of Shalmoh/Salmah" of the Hebrew poem.

If we thus follow this inference and take the *Muʿallaqah* of Imruʾ al-Qays as our Arabic analogue, we find that Arab poet referring to his beloved as a maiden of "dark seclusion"—not for her skin color but for her privileged, "darkened," or light-excluding, curtained tent-alcove *(khidr).* He invokes her, or rather reminisces and calls her back to his own mind, as his tender "egg" of that "curtain-darkened tent enclosure": *wa bayḍati khidrin* (v. 23). And when he, who is also a prince of his tribe, then "steals past guards to visit her" (v. 24), he finds her (once again) "by the tent's curtain" (v. 26).[48] The Arabic *khidr*, especially as it stands in its poetically heightened antiposition to the whiteness of the "egg" in Imruʾ al-Qays's verse, thus rightfully confirms its archaic etymological meaning, which is that of "blackness"—and which it shares in an important corroborative way with the phonetically and derivationally kindred root-variants *k-d-r, q-dh-r, kh-ḍ-r.*[49] Furthermore, through the analogy of the Imruʾ al-Qays image to that of Song of Songs 1:5, this instance of the Arabic *khidr* also suggests to us that it ought to participate not only in the Hebrew topos of "the black tents of Qedar," but, equally, in the name Qedar itself—as that name is used in creating that topical simile; for at least in this junction of texts (and images), the "Hebrew" Qedar does not lead us to the all too readily available alternate Arabic root etymology of *q-d-r* with its meaning of "to measure, compute, estimate"; "to decree, appoint, ordain"; "to have power, or ability"—not to mention that of "to cook," this latter one being clearly a denominal verbal derivation of *qidr* (cauldron, kettle).[50]

Primarily, therefore, the similarity of the two motifs as well as the etymologically generated common semanticity of Qedar, together with the Arabic root variants of *khidr*, become thus complemental, mutually reinforcing, and foregrounded. From the Arabic side, within this etymological expansion of Qedar/*khidr*, we shall, for the sake of further illustration, attend especially to the Arabic root *kh-ḍ-r,* as in *akhḍar* ("of a dark, ashy, [dark] dusty color"; as well as "of a blackish hue inclining to green"; and "black, black-complexioned"), for these meanings of *akhḍar* shall guide us back most directly to the phrasing of the topos in Song of Songs 1:5. Thus the classical Arabic lexicographers, in substantiating that meaning, took care to bring in a most telling and topically authoritative poetic text, which, indeed, seems to reflect, or rather refract, the Arabic *male* conception of the Hebrew Song's *female* "I am dark, but comely . . . / like the tents of Qedar." These lexicographers dwell on the Arabic expression, in itself topical, *akhḍar al-jildah,* meaning literally "dark, tawny of skin," but idiomatically extended to mean "pure of race," "of genuine Arab race," thus distinguishing and enhancing, if you will, the *manly* variant of "comely"—as in the adduced poetic authority, the poet al-Lahabī al-Faḍl Ibn ʿAbbās, in whose verse a no less than proverbially feminine *nigra sum sed formosa* becomes "I am black of skin, but a nobleman":

> And I am the tawny one, who doesn't know me?
> The dark-skinned one [pure of race],
> of the noble house of the Arabs.[51]

Should we now come back to Imruʾ al-Qays and follow his *Muʿallaqah* over its verses 30–41 we would realize further how that poem's lines remain attuned to the imagery and the total tenor of the lyricism of the Song of Songs, with one important difference—as we observed in the example from al-Lahabī—namely, the difference of the lover's perspective, or of the inversion of the active speaking and articulating persona. For, whereas love in the Arabian poem is seen and described from the point of view of the man, in the Hebrew poem the perspective and, even more importantly, the lover's sensibility are predominantly feminine—although there, too, the formal structure is dialogical, eclogue-like.[52]

Ultimately, we are thus left with an undeniable clarity of contrast as regards the biblical Qedar texts other than that of Song of Songs. This impels us to reread those texts and reflect upon the nature of the difference of their tone—as well as on how much they, in turn, reveal their own common denominator. Thus in Isaiah's "oracle concerning Arabia" we obtain not merely a strong triangulation (Dedan/Taymāʾ/Qedar) of a geography of Qedar that decidedly places all three points in that part of the Ḥijāz that includes the location, or the immediate proximity, of the Thamūd, but we are also told in Isaiah's prophetic ways—in which the invoked speaker is always "the Lord, the God of Israel"—that the destruction of Qedar is imminent and that such is God's decree. Once again, in the prophecy of Jeremiah, and in equally unambiguous ways, God speaks out against Qedar and, in so doing, marshals the more obvious political cause of the Babylonian Nabukhadreẓẓar.

To the bleak fate of Qedar Jeremiah links that of Ḥaẓōr, another people of implied vicinity or, which, judging by the etymology of the name, is a settled, or "fenced in," community. The destruction prophesied here—or perhaps already executed and as such described—is much worse than anything Isaiah had contemplated as the deserved fate of Qedar. The sense of ultimate curse and anathema that prevails in this "prophecy" is only comparable to that engulfing al-Ḥijr of the Thamūd, or of the salting over of "deleted" Carthage. Finally, Ezekiel's view of Qedar being more indirect and speculative, there remains Psalm 120 with its direct indictment of Qedar as those "who hate peace."

The image of Qedar that thus results is that of a wealthy people, perhaps settled, although equally dwellers in black Bedouin tents, and certainly important possessors of herds of camels and sheep. They are also allied with, or related to, such rich camel-breeders as the settled, or semi-settled, Ḥaẓōr, whose fate of condemnation and anathema they share.

The etymology of the biblical place name(s) Ḥaẓōr (and its variants) is of interest, particularly inasmuch as for our Qedar-related Ḥaẓōr—unlike the well-documented northern Ḥaẓōr of Naphtali—we lack reliable extra-biblical documentation.[53] What that etymology points to, however, is the general as well as particular idea of "enclosure," of settled and protected space, and of sedentarism opposite nomadism. To the degree to which it crosses over to Arabic etymological derivations, or to any likelihood of such derivations, Ḥaẓōr strengthens further its Hebrew root etymology and semantic range; but with this, it also serves us in our Arabic etymological task in certain important ways. Thus we realize that the Hebrew *ḥ-ẓ-r* corresponds to several Arabic phonetic combinations and permutations: to the group *ḥ-ḍ-r/ḥ-ṣ-r/ḥ-ẓ-r,* as well as, more speculatively, to *kh-ḍ-r.* The first ones all denote, and connotatively modulate, the meaning of "encirclement," "protection," and "sedentarism," while the latter, by meaning "greenness,"[54] bears in Arabic also the meaning of "darkness/ blackness."

Bearing in mind the first phonetic cluster, we are aware of the most basic and rudimentary workings of sedentarism in an environment that may have had an equal claim to nomadism: communities were formed, drew physical, not merely apotropaic, circles around themselves, and remained in place—and they called themselves, or saw themselves inside, a *ḥaẓōr,* a *ḥāḍirah* (settled country), *ḥaḍārah* (cultivated country), or *ḥaḍar* (vicinity); and they felt that they and their property were safe inside a *ḥaẓīrah* (enclosure, fenced in, protected precinct). Other groups lived in tents, in the "black" tents of the Bedouin, that is, and their only circle was the magic, apotropaic one, the *dār.*[55] Nevertheless, we do not know precisely who the prosperous but anathematized and condemned Arabian Ḥaẓōr, or "the kingdoms of Ḥaẓōr," were. We know, however, *where* they were: somewhere very near the place known in later Nabataean-Thamūdic times as the prosperous but ill-fated, condemned and anathematized al-Ḥijr. And we know, furthermore, that in matters of etymological deep structure *al-Ḥijr* and *Ḥaẓōr* ought to be related, and that, above all, if not etymological cognates, they are clear semantic equivalents.

In association with Ḥaẓōr, or without it, Qedar in the biblical prophetic texts cited above is imprinted with a sense that must be perceived as a sort of "scriptural fatalism." Its mere evocation triggers images of annihilation. But the Qedar were, no doubt, a concrete people, spanning centuries of actual historical time. From

738 B.C. they appear already in cuneiform inscriptions as Qidri, also Qadri, Qidarri, Qidari, and Qudari (Neo-Babylonian).[56] Furthermore, Pliny the Elder (A.D. 23/24–79) speaks of them as "the Cedrei" with full geographic clarity: "the Arabian tribe of the Conchlei adjoin those mentioned on the east *and that of the Cedrei on the south, and both of these in their turn adjoin the Nabataei*" [italics mine].[57]

Coming from Pliny and speaking of them as adjoining the Nabataeans, this last reference to the Qedar/Cedrei is of particular significance to us, for on the one hand it takes us full circle back into the "genealogical" mythopoeia of the birth of the Arab ethnos (or merely of one branch of it) from the loins of the two eldest sons of Ishmael/Ismāᶜīl, Nebayot/Nābit and Qedar/Qīdār/ Qaydār, while on the other hand it authenticates the existence of those already archaic Qedarites at the very time in history of Nabataean hegemony over northern Ḥijāz.

Ernst Axel Knauf's coherent study of the Ishmaelites takes the most historically sound and surefooted step out of the tentativeness and scriptural credulity that is apportioned to the topic as much in the Hebrew Bible as in the Islamic tradition. Furthermore, while constructing an actual history of the Ishmaelites, or of that Arabian people who might have been the Ishmaelites, he also brings into prominence a historical silhouette of Qedar, those Qedar who even historically may have already been known—at least to some—as Qudār.

Knauf isolates and identifies the biblical/Islamic Ishmaelites as *Šumuʾil* in accordance with the Assyrian records of them as a tribe, or rather as a "coalition" of tribes, or as a city, "in the desert" of northern Arabia. These Šumuʾil/Ishmaelites have kings (and queens), who are also "the kings, or queens, of the Arabs"—and of Qedar.[58] Knauf presents a list of no fewer than eight such Šumuʾil and Qedarene kings and queens from between 738 and 648 B.C.[59] It was then that the name Šumuʾil became regarded as corresponding to the biblical Ishmael, the son of Hagar, and upon which, in analogy to the twelve descendants of Isaac (Gen. 35:23), twelve parallel eponymous names of tribes were grafted (Gen. 25:13). As Knauf establishes, however, there could hardly have been a connection between the large tribal confederation of the Ishmaelites/Šumuʾil of the seventh century B.C. and the Hagarites of post-exilic times, referred to in 1 Chronicles 5:19.[60] It is within the confederacy of the Šumuʾil that the historical Qedar finds its place, and even more, a leading role. And it is Qedar's connection with the Nabataeans which brings it the closest to the chronological limits of our discussion.[61]

Returning now to where Pliny left us, we find ourselves at the high point of the flourishing of Thamūdic al-Ḥijr within the Nabataean "caravan empire." Chronologically, therefore—and geographically, too—the time and the place in which Pliny situates the Cedrei/Qedar are equally the time and the place of the Thamūd of al-Ḥijr: literally on the eve of the events and processes that led to the birth of the Thamūdic myth of the slaughter of the tabooed she-camel. The circle thus seems to have closed; only that from here on we do not possess any further information concerning Qedar, nor, for that matter, concerning Ḥaẓōr. Indeed, after the Roman occupation of Petra (A.D. 106) and the resulting political and economic restructuring of northern Ḥijāz, even the historicity of the Thamūd themselves, and with them of al-Ḥijr, of which we have predominant evidence precisely at this point in time, surrendered to myth and legend—at least from the Arabic point of view. And it is interesting and intriguing that the only semblance of survival of the name Qedār in this nebulous atmosphere of the gestation of the myth of Arab autochthony, or of Arab autochthonous myth, is the Qudār of Thamūdic myth. Indeed, I propose, and I strongly suspect, that Jawād ʿAlī had at the back of his mind that in this Arabian *Götterdämmerung* there took place, in a manner not far from Max Müller's "disease of language," the metamorphosis of the vestiges of the ancient, well-allied, and once-powerful Arabian people called Qedar into Qudār, the tragic and anathematized slayer of the she-camel that brought about the destruction of al-Ḥijr and the annihilation of the Thamūd. With Qudār and al-Ḥijr, which itself may not be very far from the equally anathematized Ḥaẓōr, we are thus at the Ishmaelite roots of a nation. The place and the role of Ṣāliḥ are here internally problematic—and necessarily part of the tragic flaw of the Thamūdic myth.

7

The Scream

■ Among the Arabian heirs of the Thamūd, even events of the magnitude of the Roman political and economic restructuring of northern Arabia were not historically apprehended, but instead were irrecognizably transformed into self-referential myth and symbol. We must, therefore, listen closely to the encoded idiom that speaks of that transformation. It is in this connection, too, that the myth of the cataclysmic total destruction of the Thamūd deserves its own hearing as well, if for no other reason than to unlock that myth's operative semantics of signs and symbols. We would be wise, too, to include into our concept of historicity the impact, and subsequent effect over "historical" time, of the highly probable contributing occurrence of an actual "recorded" natural cataclysm. We may thus make the further euhemeristic allowance that this cataclysm, even if its effects were not those of total obliteration, would nevertheless have been the right kind of "mythogenic moment" around which all preceding, as well as following, "manmade" historical woes and reversals of the Thamūd would, with mythopoeic ease, have organized themselves.

The most likely such cataclysmic factor would have been the occurrence of a geological or meteorological disturbance of the nature of an earthquake or a devastating storm. These two possibilities are indeed reflected in the qurʾānic text as well as in the mythopoeic narratives outside the Qurʾān. Exegetically, too, they are viewed as the actual physical agents of the destruction of the Thamūd. We have to stress here the "exegetical" character of the reading of both categories of texts, qurʾānic and non-qurʾānic, because exegesis of scriptural or parascriptural material, unless it is strictly spelled out as "revisionist" (and this too with undue pretentiousness), is by definition heavily tilted toward an aprioristic proposition of understanding. In the case of the destruction of the Thamūd, this is clearly reflected in the exegesis of the word *ṣayḥah* as meaning, with adequate semantic sufficiency, "punishment from heaven," presumably in the form of "an earthquake."[1]

Without that aprioristic exegetical proposition, however, the word *ṣayḥah* means "a scream" of great power and resonance, and only then may its semantics be contextually determined further, thus involving also its "history of usage"—which becomes the history of its understanding. Without reaching, at first, into its specific exegetic speculative semantics, we note that in the Qurʾān the word appears with direct and powerful unadornedness and with the kind of frequency that demands special interpretive attention. Thus, *wa akhadhathumu ṣ-ṣayḥatu*[2] ("and the scream took/seized them"); or *innā arsalnā ʿalayhim ṣayḥatan wāḥidatan*[3] ("we sent upon them a single scream"); or again *wa akhadha l-ladhīna ẓalamū ṣ-ṣayḥatu*[4] ("and the scream seized those that had acted wrongly").

Other than "the scream," what according to the Qurʾān's other reiterative contexts destroyed the Thamūd was a *ṣāʿiqah*[5] ("thunderbolt," "thunderclap," but also, "a cry of despair or of agony"); or a *ṭāghiyah*[6] ("storm with thunder and lightning," with the literal meaning of "a raging, tyrannical one," but also "a bellowing one"). The most explicit non-metaphoric and non-epithetic destroyer of the Thamūd in the Qurʾān is, however, *al-rajfah*[7] ("the tremor").

With its highly dramatic charge, "the scream" as the qurʾānic destroyer of the Thamūd is undoubtedly most intriguing and stimulating to the symbolic imagination. It was like that, too, to those exegetes, like al-Ṭabarī, and to the antiquarian compilers and narrators who retold the story of the Thamūd as their mythopoeia. Throughout their texts one senses their fascination with that destructive "scream," even though, in the end, they reach something resembling a semantic consensus that *al-ṣayḥah* equals the more straightforward *al-rajfah*, the "tremor" of an earthquake.

Thus in his narratively expanded exegesis of Qurʾān 7:78, al-Ṭabarī refers to the fateful "scream" no less than nine times,[8] and since only the term *al-rajfah* occurs in that sura (v. 78) (*fa akhadhathumu r-rajfatu*: "and they were seized by the tremor"), he actually reverses the supposed semantic interdependence between *al-rajfah* and *al-ṣayḥah,* telling us that, according to "scholars" *(ahl al-ᶜilm),* "the tremor is here the *scream* that shook them and sent them to destruction."[9]

Even though we should assume that to al-Ṭabarī the implied understanding of the Thamūdic cataclysm was that it had been caused by an earthquake, nevertheless that exegete-mythographer finds irresistible the suggestive ambiguity of the "scream" and the manner in which it dramatizes the horror and mystery of that cataclysm. Here we recognize the pervasive workings of the mythopoeic imagination despite the surface stance of commitment to exegetic "canonicity."[10]

In al-Nuwayrī's story it is the archangel Gabriel who screams upon the Thamūd the fatal scream. On the fourth day after the killing of the she-camel, after the perverse people's seclusion in their homes and after they had changed first to yellow, then to red, and finally to black—that is, after the ominous "respite" of their *"tamattuᶜ"*[11]—Gabriel spread over them "the wing of his wrath" and showered cinder-hot rocks upon them, while they sat hidden in their dug-out holes. Gabriel seized the earth by its extremes, and their houses and castles trembled. Then he extended the wing of his wrath over their domains "and *screamed a scream,* and this was their end. For seven days fire poured down upon them, and they turned to ashes."[12]

Al-Thaᶜlabī is more concise in his description of the calamity—but with no lesser a literary concern. He tells us, following in the main al-Ṭabarī,[13] that, after the Thamūd had meticulously and, it would appear, ritually readied themselves for the coming of death, on the fourth day of their *tamattuᶜ* "there came upon them a *scream* from heaven, in which there was the sound of every thunderbolt and the voice of every thing on earth that has a voice, and it cut through their hearts in their breasts, and they all perished, young and old."[14]

This Thamūdic mythopoeia of the scream has its possible euhemeristic content of reality as an earthquake, supported, at least hypothetically, by what little we have recovered of circumstantial historical-archaeological documentation. Here I should only call attention not so much to the Thamūd themselves as to their neighboring and kindred, and above all better documented, culture of Liḥyān.

Also of northwestern Ḥijāz, the Liḥyānites' main area of settlement was the valley of al-ᶜUlā, around al-Khuraybah, the site of the considerably more ancient Dedan. Altogether, Liḥyān/Dedan was historically a polity quite parallel to that of Thamūdic al-Ḥijr, and indeed, in the Nabataean period of the flowering of al-Ḥijr, the sheer proximity of the neighboring polities makes them, unavoidably, culturally and politically intertwined.

Werner Caskel offers a later chronology of Liḥyānite inscriptions and historical periodization than does much of the remaining Liḥyān scholarship.[15] He proposes that in their second major historical stage, which parallels chronologically the last decades of the Nabataean mercantile hegemony, the Liḥyānites had begun to free themselves of that hegemony. With the fall of Petra to the Romans (A.D. 105), the Nabataean rule over Liḥyān soon came to an end (A.D. 106). Here Caskel, basing himself on his chronology of Liḥyānite inscriptions, offers a summation of particular significance to us: "The late-Liḥyānite period begins with a catastrophe. Dedan [the town] is destroyed by an earthquake. The temple collapses, and the congregation that had gathered there is buried under the rubble, save a few who take refuge in a crypt. The rebuilding of the temple extended over thirty years, and in the year 22/127 [A.D.] it was not yet completed. It is presumed that only in 29/134 [A.D.] was it restored to its function."

Two Liḥyānite inscriptions recorded by Caskel may then be placed in this context: No. 70, which Caskel identifies as dedicatory or votive: ". . . *b. H*[Kh ???] . . . *ān* has devoted the statue to Dhū-Ghābat, in a place of refuge under his temple . . . their hiding place . . . and he granted . . .";[16] and, also votive, inscription No. 71: "ᶜAbd-Ghawth b. Zayd-Lāh (b.) Samām has offered this statue to Dhū-Ghābat because of the calamity which he visited upon the venerable majesties together with the venerable congregation of Dedan."[17]

We should note, as did Caskel, that here the god himself is the sender of the great calamity that drove the community of Dedan to seek refuge underground—which also reminds us of "who" annihilated the Thamūd. Above all, according to Caskel's chronology and interpretation of inscriptions, the history of Liḥyānid Dedan—and within it the episode of the rebuilding of the temple—introduces a factor of historicity as hermeneutically applicable. Caskel's material agrees entirely, and felicitously, with the principle espoused in the present study that mythogenesis and the symbolic retention of historical occurrences are ethnocentrically self-referential. In the case of a Liḥyānite, and implicitly also

Thamūdic, seismic catastrophe which, chronologically, would have practically coincided with the Roman occupation of Petra and thus with the downfall of the Nabataean "caravan empire," that catastrophe would in a particularly "efficacious" way have been suited to subsume in popular mythopoeic memory all the other historically far more decisive causes of the Thamūdic polity's demise. We know historically that Thamūd did not vanish into thin air—neither after an earthquake nor after the fall of the Nabataean metropolis—but rather went through a prolonged process of absorption into a broader Arabian ethnos; and we also know that after the earthquake Liḥyān not only rebuilt the temple of nearby Dedan but actually marginally flourished as a polity, having freed itself, ultimately by default, of Nabataean suzerainty. Knowing this, however, we are yet prepared to accommodate hermeneutically the complexity of mythogenesis and its symbolic univocity of the cosmic "scream." Likewise, on the same level of reality, we accept the story that on the site of ancient, then Liḥyānid, Dedan there is a large, hollowed-out stone cylinder over twelve feet in diameter and seven feet deep, which, according to local tradition, is the pail into which the Prophet Ṣāliḥ had milked his camel.[18]

8

The Arabian Golden Bough and Kindred Branches: Frazer, Vergil, Homer, and Gilgamesh

■ It is simply not possible to discuss the Arabian golden bough today and deny having been alerted to its topical potential by James George Frazer's *The Golden Bough*.[1] The very use (as textual item and as object) of this somewhat Victorian-ringing term may only be viewed now as Frazerian—although Frazer had no more than availed himself of the already existing currency given to it by Christopher Pitt, the English translator of Vergil from as early as 1743,[2] or of its imaginative use as the title of a painting by Turner of 1834, or of a reference to it in James Sowerby's *English Botany* of 1805.[3] Thus no sooner does the golden bough draw us to Frazer than it distracts us from him and leads us more discreetly (but discretion in this case basks in the virtue of proper textuality) to Vergil's dark forest at the "jaws of stenchful Avernus" (*Aeneid* VI, 201), the fearsome lake at the entrance to the Underworld, over which no bird could fly and live (VI, 238–42), and where Aeneas was to pluck the golden branch, "that fateful wand, so long unseen" (VI, 409), which was to allow him access to the Underworld.

Before entering into further, more structured paradigmatic contextualizations of our Arabian/Thamūdic myth of the golden bough, such as the *Aeneid* and the *Odyssey*, and, even more archetypally, the *Epic of Gilgamesh*, with its particular variant of the magic branch or "plant," we shall consider the more concrete historicity and "materiality" of some other-than-Arabian significant staffs, rods, and scepters—whether "golden" or merely ceremonially and symbolically empowered in ways that bring them close in meaning to the Arabian golden bough.

The textually clear Vergilian understanding of the symbolic function of the *aureus ramus*, present also in the iconography of Mercury bearing the *aurea virga* while conducting the dead into Hades,[4] has facilitated a restricted terminological clarity of the golden bough which, never quite deservedly, has become to us more Latin *(aureus ramus/aurea virga)* than Greek and which has not taken into account similar symbolic characteristics in other "staff" cultures—such as the ancient Egyptian one and, in our most immediate case, the Arabic. We thus have to supplement our picture of that one-sided "classical" golden staff and broaden our awareness of the functional, ritual, and symbolic validity of the staff even there where, as a symbolic artifact, it is not necessarily "materially" golden.

Beginning with the staff, or wand, which in text and image is expressedly "golden," we find in the *Homeric Hymns* Hermes, Apollo's "brother of the Golden wand," receiving from Apollo "a beautiful staff of wealth and prosperity, a golden one with three branches,"[5] while in the *Odyssey* Hermes, as *psychopompos*, calls up and leads into Hades the spirits of Penelope's wooers, holding in his hands "a fair wand of gold *[rhabdos]*, wherewith he lulls to sleep the eyes of whom he will, while others again he wakens even out of slumber."[6] So too the blind seer Teiresias in Homer's Hades was the bearer of a "golden staff" (*kruseon skaptron, Odyssey* XI, 91). Indeed, in three important instances in Teiresias's episodic mythic "life" his staff is mentioned: in his double metamorphosis from man to woman and from woman to man, in which also the symbol of the snake plays an important role; then in the story of his blindness; and, most important to us, in his functions in the Underworld.[7] But also Chryses, the priest of Apollo the Archer, is the bearer of a golden staff—clearly one of surrogate Apollonian authority (*Iliad* I, 11–15). His golden staff is, therefore, of "solar" origin, as was the golden staff that was Apollo's brotherly gift to Hermes. Only that Hermes, in this respect, is an Apollonian about-face: a projection into the chthonic realm of the Underworld—or a key to it. And Minos, too, "the glorious son of Zeus," retains his golden scepter in Hades (*Odyssey* XI, 568–569).

In this Graeco-Roman context it is thus not merely apposite but of the greatest significance for us to take into cognizance F. J. M. de Waele's observation that "Literary evidences, as well as some remnants of the customs and monuments, fully prove that throughout the whole of classical antiquity the dead protected themselves by carrying this golden bough"; to which he adds a note of an even more substantive, and substantiating, pertinence, namely, that such "A golden bough was found in the tomb of Kolonos."[8]

As regards the specific terminology of the Greek as well as the Latin staffs, which may or may not be "golden," de Waele allows us to venture into approximations between the classical and the Arabian terminological arguments by his cogent etymologizing of "rod" and "staff." "Rod" is the semantic and etymological equivalent of *rhabdos,* the soft, pliable branch, such as the Old Slavonic *vruba* ("willow twig"), [the Ukrainian *verba*], the Lithuanian *virbas,* etc. To it corresponds the Latin *virga.* The "staff," in its stiffness, firmness, and uprightness, on the other hand, is the Greek *skeptron,* becoming the Latin *sceptrum.*[9] In this context the Arabic *ghuṣnun min dhahabin,* literally a "bough," or "branch" of gold, should clearly, and in a primary sense, correspond to *rhabdos,* while the Arabic *ʿaṣā* ("staff") ought to approximate *skeptron,* both semantically and semiotically. But, as de Waele himself observes, "Naturally, the development of language will lead to an arbitrary use of the word *[skeptron],* in classical as well as in modern languages, the names of rigid staffs and flexible ones becoming mixed."[10] Thus, as a post-Homeric name for the staff, which, according to etymological semantics, would have been a *rhabdos,* there comes into currency, with Herodotus and Thucydides, the most ubiquitous *kerukeion,*[11] destined to become the even more current Latinized *caduceus.* As *kerukeion/caduceus,* the staff is certainly no longer willowlike and pliable, although one might say that it, too, through something resembling the Max-Müllerian regressive semantics of its original "crookedness," harbors the reminder of having come from a once pliable branch. Here too, characteristic of the *kerukeion/caduceus,* belong the entwined branches, or copulating snakes,[12] resembling the figure eight.

Inasmuch as the Homeric *rhabdos* and the later *kerukeion/caduceus* are a property of Hermes in his role as messenger and guide, especially as guide of souls into Hades, thus a *psychopompos,* during the Hellenistic and Roman periods the increasingly syncretistic Hermes became identified in all major respects with the

Egyptian god Thoth, who, more specifically in the Pyramid texts, figures equally as a *psychopompos*[13] bearing staffs of some special significance. We thus compellingly realize the existence of a broader scope of the symbolism of the staff in Antiquity, a symbolism which shows itself most strongly in beliefs and rites pertaining to afterlife.

Intrigued by the two *user* staffs flanking the *ankh* which Thoth displays quite emblematically in his capacity as *psychopompos,* we shall now turn to Ancient Egypt, that intensely staff-fixated cultural-historical "chronotope" that until now has remained outside our consideration.

In the unrivaled burgeoning of ancient Egyptian funerary culture, staffs figure among the most ubiquitous artifacts deposited in graves by the side of the deceased. From the Old Kingdom through the New Kingdom we find a strong, indeed growing, attestation of the deposition in tombs and pictorial representation on walls, and then specifically on coffins, of frequently numerous and diverse staffs—even in tombs of a broader social and administrative hierarchical reach, that is, not necessarily in royal tombs. These staffs are thus justly referred to by Egyptological scholarship as "staffs of the dead" *(Totenstäbe).*[14] In their striking diversity of form and size these funerary staffs reflect both religious-ritual and profane provenance and purposes. Their material is predominantly wood—sycamore, tamarisk, or acacia. In the Old Kingdom as well as the New Kingdom, gilded, gold-inlaid or gold-topped staffs are nevertheless frequent—although, in contrast, the Middle Kingdom evidences staffs of wood only.[15] Most remarkable, however, is the depiction of funerary staffs arranged in artfully stylized, palisade-like rows of painted friezes on the outside as well as on the inside of wooden coffins. Thus unquestionably symbolically insisted upon, and ultimately stylized into abstraction, the Egyptian funerary staff becomes characteristic of the funerary practice of the First Transitional Period.[16] A most striking example related symbolically and stylistically to the mortuary staff friezes of the wooden coffins is a bas-relief in the Temple of Isis at Philae. In it, represented as lying "on the ground," Osiris has a row of spikes of grain growing out of his body, and these are being watered by a priest. As the lower order of the relief, under the body of Osiris, a frieze-like row of staffs runs in an "egg and dart" pattern of *users* and *ankhs.* The symbolism here being that of regeneration from the earth, this lower order of the staffs, where the *ankh*, too, is reconfirmed as a staff in an androgynous manner, acquires the strongest possible semiotic efficacy of a chthonic life force.[17]

Whether deposited concretely by the side of the entombed corpse or represented in tomb reliefs and coffin friezes, the ancient Egyptian funerary staff thus reaches us as characterizing in some very obstinate ways—of which we still know very little—the richest of all the funerary cultures of Antiquity.

From among this great diversity of Egyptian funerary staffs we opt here, on admittedly hypothetical grounds, to single out further the already mentioned staff termed *user/uas*—both in its plain *(w3s)* and "wound" *(dʿm)* varieties.[18] Its length is approximately that of a grown man,[19] although it may also be noticeably shorter. It must not be entirely straight or even, and often shows the knottiness of the original branch. Topping it is a more or less diagonal short cross-branch, or cross-stick, which sometimes is stylized to resemble an excessively elongated head of a hound dog. Its opposite end always shows a pointed, short bifurcation. In funerary and celebratory representations of the Old, Middle, and New kingdoms it is primarily borne by male divinities, such as, for example, Anubis supporting a mummy.[20] Past the Old Kingdom, however, the *user* is found increasingly in funerary representations of figures of hierarchical status other than that of divinities;[21] and in isolated cases of unquestionable iconographic interest its carrier may be a fieldworker bearing offerings,[22] or a goatherd in the midst of his flock.[23] Especially considering the crudeness of the goatherd's *user* staff, the latter representation suggests to Ali Hassan, following in this C. G. Seligman, that the *user* staff itself is of an archaic, nomadic origin, and that bearing those traces it has survived into the New Kingdom.[24] It is, then, this recognized Bedouinity of the ancient Egyptian archaically pastoral staff—then turned ceremonial as well as iconographically mainly funerary—that takes us the closest to Arabian nomadism and pastoralism. It is in the latter that the indispensable staff of the Bedouin camel rider has retained, well into the time of Muḥammad, the basic characteristics of length and shape of that most ubiquitous of the staffs of ancient Egyptian funerary iconography. There it will be referred to, with much lesser terminological rigor, as *ʿukkāzah, mikhṣarah,*[25] *minsaʾah,* or simply generically as *ʿaṣā.*

As we already know,[26] the faithful executioner of Muḥammad's orders, ʿAbd Allāh Ibn Unays, was given as his reward the

Prophet's own staff, along with the Prophet's promise that, through that staff, he shall meet the Prophet in heaven. For that, "Possessor of the Staff in Heaven" *(Dhū l-Mikhṣarati fī l-Jannah)* became ʿAbd Allāh Ibn Unays's epithet of devotion and merit. He was laid in his grave with the Prophet's staff by his side.

The explicitly Bedouin camel staff comes to the fore also in what is as much an archaic Arabic proverb as a favored image of the still Bedouin, or Bedouinizing, periods in Arabic poetry: the "casting down of a weary desert traveler's staff," with the meaning of alighting after a desert journey for a necessarily long *(iqāmah),*[27] as well as restful and refreshing *(qarra ʿaynan),* biding. Even though some of its uses, especially the poetic ones, may appear to toy with transience, there is nevertheless an implicit "definitive" core to both the proverb and the image. This is summed up in the *Muʿallaqah* of Zuhayr Ibn Abī Sulmā:

> When they reached the water, welling over, blue,
> They lay down the staffs as does he that
> *settles down,* pitches tents to camp.[28]

In its earliest (pre-Islamic) usage, the "throwing down of the staff" is always "formulaic," and, as such, it is more than a one-dimensional proverb or image. It is retentively semiotic, never relinquishing the earnestness of its "act." Furthermore, it not only signals staidness and definitiveness, it may also announce an act of magic or of miraculous intervention. The latter aspects are part of its qurʾānic semiosis, which, through the persona of Moses, is either implanted into, or extracted from, the broader, archaic—as well as legendary-hermetic—semiosis of the staff itself in its, once again, Egyptian referentiality. Thus the Moses of the Qurʾān, while still in the presence of the "burning bush," even as he prepares himself for his meeting with Pharaoh, is told by the divine voice to "throw down his staff," as though to grow used to his subsequent wielding of the formidable magic of his staff; and, when the staff then turns into a snake, that divine voice tells him not to be afraid.[29] Then, standing before Pharaoh and his sorcerers, the self-assured Moses once again "throws down his staff" *(fa alqā ʿaṣāhu/alqi ʿaṣāka)*[30] and, as proof that his "magic" is stronger than the sorcerers' magic, the staff, again, turns into a snake.

Building on this qurʾānic topicality and, as far as the symbolism of the staff is concerned, ultimately on its almost coterminous

Egyptian referentiality, the Arabic court poet of the imperial Abbasid age, Abū Nuwās (d. 199/814 or 200/815), has already entirely metaphorized that qurʾānic episodal "scheme." Addressing in his verses an act of local rebellion in Egypt, he presents us with a scene in which it is in the name of the Caliph and "Commander of the Faithful" (Amīr al-Muʾminīn), not in that of the qurʾānic "voice from the bush," that the governor of Egypt, al-Khaṣīb ("the Fertile One") is "figured" into the role of Moses carrying in his hand the *staff* that will turn into a snake. Turning to the rebellious Egyptians, the Abbasid poet thus argues his now merely political case, while still mindful of the old symbolic and "scriptural" resonances of his images:

> For if in you there still be Pharaoh's falsehood,
> The staff of Moses [yet] remains in Khaṣīb's hand.
> The Commander of the Faithful threw at you a snake
> That shall devour and drink up the snakes of your land.[31]

But a further connotative strain must here be observed, namely that of fertility and its gifts and bounty. For the staff of Moses is here in the hand of a man who is himself "a fertile one" *(khaṣīb)*, entrusted to restore order to the land of proverbial, and even symbolic, fertility. His staff is fertile, life-giving, and of power. Such is the Egyptian legacy of the staff passed on to the Arabian lore: both funerary and life-giving.[32]

Returning now to the point before our excursus on the materiality, symbolism, and philology of the staff, we must admit that our contextualizing of the symbolic matter of the Thamūdic golden bough, that is, our move to Vergil, is itself guided by Frazer from the very opening page of his monumental work. But Frazer, as a guide to sources, is very deceptive, an intellectual trickster, one could say. His deceptiveness, however, is in the end, after the effort of twelve majestic volumes, disappointing. At least it is disappointing to those who are in pursuit of the Vergilian golden bough, not the Frazerian substitute. For to Frazer, we soon realize, the Latin poet's story of the branch of gold is merely a felicitously struck-upon name of great fascinating power—as much to himself as the "incept" as it is to us as a concept. He does not intend to dwell on the proper realm of that power, however. He makes the name his own and moves on to his true subject, or subjects, through the narrowest of escape routes—an exegetical-philological loophole: he uses Vergil's comparison of Proserpine's golden branch or bough with the mistletoe's strange hue of wintery leafage upon "an alien tree" (VI, 206).[33] This allows him to develop his own most ambitious and fascinating argument concerning priestly kingship, one that is, however, conspicuously tangential to the symbolic purpose and efficacy of the golden bough of Vergil's *Aeneid*. That argument, in turn, requires a formidable digression from Vergil, and this is then facilitated most conveniently by a tangential, or rather more strictly "marginal," exegetical connector. He builds on a brief, and single, gloss to the Sixth Book of the *Aeneid* by the fourth-century scholiast Servius. According to that gloss the golden branch of Aeneas, admittedly proper to the mysteries of Proserpine, was, "as public opinion has it" *(publica tamen opinio hoc habet)*, the bough which every claimant to the office of Rex Nemorensis, the priest-king of Diana's grove of Aricia, had to possess and, possessing it, slay the reigning priest-king in combat.[34]

From here on, armed not so much with the golden bough as with the opportune, folklore-specific mistletoe, Frazer constructs his overarching argument of priestly kingship, of the right of succession to such kingship, and—in a rambling manner that is itself almost vegetatively rank—of the taboos of power. To this one should add that Frazer also misinterprets Turner's 1834 painting, *The Golden Bough*, which does not reflect the scene of Nemi but rather, more legitimately, that of Aeneas and the Sibyl at the lake of Avernus.[35]

There is thus something conveniently utilitarian, and even opportunistic, in Frazer's choice of the Vergilian *locus classicus* of the term "golden bough" that leads him to choose that mysterious object for the general title of his sprawling opus. For in Frazer the problem of the golden bough as it figures in Vergil remains unexplored save for the briefest of references[36]—or at best it is left irretrievably buried under the symbolic and anthropological-ethnographic debris of his various other interests.[37] Thus the subject of Vergil, that is, the subject of the only legitimate evidence of a "golden bough" in all of Frazer's opus, lies hidden in his most extensive excursus into the mytho-legend of Balder the Beautiful and "the fire festivals of Europe." There it coruscates momentarily with its own light, only to disappear in broader theoretical strategies linked to the folklore and the symbolic ramifications, implications, and insinuations of the mistletoe. In Frazer's brief reference to

Aeneid VI proper, when he mentions almost incidentally that the golden bough, in the hands of Aeneas, is a kind of "open Sesame" to unlock the gates of hell, his tone is studiedly lighter and does not promise further elaboration. The only "actual" golden bough of Frazer's gigantic burden of sources, that of Vergil's *Aeneid,* thus appears as quite secondary to his main concerns. The reader's uncertainty as to Frazer's interest in the "bough" is not much tempered by his introduction of two further, even briefer and more marginalized, references that echo the Vergilian symbol of the golden bough: one of Orpheus with his lyre in one hand and willow branches in the other, depicted in a fresco representing the Netherworld;[38] and the other in the scene of Adonis parting from Aphrodite, as depicted on a sarcophagus in the Lateran. In that scene Adonis holds a branch "which has been taken to signify that he, too, by the help of the mystic bough, might yet be brought back from the gates of death to life and love."[39]

These three scenes of strong symbolic cohesiveness, certainly quite properly noticed and assessed by Frazer, nevertheless seem to have surfaced too late in that author's firmly entrenched leading idea and procedural scheme. At the point of their entering the discussion, the mistletoe already reigns supreme as Frazer's organizing symbol. Meandering through his tomes' innumerable digressions, the mistletoe *was*, and remained, the golden bough (or its substitute), representing "on homeopathic principles . . . the best possible care or preventive of injury by fire"; and considerations such as this, to Frazer, "may partially explain why Virgil makes Aeneas carry a glorified bough of mistletoe with him on his descent into the gloomy subterranean world." With "illuminating glitter" that mistletoe/golden bough would then equally "be a lamp to his feet as well as a rod and staff to his hands."[40]

After this mixing of purposes, tools of argumentation, and symbols, and literally after proposing the less than likely (even when operating within the matter of myth) envisaging of a branch of mistletoe (which must also be the golden bough) as being of the size and resiliency that would make it serve as a wanderer's "rod and staff," Frazer returns to his main concerns. These revolve around the meaning of the mistletoe more proper to folklore and ethnography—to his "tree-spirit in the oak"—and, ultimately, to the superposition of his interpretation of the myth of Balder the Beautiful upon that of the priest-king of Nemi. His own question of "What was the Golden Bough?"[41] which he asked in his disquisition almost two full volumes prior to this point, appears now almost as though it were never meant to be answered.

Our difficulties with Frazer are, however, due less to his idiosyncratic use of *Aeneid* VI than to our own discomfort over reading the mythopoeia around the Arabian *ghuṣnun min dhahabin* almost reflexively as a response to his golden bough/mistletoe. We realize that our reading of the Arabian golden bough suffers, as it were, from a psychological dependence on that much larger, oppressively pre-argued text, even though we know that, in the Arabic case, we are in possession of something Frazer, despite having made of it the title of his whole enterprise, never quite possessed: that unmistakable, unmodified by Vergilian similes or far-flung analogies, lexically and terminologically precise evidence of the golden bough's existence. So laconic in its precision, so bare, one might say, is the Arabian golden bough that in those respects it takes "technical" primacy of semiotic impact even over its extended textuality and chronological precedence in Vergil.

Had Frazer not been so zealously set on bolstering ethnographically his argument of the priestly king with the labyrinthine folklore of the mistletoe he might have with ease stayed with the terminological (and symbolic) clarity already present in Vergil's *aureus et foliis lento vimine ramus* [*Aeneid* VI, 137], as indeed it was given to him in Christopher Pitt's translation of "A mighty tree, that bears a golden bough"[42]—itself in no way a rendition entirely faithful in tone and imagist conveyance. There the golden bough is already in a Pirandellian way the title in search of its author. Ultimately, one can safely imagine that, had Frazer possessed the further literal evidence of the golden bough of the Arabian *ghuṣnun min dhahabin,* he would still have chosen to view it as the incidence of a "meandering" northern mistletoe stranded in desertic Arabia.

We shall now leave aside, at least temporarily, the Frazerian golden bough and turn with a much greater sense of comfort to Vergil's sixth book of the *Aeneid*. The story of Vergil's *aureus ramus* has certain central, as well as tangential, characteristics that are significant to us. In it the branch of gold is tied in symbolically to the Netherworld with the kind of full directness that is unusual for a symbol. And it is furthermore correct to say that there it belongs to the world of the grave—that is, to be more precise and faithful to the Vergilian sense, it leads to the world of those that have been given, or ought to be given, a physical and ritual burial. To that world the golden bough is the absolute key. Aeneas obtains that key: he cuts the golden bough at the place, and off the tree, revealed to him by the Sibylline oracle. This he does in fulfillment of the conditions set by Proserpine, the goddess-queen of the Underworld, who herself is a temporary, or half-year, dweller in her dark realm.

Aeneas's desire to enter the world of the dead is, professedly, that of filial piety—to see once more his father Anchises; but it is also quite clear that behind that desire there lies an even deeper one: to know the fate that awaits not him alone but the state and realm that he is about to found. This is signaled from the outset of his quest through the words which he addresses to the Sibyl: *tuque, o sanctissima vates, / prescia venturi, da—non indebita posco / regna meis fatis—Latio considere Teucros* (And you, O most holy prophetess, foreseeing the future, grant—and I ask no powers outside the scope of my destiny—that the Teucrians may rest in Latium [*Aeneid* VI, 65-67]).

Throughout his descent into the Underworld Aeneas is accompanied and guided by the Sibyl, who is the carrier of the golden bough. The golden bough, however, is needed only to give Aeneas passage through those realms of the Underworld that are meant for those damned and punished. As he comes to the "door" that separates the realm of the damned from the realm of the blessed, he performs what should be understood as a ritual ablution (v. 636) and then "fixes the branch upright on the threshold" *(ramumque adverso in limine figit).* His rites are thus performed, and the golden bough delivered to Proserpine—by which we are also confirmed in the certainty that Aeneas has reached his destination. The golden bough will not be mentioned again in what remains of Aeneas's sojourn in the Underworld.

Aeneas now enters the second (or rather third) realm, the Groves of the Blessed and the Halls of Bliss (v. 639). It is here that he finds his father, Anchises, who transmits to him the prophecy of the future of his lineage. The earlier "prophecy" of the Sibyl has been only this latter prophecy's semiotic cue. This prophecy, we realize, is the substance behind the semiotic message of the golden bough—as much as being the key that unlocks the gates to the Underworld is the golden bough's instrumental signal. What this means is that with the enunciation of the golden bough in *Aeneid* VI, we know, or expect to be led to the knowledge of, two interdependent things: the descent to the Netherworld and the revelation of a transcendent prophecy.

Vergil, however, was working neither in a literary nor in a deep-symbolic space of unique ideas. His predecessor and model in both these respects was the *Odyssey*, where in Book XI a close-to-analogical structuring of signs and symbols exists—this aside from the "frame story" of the descent to Hades, or rather, to be more precise, of Odysseus's *nekyia*.[43]

In the Homeric epic, Odysseus, instructed by Circe, sails to the perpetually fog-bound land of the Cimmerians at the frontiers of the world. There, in an omphalos-like site of access to the Netherworld, Odysseus "drew his sharp sword . . . and dug a pit about a cubit long and a cubit wide and into it poured sacrificial libations for all the dead" (*Odyssey* XI, 25–26)—and we, keeping in mind our Arabian contexts, are not at all incidentally reminded that Muḥammad, too, dug up with the sword the pit/grave that revealed to him the golden bough and brought back the memory of the Last of the Thamūd.

Odysseus then sacrificed sheep and let their blood run into the pit, and thus standing on the threshold of Hades called up the "souls" of the dead, his main purpose in this being the summoning and questioning of the spirit of Teiresias, that is, asking him to *prophesy*.[44] When the seer Teiresias finally appears at the pit, he bears "a staff of gold" (vv. 90–91) and, upon drinking of the sacrificial blood from the pit, "prophesies" to Odysseus of his return to Ithaka, where, till the end of his days, he will live surrounded by his prosperous people (vv. 100–137).

Now properly in Hades, not on its threshold, there also appears to Odysseus "Minos, the glorious son of Zeus, golden scepter in hand, giving judgment to the dead from his seat, while they sat and stood about the king through the wide-gated house of Hades."[45] Although clearly of a derivative semiotic importance in its fuller context, the "golden scepter" of Minos as the attribute of royal or judicial authority is nevertheless noticed and singled out among the things Odysseus encounters in Hades.

To be differentiated in Odysseus's Hades are the two dimensions of knowledge: the knowledge of the future and that of the past. The prophecy about the future comes only from Teiresias, the blind seer who carries the golden staff, while the information, or the narrative, about events of the past is given Odysseus by his now Hades-dwelling mother. There is no confusion of, or interference between, these two dimensions. Because of this, too, we become more aware of the symbolic and chthonic attributes of both and of their directing, or affective, semiotics.

There is between *Aeneid* VI and *Odyssey* XI one further motif recurrence—or call it structural parallelism—that ought to be significant to us and is characteristic of the ritual and symbolic procedure in both texts as regards gaining entry into the Underworld. It is the obligatory insistence that, as a precondition to entering the realm of Hades, the "intruding" hero fulfill the requirement of ritually burying his missed, or unminded, dead companion. Precisely because this motif is given in both epics symbolic weight and prominence that go far beyond its seemingly adventitious and digressive appearance in the respective narratives taken in isolation, we receive a reinforced sense of some implicit link between the golden bough, the main *artifact of descent* into the realm of the dead to obtain prophecy of some transcendent legacy and destiny, and the signaling presence of an almost intrusively incidentally appearing "motif" of the grave.[46] This motif of the grave, in order to possess a broad signaling validity, does not even explicitly beg for justification—other than some "self-understood," archaic, and fully ritualized act of purification and apotropaism. In that, it is the prefiguration of the "pit" itself and of the ritually sanctioned descent into it,[47] a descent in which the golden bough will have its place.

Thus in *Odyssey* XI, 51-80, Elpenor extracts from Odysseus the promise to bury him, while in *Aeneid* VI, 149-189, Vergil, in a manner that is not merely an imitation but betrays a strong hermeneutical intent opposite the Homeric text, makes Aeneas give a ritually distinctly archaizing heroic burial to his companion Misenus. Only through such burial will the danger be avoided that "the gods' curse" fall upon Odysseus (*Odyssey* XI, 73) and only so the defilement of Aeneas's fleet by unattended death will be cleansed (*Aeneid* VI, 150); and, holding fast to Vergil's hermeneutics, we follow the Sibyl's admonishing counsel to Aeneas, "only so shall you survey the Stygian groves and realms the living may not tread" (*Aeneid* VI, 154-155). We thus know that, in deriving his Misenus from the *Odyssey*'s Elpenor, Vergil not only intends to give a ritual and symbolic sense to the burial of Misenus but that, by doing so, he also gives, from within his own text, a strong interpretive reading to the Homeric Elpenor—the latter reading remaining most needed and critically missed in both scholiae and criticism.[48] And yet, it is because of Misenus (and partly also because of Palinurus) that we know more of Elpenor.

The difficulty that Misenus encounters with criticism, classical and modern alike, is due to the fact that in the Vergilian epic his persona appears overshadowed by his own "shadow image," or *Doppelgänger,*[49] that is, by Palinurus, who, rather than Misenus, is with critically uncalled-for ease taken to be Elpenor's primary analogue. In the structural sense within the *Aeneid,* and in his equally structurally appraised projection back to the *Odyssey,* however, Palinurus is not the primary analogue to Elpenor, despite their similarities—including that of etymology-toying alliteration. He is only a secondary motival "restatement." For, although in the *Aeneid* both Palinurus and Misenus, like Elpenor of the *Odyssey,* are unburied heroes that require a heroic burial, it is only Misenus's burial, like that of Elpenor, that is clearly tied to the fulfillment of heroic destiny. Palinurus, on the other hand, only begs Aeneas to give his body a burial. He does not call upon "the wrath of the gods" nor threaten with the "defilement of the fleet." Thus in both the *Odyssey* and the *Aeneid* the ritual obligations for the descent into the Netherworld are satisfied—one of these being the satisfaction or, respectively, the promise in due time fulfilled (*Odyssey* XII, 9–55), of the heroic burial. In an important manner this is made hermeneutically clear through Vergil's introduction of Misenus, who thus, intertextually, "explains" Elpenor almost as a gloss. Palinurus does no more than add further detail, as it were, to the persona of Misenus. One could go as far as to insist that structurally—and symbolically—Palinurus is irrelevant; or, considered without further discrimination as an element of Vergilian epic narrative and its sources, he is a beneficiary, together with Misenus, of the distribution "of that which the Homeric *nekyia* communicates of Elpenor."[50] Even Norden, somewhat hesitantly, admits that "if one of the two episodes [i.e., of Misenus and Palinurus] be at all secondary, it would be the episode of Palinurus."[51] And, since obtaining the golden bough is in the *Aeneid*'s *nekyia* a matter of key factitive and symbolic pertinence, the episode of Misenus being part of it should in itself suffice. This cannot be said of the episode of Palinurus.[52]

If we are also certain of being able to establish a strong archetypal and structural affinity between the epic of Gilgamesh and the Graeco-Roman "golden bough" sources,[53] we must, nevertheless, first register the mythopoeically procedural differences between the two. For Gilgamesh obtains his magic bough (or "plant") not at the beginning but at the end of his journey to the land of Dilmun, or the distant world at the edge of things that lies past "the waters of death," where Utnapishtim, the mythic forerunner and textual model of the biblical Noah, lives a life of eternal existence, thus godlike, but also of total isolation, save for the presence of his equally immortalized wife. The world to which Gilgamesh journeys, or into which he intrudes, corresponds closely to that of Hades, and his quest is explicitly a quest for immortality. Although not ending in a "prophecy," it too ends—as far as Tablet XI of the epic can carry us—in the fulfillment of a polity-founder's destiny. A certain air of lyrical diminuendo characterizes the end of Tablet XI, not, however, a tone of dispirited resignation. We also easily imagine that a closure of the epic has been achieved, or that the closure is near.[54]

For the archetypal and structural ties between the epic of *Gilgamesh* and its Greek and Latin genre companions, the *Odyssey* and the *Aeneid*, to be understood properly—or for them even to be accepted as such—one must place the quest of Gilgamesh within a structural paradigm offered more clearly by these two later genre-"variants." Thus the part of the quest of the Homeric hero which leads him into the Underworld and the parallel segment of the quest of his Vergilian counterpart both begin with a "guidance" or an "initial prophecy." In the *Odyssey* this is provided in the person of Circe,[55] and in the *Aeneid* in that of the Sibyl.[56] In the *Gilgamesh Epic*[57] there appears, at the precise structural point at which, respectively, we had encountered Circe and the Sibyl, the more ambiguous "divine barmaid" Siduri, "who dwells by the edge of the sea."[58] She at first tries to dissuade Gilgamesh from even contemplating his perilous quest:

> Gilgamesh, whereto do you run?
> The life which you seek you will not find;
> (For) when the gods created mankind,
> They allotted death to mankind,
> (But) life they retained in their keeping.
> You, O Gilgamesh, let your belly be full;
> Day and night be merry;
> Make every day (a day of) rejoicing.
> Day and night do dance and play.
> Let your raiment be clean,
> Your head be washed, (and) yourself be bathed in water.
> Cherish the little one holding your hand,
> (And) let the wife rejoice in your bosom.
> This is the lot of [mankind . . .].[59]

This advice from Siduri to Gilgamesh has led Gilgamesh scholarship to the awkwardly flattened-out characterization of its stemming from "a hedonistic philosophy of life,"[60] or, as the archetypal psychologist and *Gilgamesh* interpreter Rivkah Schärf Kluger, herself just barely avoiding the cultural-historically minimalizing designation of hedonism, phrases it, "She [Siduri] wants to pull him back into a full natural life, to involve him again in the Epicurean *carpe diem,* 'pluck the day.' That is her advice, and it sounds terribly modern. 'Enjoy life as long as you can, for afterwards you will be dust under the earth.' Which is a discarding of all other aspects of inner values."[61] Both the philologists' and the Jungian analyst's hermeneutics, however, fail to grasp the symbolism at play in the motif and the dictates of archaic epic structure that combine to give this text its operative meaning. Siduri's advice to Gilgamesh "sounds terribly modern" indeed, but the context into which it belongs, its own formally controlling epic time and space, does not allow it to rest well in our facile "modernity." It clings too tenaciously to being "terribly" archaic. Visualized in a structural diagram, it is a heroic crossroads, where, in his quest, the hero is to choose between the narrow path and the broad highway, between taking the road to the right or to the left. It is thus part of his heroic test. Joseph Campbell thus quite properly notes that in Gilgamesh "the passage represents an initiatory test, not the moral philosophy of the ancient Babylonians."[62]

Furthermore, in a manner quite noticeable to those familiar with pre-Islamic Arabic archaisms, from the point of view of the earliest testimony of classical (pre-Islamic) Arabic poetry, not even such an understanding of Siduri's words would fully comprehend the archaic heroic stance. Here the fourteen verses of Tablet X, column iii do not merely remind us of, but literally produce a textual model for the "censuress" *(ʿādhilah),* a rigorously formalized thematic segment of the pre-Islamic *qaṣīdah* (ode) whose occurrence has strict structural and hermeneutic implications. In the *qaṣīdah* this *ʿādhilah* is the early Arab poet's "second voice." As such she is also, above all, that poet's admonishing, discomforting, and "corrective" voice. She is thus designated to be "non-heroic," that is, to be the non-individualistic, communal voice: the speaker for those controlled and controllable values challenged and endangered by the "hero," or by the individual. Through this "other voice" we are given to understand that the hero, bound for adventure, is imperiling not only himself but also the communal assumptions of life. As a "dramatizing" scheme, or as an allegorization of agents within the poem, the pre-Islamic Arabic *ʿādhilah*, the feminine counter-voice which, conveniently, may also become the likely voice of the poet-hero's keeper of the hearth, is thus above all an inner voice that reflects the hero's social more than personal "second" awareness of himself, of his *stasis* within that which is held to be the tolerable, or even acceptably desirable, communal norm. While representing warning and guidance, this "other" voice must, however, be defied and transcended if the poet is to achieve heroic status and live out his destiny. Ultimately, therefore, the hero even instills *value* in a system of things he has transgressed or rejected. He reanimates the monotony of the weave of the social fabric through engrafting it with the exhilaration of legend and myth, or at least he inspirits it with a personal gesture. Otherwise, the *ʿādhilah* is also the earliest Arabic literary expression of allegorized psychomachia. Textually, however, vis-à-vis the Old Babylonian Version of *Gilgamesh,* she is insinuatingly close to "the divine barmaid" Siduri.[63]

Thus in a poem of heroic boast by the pre-Islamic bard ʿAntarah, in which that tribal hero is called to assist his kin in battle, the closing section—and motif—is that of the *ʿādhilah.* In it ʿAntarah scorns the *ʿādhilah*'s attempt to warn him of the dangers of warlike life:

17. From morning on she filled me with the fear of death
    As though I had never chanced it.
18. "Death is a desert waterhole," I answered her,
    "And I must drink from it my full cup.
19. Shame be on you, you misbegotten, and know
    That I shall die all the same, even if not slain in battle."[64]

To the heroic brigand poet ʿUrwah Ibn al-Ward the "censuress" who disapproves of his hazardous life may be his woman, or wife. His answer is that "she go easy with her blame," and "leave his soul alone to its own will." He assures her that only by giving all he possesses, and even his life, will he acquire living glory, because

3. Tales remain, while a young brave does not live forever,
    [His soul] turned into an owl that circles over
        heaped-up cairns,[65]
4. In colloquy with the stones, complaining
    To all known and unknown.[66]

A pre-Islamic poet whose poems rarely lack the motif of the "censuress" is Ḥātim al-Ṭāʾī. This poet's path to glory and to the immortality of his name was his boundless generosity. His "censuress," therefore, centers her blame on his self-destructive openhandedness:

1. O censuress, how she accosted me with blame,
   As though I wronged her when giving of my flocks.
2. O censuress, generosity will not destroy me,
   Nor will blame secure eternal life
      to a miser's soul.
3. But a young man's noble ways shall be recalled,
      though his bones
   Lie hidden in the grave, his remains wasted.[67]

It is a later poet, however, the ʿAbbāsid conceptualizer Abū Tammām, who gives us the interpretive summation of the archaic Arabic *ʿādhilah* motif:

3. O my censuress, harsh is the voyager's night,
   But harsher still is the voyager's lot.
4. Leave me with life's trepidations to humor them,
   As life's greatest fears are trailed by new desires.
5. Did you not know that to stand fast
   In nightly journeys, in misfortunes's face,
      is friend and brother of success?
6. Leave me to my unbending ways. Let them be
      either my fortune, or else
   Let mourning women moan over me![68]

Returning now to Tablet X of the Assyrian version of *Gilgamesh*, we note that it is only there that we find a different, or more complete, image of Siduri. There, Gilgamesh beseeches "the divine barmaid" to tell him which is the way to Utnapishtim (X, ii, vv. 15–19). She at first tries to dissuade him from daring to pursue such an unattainable goal:

21. "Gilgamesh, there has never been a crossing;
27. (And) when you arrive at the waters of death,
       what will you do?"

Then, however, Siduri gives in to Gilgamesh's determination and reveals to him that "there is Urshanabi, the boatman of Utnapishtim" (v. 28), and that he is the one who can ferry him to where Utnapishtim lives eternally. Thus Gilgamesh, ferried by Urshanabi, arrives at the waters of death (X, iii, v. 50).[69]

A structural and thematic identification of Siduri, "the barmaid who lives by the edge of the sea," is now possible. Within an obviously Proppian scheme, this remote "divine barmaid" emerges—motivally and narratologically—as akin to both Homer's Circe and Vergil's Sibyl, but also close, or supplemented by, the nymph Calypso of *Odyssey* V. Furthermore, Siduri enters the Sumerian narrative at a point that is closely analogical to the points at which Circe and the Sibyl enter their respective narratives—that is, if, within the narrative techniques of orality, we take the Homeric Calypso to be Circe's extended persona. This way we do not contradict, but merely extend, the historicist source-criticism already outlined by Wilamowitz (1884) and more recently summarized by Gregory Crane.[70] Of the two Homeric Siduri parallels it is, however, more important for us to deal with Circe first.

According to the Old Babylonian redaction (or what we possess of it), Siduri's structural as well as motival function is to serve as threshold before, or facilitator of, a heroic endeavor and, being herself "divine" or "semi-divine," as an ensurer of some degree of success of that mission. Thus she enables Gilgamesh to find the boatman who will take him across "the waters of death." With this Siduri also fulfills the important condition of her own Sibyl-like liminality, which, too, is a radical precondition of "prophecy." In ways that are both mythopoeically transparent and structurally deterministic, Siduri thus knows, and is capable of revealing, the secret of the access to immortality. In that capacity, like the Sibyl of *Aeneid* VI, she can direct Gilgamesh to the boatman Urshanabi, who, himself, is none other than a Sumerian/Babylonian Charontes.

Returning now to Calypso, "she who conceals" (*kalypt* meaning "to cover," "to conceal"),[71] who, as the daughter of Atlas, is also destined to live in a most distant land, the island Ogygie, which is "the navel of the sea," we shall best refer to Arthur Ungnad's essay "Gilgamesch-Epos und Odyssee" (1923), in which that early participant in the debate over the *Odyssey* parallel pays special attention to establishing points of contact between the Homeric nymph and Siduri. He does not speak of Circe, however, but rather sees a connection between Gilgamesh's reaching Siduri's island and his embarkation from there to the even more distant place of paradise-like repose inhabited by Utnapishtim and Odysseus's embarkation from Calypso's island to the land of the Phaeacians and the palace of Alcinous. Ungnad sums up his "points of contact" by suggesting that "the journey of Gilgamesh to the Underworld and that of Odysseus could hardly be viewed as internally unconnected."[72] The problem here, however, is that in Homer it is Circe, not Calypso, who offers us the more decisive parallel with Siduri and the quest of Gilgamesh.

It is precisely here, therefore, that we realize how much Calypso and Circe are to be brought into one persona when speaking of their broader relationship or parallel with "the divine barmaid" Siduri's role in the quest of Gilgamesh. Thus, if Alcinous in the *Odyssey* represents a similar station (and *locus*) to that of Utnapishtim in *Gilgamesh,* then, indeed, we are allowed to compare (as does Arthur Ungnad) Calypso with Siduri. But it is only through Circe that Odysseus is directed to those domains, or dimensions, of the Underworld that are of abiding significance in the symbolism of his experience, not just the respite of a placid, visionary episode of his encounter with Alcinous.

Before proceeding to Gilgamesh's encounter with Utnapishtim the Distant, reference must be made to a further intervening structural and motival element which, to varying degrees, is common to all three of the epics discussed. We have already noted the almost mechanical, ritualized requirement in both the *Odyssey* and the *Aeneid* of the appearance of the motif of the titular hero's friend, or companion, who, having died a senseless death, becomes, precisely because of the senselessness of his death, all the more strongly a reminder of mortality to the hero who is about to cross the threshold of the Underworld.[73]

Endowed with considerably more pathos, yet without disrupting the essential parallelism of relationships, is the *Gilgamesh* scene/motif of the titular hero's dead friend Enkidu. It introduces Gilgamesh's request to be led to the Sumerian epic's version of the *nekyia*—the secret of Utnapishtim—and is then also repeated in the same formulation in Utnapishtim's address to Gilgamesh.[74] By bringing together the three epics at the converging point of the death of the three (or four, including Palinurus) companions of the respective titular heroes we become more fully aware of the nature of Vergil's hermeneutical reading of the *Odyssey*'s Elpenor episode and of how close in the structural and symbolic sense it brings us to the much more archaic *Gilgamesh*.[75] It is, furthermore, in the Sumerian structure that the "burial" of the friend is also strongly implied as carried out prior to the passage to Utnapishtim; and, although the damaged text does not give us a definitive picture of the burial, Gilgamesh's highly lyrical and emotive elegy for Enkidu presupposes that the burial rites have either already been performed or that the elegiac song and dirge of Gilgamesh are themselves part of those rites.[76]

The structures of three epics have thus come together and, as a result, in sharing in the allocation of certain common motival arrangements, have spoken to us with a heightened supratextual force of the semiotics of form. And what may be called the Sumerian epic's main mythos as well as its highest concentration of symbolic intensity thus comes introduced onto a fully prepared ground. Now Gilgamesh finally faces Utnapishtim the Distant and directs to him the question for whose sake he had crossed the waters of death:

> 7. "[Tell me], how did you enter into the company of
> the gods and obtain life (everlasting)?"

To which Utnapishtim replies in a manner that in this first context of the question is bound to remain highly enigmatic:

> 9. "Gilgamesh, I will reveal to you a hidden thing.
> 10. Namely, a secret of the gods will I tell you."[77]

For at this point the story of the deluge begins to develop (vv. 11-154) into an unmistakable "story of Noah"—although without even a trace of the biblical genealogical, and tribal-ideological, framing apparatus.

What interests us, and what interested the *Gilgamesh* mythologist (or mythologists), is the Sumerian proto-Noah's, that is, Utnapishtim's, own obtaining of godlike immortality, his own quest that must now be repeated by Gilgamesh; and it is only with Gilgamesh that we regain here the "culture hero" figura. Thus in verse 187 of Tablet XI we are told that to Atrah[kh]asis, "the exceedingly wise one," that is, to Utnapishtim, the god Ea, who "alone understands every matter" (v. 175), had "shown a dream, and so he learned the secret of the gods" (v. 187). But we are not told with any specificity "what was the secret of the gods." Was the punishment of the "flood" because of Utnapishtim's acquisition of "the secret"? Does the god Enlil's final acceptance of Utnapishtim's salvation from the flood mean the acceptance that "the secret of the gods" should now be in Utnapishtim's hands when he, Enlil, pronounces over him and his wife:

> 193. "Hitherto Utnapishtim has been but a man;
> 194. But now Utnapishtim and his wife shall be like
> unto us gods."[78]

Enlil, however, restricts and in a semiotic sense specifies the place, and ultimately also the nature, of Utnapishtim's eternal existence:

> 195. "In the distance, at the mouth of the rivers,
> Utnapishtim shall dwell!"[79]

Not at all the imagined hero, but lying idly on his side or on his back (v. 5), in total isolation from the realm of the mortals, that is, from those "living," and only accessible through his Charontes-like boatman: thus "exists" the man from whom Gilgamesh hopes to learn the secret of immortality.

The flood story told, Utnapishtim subjects Gilgamesh to the conditions of the first promise, or test, of immortality: he imposes upon him the test of not sleeping for six days and seven nights. Having failed this test, Gilgamesh readies himself for his return to the land of mortality (vv. 234-257) "through the gate through which he came" (v. 207). Utnapishtim's wife's pity for Gilgamesh, however, moves Utnapishtim to call Gilgamesh back and to utter to him the words he had once before spoken in his enigmatic introduction to the story of the flood. But now the enigma will be unveiled. The "secret of the gods" shall be brought up from the chthonic depth of the sea. Once again, Utnapishtim thus spoke to Gilgamesh:

> 266. "Gilgamesh, I will reveal to you a hidden thing,
> 267. Namely, a [secret of the gods will I] tell you:
> 268. There is a plant like a thorn . . . .
> 269. Like a rose (?) its thorn(s) will pr[ick your hands].
> 270. If your hands will obtain that plant, [you will find new life]."[80]

Upon hearing this, Gilgamesh ties heavy stones to his feet and is pulled by those stones into the abyss, where he sees the plant.

He plucks the plant, cuts the stones from his feet, and comes up to the shore. There he shows it to Urshanabi:

> 278. "Urshanabi, this is a wondrous (?) plant,
> 279. Whereby a man may obtain his former strength (?) . . . .
> 281. Its name is 'The old man becomes young
> as the man (in his prime).'"[81]

Gilgamesh intends to take that wondrous plant back to Uruk, but on the way he stops by a pool with cool water. He puts the plant by the water's edge and bathes; but a serpent emerges from the water, is attracted to the plant by its fragrance, snatches it, and disappears once again in the deep. When it reappears, it has sloughed its skin. The wondrous plant/branch is lost forever to Gilgamesh, and the snake is its heir (vv. 284-289).

> 290. Then Gilgamesh sat down and wept.[82]

Gilgamesh's return to Uruk is, nevertheless, of symbolic significance, for, unlike the successful possessor of immortality, Utnapishtim, whose existence is blessed within an otherworldly setting of Elysian Fields of inaction and of implicit aimlessness, Gilgamesh returns to Uruk as a mortal who is, nonetheless, a builder of his own permanence in a well-founded, secure polity. In its closure, therefore, as well as in all its main motival-symbolic and structural points of contact with *Odyssey* XI and *Aeneid* VI, the *Gilgamesh Epic* speaks of things that in diverse, admittedly discreet ways are tied in with our discussion of the golden bough. Above all, the second citing in the *Gilgamesh Epic* (vv. 266-268) of the "secret of the gods," which Utnapishtim possessed and which Gilgamesh strove to gain, helps to free the Sumerian epic's key symbol, the plant/branch (which is its golden bough variant and which can secure passage through the gates of mortality), from its semiotic opacity as a mere incongruous attachment to the "biblically" articulated Noah story.[83] It gives it instead congruity and semiotic validity precisely because it finds its rightful motival company in the golden bough of *Aeneid* VI and the golden staff of Teiresias. In the end, all three heroes, Gilgamesh, Odysseus, and Aeneas, emerge out of their encounter with death/eternity, the time elapsed and the time to come, as builders, rebuilders, and founders.[84]

Conclusion

■ Unlike the Vergilian/Frazerian golden bough, and unlike the "plant to make old young again" of Gilgamesh, the Arabian golden bough does not come down to us with any textual intentionality as an offshoot of vegetative nature or even as an image out of a magic parasitic flora, as Frazer would see such things—even though it, too, by being named *ghuṣnun,* that is, a branch, must plant in our minds the idea of vegetation. Beyond that, its "text" does not let us know much about its characteristics. It is merely a branch of gold that lies in a grave buried together with its ancient tragic possessor. It, too, could be a dead twig, if it could be said that a twig of gold is dead, or can die, being both chthonic and solar. Furthermore, unlike its Vergilian namesake, it was not purposefully sought and obtained as a precondition to entering the "pit." It is a part of that "pit." That is, it is not a key that from without unlocks it, as does Vergil's golden bough, which only legitimizes the hero's further *katabasis,* at whose end there lies the great prophecy of Rome—the future. In a votive gesture, the Vergilian golden bough is relinquished at the threshold of that future, for, like all keys, it unlocks but does not itself cross the threshold, beyond which it is no longer needed. The Thamūdic golden bough, on the other hand, unlocks a tragic myth, that of the Thamūd, from within the dimension of the past alone. It does not make an immediate allowance for the prophecy that must be the future. It offers only the knowledge of its own past. What happens thereafter depends on the one who digs open the grave and finds the golden bough—who knows it, "recognizes" it. Its prophecy is not the explicitly articulated future of the building of a city, of a felicitous and beneficent homecoming, or of a precisely drawn trajectory of an empire—as is the case in the Sumerian, Greek, and Latin epics. It must be mediated. The knowledge of its own past, its myth, is all it offers and demands. But it deposits these things into the strangest and most fateful hands.

The Arabian golden bough, as we know from the circumstances of its unearthing, is not an object devoid of its own time frame: it comes out of a mythical, but nevertheless "specific," time frame. It thus harbors its own paradox. Then, too, coming from the past of myth, it is also a carrier of a message, a reminder of a tragic flaw in the polity of the Thamūd. And, coming from a grave that is not "accidental," as the *ḥadīth* text would have it, but linked by name and place to the main bearer of the Thamūdic tragic flaw—as it is linked to a city that itself is a relic, a city of the dead not just mythically—it is meant to speak of things out of the past. Only then, not in the end but at the precise moment of its unearthing and "recognition," does it touch on things to come, even though, on the surface, the latter seems a less apparent projection.

All in all, if only because of being rendered "inanimate" through its entombment, the Arabian golden bough suggests a certain analogy with the golden staff of Teiresias. It is found in the Underworld, or the world of graves and dead cities, and it does not suggest any direct efficacy. It harbors, or shelters, symbolic meaning rather than effecting it.

On the other hand, the twig of gold plucked by Aeneas from an oak tree at the shore of the Avernus, with its power to open the gates of the Underworld and to give the knowledge of destiny, is eminently performatory. So too is, or might have been, the still chlorophyll-green (one assumes) "plant" of Gilgamesh, which he brings out of the waters' depth in the horizontally remotest, not chthonically "deepest," Sumerian Elysian Fields—although at this point refractions of spatial symbolic geometry no longer affect symbolic "location."

A further differentiating point in the case of the Arabian golden bough is that, unlike the Latin and Sumerian variants, it is neither the goal nor the means of a "quest" within which it would bear a meaning sufficiently defined to satisfy narrative expectations. In its "static" appearance, it indeed lies closer to the iconic symbolism of the Greek staff of Teiresias; although even here it escapes—if no more than through its textual paucity—an easily graspable meaning, the kind of meaning that Teiresias's staff acquires through the cumulative hermeneutics of Greek mythological intertextuality.

The Arabian golden bough stirs, at first, only a disturbing awareness of an archetype and symbol which is very deeply encoded, but then, paradoxically, almost irritatingly cast up to the semantic surface. In a sense that invites an analogy with archaeology, the Arabian golden bough must be "dug up"—not with a spade, however, but with a sword—rediscovered and retextualized. Then the symbol will grow into myth and the myth will show its archetypal bedrock. Otherwise the golden bough found by the Prophet Muḥammad remains without its own story—beyond the denuded incidence of the "finding," which will remain owing its prehermeneutic meaning to no more than the singularity of the "finder."

We, therefore, have to ask further questions as well as be reminded of avenues of understanding explored beforehand. Thus we have already established that there was a tragic flaw in the polity of the Thamūd, and that out of the opacity and near incidentalness of the tragic actors/victims of the cataclysm that resulted from that flaw there emerge only two abiding figures: Ṣāliḥ of the She-Camel and Qudār, the She-Camel's slayer. Of these two, Ṣāliḥ, the victor who, paradoxically, loses not only his community but also his land, vanishes in an almost pastoral, melancholy dénouement that is quite Abrahamic in its reenactment of the migration toward Palestine. The vanquished Qudār, however, remains in the land of the Thamūd, buried there together with a golden bough, as the true reminder of the tragic legacy.

Thus rests the myth, or the legend, of the curse upon the Thamūd, until it is called up again by Muḥammad, the Prophet of the inheritors of that legacy. How much Muḥammad is the spokesman for that autochthonous Arabian/Thamūdic legacy becomes even clearer when we compare the two strains of Arabic mythopoeia (both qurʾānic and extra-qurʾānic), namely, the Thamūdic Arabian strain and that other, tangential and consciously adoptive strain that revolves around the Old Testament/ Gospel amalgam. Thus, whereas Muḥammad by unearthing the golden bough establishes contact with "the last of the Thamūd," al-Thaʿlabī relates that it is Jesus of the house of David, the son of Maryam, who has a similar access to the pale of the other (his own), parallel autochthony: before his disciples Jesus recognizes the dust that had once been the heel of Sām, the son of Noah, and brings him back from his grave so that he may narrate to the disciples the story of the flood. Then Jesus returns him to his grave.[1]

It is also the burden of this legacy—its unearthing and recognition—that brings us again to the actual historical moment of the Raid on Tabūk; and under the burden of that Thamūdic legacy, too, we witness that historical moment turn into the reenactment of the overarching myth.

This means, furthermore, that we are approaching the end of Muḥammad's Medinan period. Almost all the mythopoeia of the tragedy of the Thamūd has by then been told and retold in the Meccan portions of the Qurʾān—except one, that of the finding of Qudār's/Abū Righāl's grave and of the golden bough in that grave. This episode, however, is not qurʾānic. It remained a symbolic afterthought out of the darkest of Arabian autochthony, and Muḥammad, as its unmediated narrator, reserved it to himself. It became his personal encounter with Arabian myth and, even more, his own mythopoeia. In it, as we already know, Muḥammad reenacts the agonies and uncertainties of Ṣāliḥ in his own prophetic mission;[2] and in this reenactment it was not at all accidental, but necessary, for him to produce an encounter with Qudār.

The structure of that reenactment/encounter thus reveals to us two equations. One is between Muḥammad and Ṣāliḥ as two separate prophetic identities, where Ṣāliḥ is drawn from the ahistorical time of myth, autochthony, and a cyclic moral parable that reflects the archaic sense of religion as trial in obedience. In it Muḥammad is the fully historical agent who, nevertheless, senses the burden of that cyclic prophetic ahistoricity that weighs upon him to the degree that it brings about between the two prophetic personae—precisely during the Raid on Tabūk—an almost perfect ideosynthesis. The other equation is between Muḥammad and the composite figure of Qudār as both Qudār the taboo breaker of the Thamūdic myth of the slain she-camel and as Qudār/Abū Righāl, the mysterious bearer of a golden bough. These equations, each one with its composite mythopoeically acting persona, are what in the end give meaning to Muḥammad's producing the "surprise" of the golden bough and of the conjuring of the myth or memory of Qudār/Abū Righāl.

From the point of view of the symbol, we must not entertain any doubt that the possession of the golden bough marks Qudār/Abū Righāl for special destiny—as much as it is meant to remind us that in his own past mythic sphere he was the executor of a special and tragic destiny. Our hermeneutical effort cannot possibly stop at the almost piquing textual banality of "a certain" Abū Righāl's grave and golden bough being found by Muḥammad in circumstances that, if devoid of context, might easily be taken to be self-serving or merely anecdotal and perfunctory. We have already explored the ambiguities of Qudār's likely entry into the Thamūdic myth—and of his place in it. We know that as the villain of that myth he was nevertheless consistently spoken of in a tone not entirely removed from the heroic: the evil hero, the tragic hand of mythic predestiny—in other words, as a figure without whom Ṣāliḥ would not have fulfilled his own mythic destiny as the prophet of the cyclic extinction/salvation paradox: a people's exemplary annihilation and, within that annihilation, a wholly paratactic, figural as it were, resumption of prophetic manifestation in each new cycle. Such prophetic cycles are thus in themselves, as far as their own political, social, and, ultimately, human or biological circumference is concerned, cycles of tragedy in which the victor, as his respective cycle's chosen survivor, is no more than a link, the securer of the cyclic constant of its symbolic inheritance. If within this scheme Qudār is the strongly insinuated "adversary" of Ṣāliḥ's cycle, he is, however, not that cycle's antihero in the understanding familiar to us through processes of modern social banalization. If he is at all, in some use of the term, an antihero, he is one of myth and epos, enshrouded in tragedy, and above all in pathos, close enough to the Teutonic Hagen of the Nibelungen, and for us yet to be understood in such broader environs.

The "equation" of the two Qudārs also reveals to us two "existences" of him whom we know as Qudār: one archaic and radically archetypal within the framework of the myth of the downfall of the Thamūd; and the other in Muḥammadan prophetic legend spun into the mythopoeia found in the narrative of the Raid on Tabūk.

In the Thamūdic myth alone, Qudār must, however, necessarily be reclaimed from the Qurʾān- and *ḥadīth*-generated diatribal exegesis that surrounds him. His special role in the drama of the Thamūd, or, more specifically, in that of the Thamūdic polity, where he appears invested with all the accolades of a heroic figura, and his symbolic, predestined, and thus thoroughly mythic, antiposition to Ṣāliḥ ought to be seen as his entitlement to be the one to bear the golden bough into his grave. Not quite alien to such semiotics, the quasi-Abrahamic Ṣāliḥ in his "pastoral," distinctly patriarchal role—which, nevertheless, also combines with the role of a prophet of doom—may then be imagined as the bearer of the myth's other symbol of entitlement and destiny: not the golden bough deposited in the Thamūdic grave but, one should symbolically imagine (and supplement), the pastoral staff of the wanderer, the ever turning and returning cyclic interloper, the prophet/servant of a different autochthony of which Qudār himself knew nothing but in which he was nevertheless called upon to play a fateful role.

As Qudār thus remained inseparable from the soil of the tragedy of the Thamūd throughout the fullness of his mythical time, on the other hand, Ṣāliḥ, his work done, has wandered off estranged or, at best, in melancholy detachment. Nevertheless, it was Ṣāliḥ's ultimate cyclic "return" in Muḥammad's self-conscious reenactment of his "figura" in a preordained cyclic prophetic scheme that brought about the discovery, or rediscovery, of "the last of the Thamūd," and with him of the golden bough. Some sort of symbolic fruition has thus come about: Qudār's grave in Thamūdic soil—and in that grave his golden bough—becomes not only the sign remindful of the closure of the foregoing cycle of Thamūdic legacy but, in the act of Muḥammad's unearthing the Thamūdic golden bough, it also points to the interlocking of that archaic cycle with that legacy's newly emerged inheritor—and thus with a new cycle. Muḥammad's "finding" of the golden bough of the Thamūd must therefore not be dismissed as a passing hagiographic incident cast in a demythologizing, anecdotal style. Nor should it be viewed as a naïvely self-serving ruse that undervalues, or lacks awareness of, the "strong" symbol that it has touched upon.

Concerning Qudār, and thus the Arabian golden bough itself, we must finally posit certain questions and assumptions: If Qudār/Abū Righāl was thus *marked,* aside from his physical characteristics of redness and "demon-like" blue eyes,[3] by the possession of the golden bough of the Thamūd, does this not imply that he is also the bearer of what should be viewed as his specific destiny of mytho-historical encounter with him who shall return to his grave and unearth the buried symbol? For here we notice once again that, in his station at the ruins of al-Ḥijr, Muḥammad does not find his own validation in an "encounter" with his cyclic other self, Ṣāliḥ—except through the recognizably Ṣāliḥ-patterned agonies which he experiences during his march on Tabūk. Instead, however, Muḥammad symbolically meets with Qudār and comes to acknowledge his golden bough, and to be acknowledged through it.

The further question/postulation then is: If Muḥammad the Prophet were to be cast in entirely detached and objectivized archetypal-symbolic and mythical terms, he would undeniably fit into the paradigmatic mold of the culture hero, inasmuch as he was a founder, a builder, and a lawgiver—all three on a distinctly "mythical" scale. In such a mythologized epiphany the transfer of the golden bough of the Thamūd to the one who recognized it would also mean that it recognized him. As much as Qudār would be thus redeemed, Muḥammad would be validated. And, against so many impediments placed in our path by Frazer himself, we would be reminded here that the golden bough, not necessarily the mistletoe, may also be the scepter that symbolically secures the succession of priestly kingship. After all, Muḥammad, the heir of Thamūdic Arabia, is also history's most salient case of priestly-prophetic "kingship."

NOTES

Introduction

1. See the fluctuating aspect of that critical receptivity in Jaroslav Stetkevych, "Arabic Poetry and Assorted Poetics," in Malcolm H. Kerr, ed., *Islamic Studies: A Tradition and Its Problems* (Malibu, California: Undena Publications, 1980), pp. 103–23.

2. Northrop Frye, *The Great Code* (New York/London: Harcourt Brace Jovanovich, 1982), p. xviii.

3. Thus the prophet Zakarīyā's, his wife's, and his son Yaḥyā's relationship to God is that of *raghaban wa rahaban*—of "aspiration and awe" (Qur'ān 21:90). Current in the Qur'ān are also the terms *rāhib* in its plural form, *ruhbān,* with its accepted meaning of "anchorites" (Qur'ān 9:31), and *rahbānīyah* ("anchoritism"/"monasticism") (Qur'ān 57:27). The term *rāhib* should, however, be connected "institutionally" with our archaic meaning of *rahbah;* for *rāhib* ought to have meant something like a "supplicant" (at court) and a "servant" in one sense, and in another sense an *ʿabd or kāhin* (a servant/minister). In both senses he *(rāhib)* is one who "approaches in awe"—thus, initially, not the one who "withdraws." This relation of *raghbah* to *rahbah* then receives in al-Jāḥiẓ's (d. 255/868) incipient political thought its synonymic hermeneutics through the tension in the "pairing" of *mahābah/maḥabbah* ("awe"/"love"). See Abū ʿUthmān ʿAmr Ibn Baḥr al-Jāḥiẓ, *Al-Bayān wa al-Tabyīn,* 4 vols., ed. ʿAbd al-Salām Muḥammad Hārūn, 5th ed. (Cairo: Maktabat al-Khānjī, 1405/1985) 3:115.

4. Qur'ān 11:49.

5. Qur'ān 26:214; 9:24; 58:22.

6. *Mathalu l-jannati l-latī wuʿida l-muttaqūna fīhā anhārun min māʾin ghayri āsinin . . . wa anhārun min khamrin ladhdhatin li-sh-shāribīna . . .,* Qur'ān 47:15.

7. *Inna l-abrāra la fī naʿīmin / ʿalā l-arāʾiki yanẓurūna / taʿrifu fī wujūhihim naḍrata n-naʿīmi / yusqawna min raḥīqin makhtūmin / khitāmuhu miskun wa fī dhālika fal-yatanāfas il-mutanāfisūna / wa mizājuhu min tasnīmin / ʿaynan tashrabu bihā l-muqarrabūna,* Qur'ān 83:22–28. To be noted here further is the term *al-muqarrabūn* (v. 28), literally "the ones brought near," but originally (terminologically) "courtiers," "favorites," etc., as borrowed from imperial/royal courtly institutions and customs.

8. See Suzanne Pinckney Stetkevych, "Intoxication and Immortality: Wine and Associated Imagery in al-Maʿarrī's Garden," in Fedwa Malti-Douglas, ed., *Critical Pilgrimages: Studies in the Arabic Literary Tradition. Literature East and West* 25 (1989): 31–43.

9. Ignaz Goldziher, *Muslim Studies,* ed. S. M. Stern, trans. C. R. Barber and S. M. Stern (Albany: State University of New York Press, 1967), p. 202 ("What Is Meant by 'Al-Jāhiliyya'").

10. This verse (Qurʾān 48:26), which refers itself to the changing moods that led to the truce, and treaty, of Ḥudaybīyah, also antiposes to *ḥamīyat al-jāhilīyah* the term *sakīnah* ("tranquility," "calmness," "gentleness"), which, let there be no doubt, is in this case a self-conscious choice of synonym for the pre-Islamic Bedouin "balancing" virtue of *ḥilm* ("gentleness," "clemency," "mildness," "forbearance," "indulgence," "patience," "understanding," "discernment") opposite *jahl.* Just as the specific *jahl* does not occur in the Qurʾān, neither does *ḥilm*—although one of the important epithetic names of Allāh is its adjectival derivative, *ḥalīm.*

11. Suzanne Pinckney Stetkevych, *The Mute Immortals Speak: Pre-Islamic Poetry and the Poetics of Ritual* (Ithaca: Cornell University Press, 1993), pp. 207–10.

12. Luwīs ʿAwaḍ, *Usṭūrat Ūrist wa al-Malāḥim al-ʿArabīyah* (Cairo: Dār al-Kātib al-ʿArabī li al-Ṭibāʿah wa al-Nashr, 1968), pp. 7, 45, 88. Technically, the relationship between the clans of Bakr and Taghlib is that of paternal cousins *(abnāʾ al-ʿamm).* This is also reflected in Luwīs ʿAwaḍ's discussion (p. 7). My present intention is to uncover the archetype rather than to dwell on the genealogical complexities, especially of the name Taghlib. I would only, at this point, side with Nöldeke's (*ZDMG*, xl [1886], p. 169) philologically sound consideration that Taghlib is originally a collective term which qualifies the whole tribe as "prevailing," or "victorious." The "matrilineal" speculation based on the understanding of *taghlib* as "*she* prevails" (W. Robertson Smith, *Kinship and Marriage in Early Arabia* [Oosterhout N. B., Netherlands: Anthropological Publications, 1966], pp. 13ff., and 253ff.), as reflected in some early Arabic verse, is also tempting, although it is philologically not decisive and genealogically suspect. For the classical Arabic genealogies and their sources, see art. "Taghlib" by H. Kindermann in *The Encyclopaedia of Islam* (First Edition), and art. "Bakr b. Wāʾil" by W. Caskel in *The Encyclopaedia of Islam* (New Edition).

13. See further, S. Stetkevych, *The Mute Immortals Speak,* pp. 199–205.

14. Goldziher, *Muslim Studies,* pp. 202–03. Otherwise, while acknowledging "that in the old language, too, we find the concept of knowledge *(ʿilm)* contrasted to *jahl,* . . . this opposition is founded on a secondary meaning of *jahl.*" Same, p. 203.

15. *Laʾin kuntu muḥtājan ilā l-ḥilmi innanī*
ilā l-jahli fī baʿḍi l-aḥāyīni aḥwaju
Wa mā kuntu arḍā l-jahla khidnan wa ṣāḥiban
wa lākinnanī arḍā bihī ḥīna uḥraju
Fa in qāla qawmun inna fīhī samāḥatan
fa qad ṣadaqū wa dh-dhullu bi l-ḥurri asmaju
Wa lī farasun li l-ḥilmi bi l-ḥilmi muljamun
wa lī farasun li l-jahli bi l-jahli musraju
Fa man shāʾa taqwīmī fa innī muqawwamun
wa man shāʾa taʿwījī fa innī muʿawwaju

Abū ʿUmar Aḥmad Ibn Muḥammad Ibn ʿAbd Rabbih al-Andalusī, *Kitāb al-ʿIqd al-Farīd,* 3d ed., 7 vols., eds. Aḥmad Amīn, Aḥmad al-Zayn, Ibrāhīm al-Abyārī (Cairo: Maṭbaʿat Lajnat al-Taʾlīf wa al-Tarjamah wa al-Nashr, 1367/1948) 3:14. This source refers to the author of these lines as "and another [poet] said" *(wa qāla ākharu).* Without giving a precise textual reference, Goldziher [*Muslim Studies,* p. 204] quotes only lines 1, 4, and 5 of this short poem (or, itself, a poetic fragment), as does his likely source, Abū ʿUbayd Allāh Muḥammad Ibn ʿUmrān al-Marzubānī, *Muʿjam al-Shuʿarāʾ* (Cairo: Maktabat al-Qudsī, A.H. 1354), pp. 429-30.

The translation given on pages 8-9 of the present text, and all other translations appearing without other attribution, are my own.

16. Muṣṭafā Nāṣif, *Qirāʾah Thāniyah li Shiʿrinā al-Qadīm* ([Tripoli, Libya]: Manshūrāt al-Jāmiʿah al-Lībīyah, Kullīyat al-Ādāb, n.d.).

17. See Jacob Lassner, *The Demonization of the Queen of Sheba* (Chicago: The University of Chicago Press, 1994).

18. See Jaroslav Stetkevych, "Confluence of Arabic and Hebrew Literature," *Journal of Near Eastern Studies* 32, nos. 1 & 2 (Jan.-April 1973), p. 220.

19. Further on the myth/legend of the Seven Sleepers of Ephesus, see below, chapter 2 n. 7.

20. See further, Jaroslav Stetkevych, *The Zephyrs of Najd: The Poetics of Nostalgia in the Classical Arabic Nasīb* (Chicago: The University of Chicago Press, 1993), pp. 168-70.

21. See also S. Stetkevych, "Intoxication and Immortality," pp. 40-41.

Chapter 1

1. Virgil [Vergil], *Eclogues, Georgics, Aeneid,* Trans. H. Rushton Fairclough (The Loeb Classical Library), 2 vols. (Cambridge, Massachusetts/London: Harvard University Press, 1994/1986), Vol. 1 [*Aeneid* VI, 186-89, 203-04], pp. 518/519-520/521.

2. Abū Jaʿfar Muḥammad Ibn Jarīr al-Ṭabarī, *Tafsīr al-Ṭabarī: Jāmiʿ al-Bayān ʿan Taʾwīl Āy al-Qurʾān,* 16 vols., eds. Maḥmūd Muḥammad Shākir and Aḥmad Muḥammad Shākir (Cairo: Dār al-Maʿārif bi Miṣr, 1957) 12:538-39; Ibn Kathīr [ʿImād al-Dīn Abū al-Fidā Ismāʿīl Ibn ʿUmar al-Qurashī al-Dimashqī], *Al-Bidāyah wa al-Nihāyah fī al-Tārīkh,* 14 vols. (Cairo: Maṭbaʿat Kurdistān al-ʿIlmīyah li Nashr al-Kutub al-ʿĀliyah al-Islāmīyah, A.H. 1348) 1:137, and *Qiṣaṣ al-Anbiyāʾ* ([Cairo?]: Dār Nahr al-Nīl, n.d. [1981?]), p. 123; Ibn Isḥāq Aḥmad Ibn Muḥammad Ibn Ibrāhīm al-Thaʿlabī, *Kitāb Qiṣaṣ al-Anbiyāʾ al-Musammā bi al-ʿArāʾis* (Cairo: Al-Maṭbaʿah al-Kāstalīyah, A.H. 1298), p. 62; A. J. Wensinck and J. P. Mensing, et al., *Concordance et indices de la Tradition Musulmane: Les Six Livres, Le Musnad dʾal-Dārimī, Le Muwattaʾ de Mālik, Le Musnad de Ahmad Ibn Hanbal* (Leiden: E. J. Brill, 1962 [photo-offset of 1936-1943 edition]) 4:519 (from Abū Dāwūd, ch. 41 [*imārah*]).

3. What we characterize here as a "folkloric manner" in a *ḥadīth* is also recognizable as a stylistic trait of a number of the shorter qurʾānic suras, such as 77:13-14; 82:17-18; 83:8-9, 19-20; 86:1-3; 90:11-13; 97:1-3; 101:1-3, 9-11; 104:4-6.

4. The importance of this "place of burial" in the disentanglement of the complexity of the persona of Abū Righāl will be discussed in chapter 4.

5. Entirely, or in part, this episode is told by al-Ṭabarī, *Tafsīr* 12:538; Ibn Kathīr, *Al-Bidāyah wa al-Nihāyah* 1:137, and *Qiṣaṣ al-Anbiyāʾ*, pp. 122-23; and

al-Thaʿlabī, *Kitāb Qiṣaṣ al-Anbiyāʾ*, pp. 61–62, although without the introduction of Muḥammad's passing by a grave and asking his people the rhetorical question. Instead, al-Thaʿlabī's narration of the incident comes entirely integrated into the story of Ṣāliḥ and the Thamūd. It is altogether odd, or rather symptomatic, that S. A. Bonebakker, in his entry on Abū Righāl, should have totally failed to take notice of the existence of as strange an object as a golden bough found in the grave of Abū Righāl. See S. A. Bonebakker, art. "Abū Righāl," *The Encyclopaedia of Islam* (New Ed.), ed. H. A. R. Gibb et al. (Leiden: E. J. Brill; London: Luzak and Co., 1960–).

6. Al-Thaʿlabī, *Kitāb Qiṣaṣ al-Anbiyāʾ*, p. 62.

7. Muḥammad Ibn ʿUmar Ibn Wāqid, *Kitāb al-Maghāzī li al-Wāqidī*, 3 vols., ed. Mārisdin Jūns [Marsden Jones] (Oxford: Oxford University Press, 1966) 3:1008.

8. For a discussion of the ultimate implications of the qurʾānic cyclic scheme, see my "Arabic Hermeneutical Terminology: Paradox and the Production of Meaning," *Journal of Near Eastern Studies* 48 no. 2 (April 1989), p. 84.

9. Al-Ṭabarī, *Tafsīr* 12:524–47; Ibn Kathīr, *Al-Bidāyah wa al-Nihāyah* 1:130–39; and, more closely keyed to the Qurʾān, Ibn Kathīr, *Qiṣaṣ al-Anbiyāʾ*, pp. 112–27; Shihāb al-Dīn Aḥmad Ibn ʿAbd al-Wahhāb al-Nuwayrī, *Nihāyat al-Arab fī Funūn al-Adab*, 31 vols. (Cairo: Dār al-Kutub al-Miṣrīyah, 1342/1924–1374/1955; Al-Hayʾah al-Miṣrīyah al-ʿĀmmah li al-Kitāb, 1412/1992) 13:71–86; al-Thaʿlabī, *Kitāb Qiṣaṣ al-Anbiyāʾ*, pp. 57–62; Muḥammad Ibn ʿAbd Allāh al-Kisāʾī, *Qiṣaṣ al-Anbiyāʾ*, ed. Isaac Eisenberg (Leiden: E. J. Brill, 1922/23), pp. 117–21. See also the English translation, *The Tales of the Prophets of al-Kisāʾī*, Translated from the Arabic with Notes by W. M. Thackston, Jr. (Boston: Twayne Publishers/G. K. Hall and Co., 1978), pp. 117–28.

Chapter 2

1. *ʿAdam idrāk li al-zamān wa al-makān*, see Jawād ʿAlī, *Al-Mufaṣṣal fī Tārīkh al-ʿArab qabl al-Islām*, 10 vols. (Beirut: Dār al-ʿIlm li al-Malāyīn/Baghdad: Maktabat al-Nahḍah, 1969) 1:75.

2. Bernard F. Batto, *Slaying the Dragon: Mythmaking in the Biblical Tradition* (Louisville, Kentucky: Westminster/John Knox Press, 1992), p. 123.

3. Abū Jaʿfar Muḥammad Ibn Jarīr al-Ṭabarī, *Tārīkh al-Ṭabarī: Tārīkh al-Rusul wa al-Mulūk*, 11 vols., ed. Muḥammad Abū al-Faḍl Ibrāhīm (Cairo: Dār al-Maʿārif bi Miṣr, 1960) 1:314.

4. Al-Nuwayrī, *Nihāyat al-Arab* 13:73; and al-Kisāʾī, *Qiṣaṣ al-Anbiyāʾ*, p. 111 [English translation, p. 118]. This quotation from the Qurʾān (*jāʾa l-ḥaqqu wa zahaqa l-bāṭilu inna l-bāṭila kāna zahūqan* [17:81]) is unrelatable to the story of the Thamūd, unless it is to be taken as a "figura." In its correct, not mythopoeically adapted, context it merely announces, or confirms, the institution of the obligatory daily prayers.

5. Al-Nuwayrī, *Nihāyat al-Arab* 13:73.

6. We easily recognize in the Thamūdic (or would-be Thamūdic) Kānūh, as Ṣāliḥ's father is named in the Arabic mythopoeic texts, a cognate of the Hebrew, as well as Aramaic, *kohen* (priest)—together with the

archaic Arabic term of *kāhin* (priest), which perhaps ought to occupy the primary place in our etymological awareness. Furthermore, in the entire scene in which Kānūh is introduced, we are given an Arabic variant of the archetypal motif most iconically represented in the Christian annunciation. In the Thamūdic/Arabian case, however, it is the male who is the receiver of "the good tidings," bearing in it a sign that is both physiological and a testimony to having communicated with divinity. Also compare Kānūh's annunciation with that of Sarah (Genesis 18:9–15, and Qurʾān 11:69–74), as well as with Zachariah (Luke 1:8–24) and Mary (Luke 1:26–38). In a special way, treading the thinnest of lines between being outright earthy and mystical-symbolic, the episode of the particular glow that radiates from the eyes of Kānūh and issues from the fecundating stirrings in the marrow of his spine should be placed side by side with the hagiographic story told by Ibn Isḥāq, the source of Ibn Hishām, of how the Prophet Muḥammad was fathered and conceived. In it, as Muḥammad's father, ʿAbd Allāh, approaches his wife Āminah, the woman to become Muḥammad's mother, he too bears a sign on his face: the "light" of a blaze on his forehead. After the union, which leads to Muḥammad's conception, the blaze disappears. See Abū Muḥammad ʿAbd al-Malik Ibn Hishām, *Al-Sīrah al-Nabawīyah,* 4 vols. (Cairo: Dār al-Fikr li al-Ṭibāʿah wa al-Nashr wa al-Tawzīʿ, 1980) 1:173–74; and, with only minor textual variation, Abū Muḥammad ʿAbd al-Malik Ibn Hishām, *Al-Sīrah al-Nabawīyah li Ibn Hishām,* 6 vols., ed. Ṭāhā ʿAbd al-Raʾūf Saʿd (Beirut: Dār al-Jīl, 1411/1991) 1:292–93. This Muḥammadan hagiographic parallel with Kānūh, his wife, and the conception of the Thamūdic prophet Ṣāliḥ is of particular importance to us, for it will substantiate and clarify our further analogies pertinent to Ṣāliḥ and Muḥammad.

7. Kānūh's refuge in a magic cave and his sleep in it for one hundred years is to be put into the Qurʾān's own mythopoeic context of the Companions of the Cave *(Aṣḥāb al-Kahf),* Qurʾān 18:9–26, and their sheltered three hundred and nine year sleep. The qurʾānic version of the story of the Sleepers has in turn its origin in the legend of the "Seven Sleepers of Ephesus," which, in its internal textual reference points, dates back to the mid-third century, the time of persecution of Christians under the Emperor Decius. In its Christian context the legend acquires a distinct hagiographic character, and in the sixth century a shrine of the Sleepers of Ephesus is known to have existed as a place of worship. According to the Qurʾān (8:21), too, a mosque is erected over the Companions of the Cave. See especially P. Michael Huber, *Die Wanderlegende von den Siebenschläfern* (Leipzig: Otto Harrassowitz, 1910), p. 237–38; and, generally, *The Encyclopaedia of Islam* (New Edition), art. "Aṣḥāb al-Kahf."

8. Al-Nuwayrī, *Nihāyat al-Arab* 13:73.

9. Qurʾān 5:34. It is interesting to note that what in the Qurʾān is a "story" of burial is here a story of awakening, or, as it were, of resurrection. Then, too, see al-Nuwayrī, *Nihāyat al-Arab* 13:74; and al-Kisāʾī, *Qiṣaṣ al-Anbiyāʾ,* p. 112 [English translation, p. 119].

10. In his *Vögel als Boten* (Göttingen: Vandenhoeck und Ruprecht, 1977), Othmar Keel devotes much attention to the mythological figuration of the raven/crow as the guide- or orientation-bird. He begins with the Early-Dynastic II (ca. 2600 B.C.) Mesopotamian cylinder seal from Fara (Shuruppak), which is interpreted as representing Gilgamesh holding in his hand the

plant, or branch, of youthful immortality, seated in a boat opposite Utnapishtim. Behind him there stands a boatman (Urshanabi [?]), while over the boat's stern there either flies or perches a raven (pp. 83, 85). Callimachus of Cyrene (d. ca. 240 B.C.), in his *Second Hymn,* addressed to Apollo, praises the god, who, as a raven, guides his people to Libya. Inasmuch as the journey involved the crossing of the sea, Apollo the Raven is in it clearly the "orientation-bird" (p. 83). So too was Alexander the Great guided by two ravens to the Ammon oracle in the oasis of Shiva (p. 82). Keel provides equally persuasive examples from early (first century B.C.) Indian maritime travels in which the raven was taken on the ships because of its ability to orient, that is, guide, the seafarers.

Continuing after Callimachus with Ovid, we return to the raven as the messenger of the god Apollo, and thus as the inhabiter of a Paradise-like sphere. There this Greek mythical raven had once been whiter than snowy doves, swans, and even geese. As Apollo's bird, it had the misfortune, however, to have once come upon an indiscretion of the beautiful Coronis of Larissa, a maiden whose love Apollo had taken for himself and of whose faithfulness he entertained an unjustified illusion. When, in his straightforwardness as messenger, the raven, against every better judgment, informed Apollo of Coronis's unfaithfulness, the god in his rage not only killed the girl but also changed the raven's color to black and banished it forever from the company of all white birds (Ovid, *Metamorphoses,* trans. Rolfe Humphries [Bloomington: Indiana University Press, 1964], pp. 45–48 [2: 539–631]). From then on the raven remained the bird of ill omen and of separation.

In the Mithraic myth the raven is confirmed in its Apollonian connection. There the "servitor of the Sun" sends the raven to Mithra as the messenger that bears the command to slay the bull. In the comparison between the two ravens, the Apollonian and the Mithraic, we have to keep in mind the "Apollonian" unified solar divinity as against the Mithraic division into two complementary divine personae. Not entirely to be separated from being the solar messenger, in the Mithraic mysteries, too, the raven constitutes the first of the seven stages of initiation. See Franz Cumont, *The Mysteries of Mithra,* trans. Thomas J. McCormack (New York: Dover Publications, Inc., 1956), pp. 152, 154–55.

Bearing still recognizable Apollonian characteristics, in the Arabic mythopoeia which grew, one might say, exegetically, out of the qur'ānic narrative paucity of the Noah story, the raven/*ghurāb* is also the "failed" messenger bird. The cause of its failure, however, is not excessive zeal, as was the case of Apollo's raven, but its being remiss in bringing Noah the news of the abatement of the flood. It became distracted by a carcass floating on the flood waters and failed to return. For that it was punished to remain a bird of distance and separation from man—as well as being condemned to announce the inevitability of separation among men. The opposite is then the role and the mythopoeic and literary fate of Noah's other messenger, the dove. See al-Thaʿlabī, *Qiṣaṣ al-Anbiyāʾ,* p. 50; Kamāl al-Dīn al-Damīrī, *Ḥayāt al-Ḥayawān al-Kubrā wa bi Hāmishihā ʿAjāʾib al-Makhlūqāt wa al-Ḥayawānāt wa Gharāʾib al-Mawjūdāt* by Zakariyā Ibn Muḥammad Ibn Maḥmūd al-Qazwīnī, 2 vols. (Beirut: Dār Iḥyāʾ al-Turāth al-ʿArabī, n.d. [photo offset of the ed. Cairo: Maṭbaʿat al-Ḥijāzī, A.H. 1353]) 2:172–74.

11. "Hallowed" is here *maʿṣūm* and "venerated and exalted," *mukarraman muʿaẓẓaman*, both being with full intentionality used as "prophetic" epithets, thus resonating with Muḥammad's "names"/epithets. Al-Nuwayrī, *Nihāyat al-Arab* 13:75.

12. That is, *alladhīna yufsidūna fī-l-arḍi*. See al-Nuwayrī, *Nihāyat al-Arab* 13:76; and Qurʾān 26:152; or 27:48. An important general observation in this context should be that "bringing corruption to the land" appears to be the main accusation cast against the Thamūd. This should allow us to place its symbolic meaning within the broad archetypal scope of vegetation symbolism, the "wasteland," the Fisher King, etc..

13. Al-Nuwayrī, *Nihāyat al-Arab* 13:77.

14. Too many lateral issues of incidental and tangential symbolism (but even then of a possible cumulative coherence) are surging here for us to even try to give them justice within the limitations of our present essay. It is sufficient to note how archetypal is Ṣāliḥ's "setting out toward the wilderness," and how it falls into patterns such as those of John the Baptist and Christ. Equally archetypal is Ṣāliḥ's entering the cave, his prophetic sleep/gestation of forty years, and even his "golden bed" and the lamp-candelabra. With regard to the last, we may think of the Fisher King of the Grail saga, but also of the buried golden bough itself.

15. Al-Nuwayrī, *Nihāyat al-Arab* 13:78.

16. Al-Nuwayrī, *Nihāyat al-Arab* 13:79.

17. Al-Nuwayrī, *Nihāyat al-Arab* 13:79. As much as we know of the "miracle of Noah," which is the building of the Ark, we know nothing of a specific "miracle of Hūd." In Qurʾān 11:53, 54 the people of ʿĀd even say to Hūd's face: "O Hūd, no clear sign have you brought us." Only Hūd's prophecy of ʿĀd's annihilation and their replacement by another people can, therefore, be the "miracle." The actual "story" of their annihilation is given, once again, more picturesquely and exhaustively in al-Nuwayrī, *Nihāyat al-Arab* 13:56.

18. Thus in Qurʾān 7:73; 91:13; etc.

19. Compare, for example, the narration of al-Nuwayrī (*Nihāyat al-Arab* 13:79) with that of al-Ṭabarī (*Tafsīr* 12:525).

20. Al-Nuwayrī, *Nihāyat al-Arab* 13:79.

21. Such is the account of al-Thaʿlabī's *Kitāb Qiṣaṣ al-Anbiyāʾ* (p. 58), and the same meaning may also be construed from al-Ṭabarī's *Tafsīr* (12:526). In al-Nuwayrī's *Nihāyat al-Arab* (13:80), on the other hand, even the watering of the She-Camel on alternate days remains one of the specific conditions presented by the Thamūd.

22. Ṣāliḥ's words in the narration are a quotation from Qurʾān 7:73.

23. Aside from there being a good reason for the exploration of Qudār's etymologies based on morphologically determined semantics, and even on "folk-associative" usages, our main approach must ultimately be that of concrete etymology within the root *q/k-dh/d-r* and *kh-ḍ-r*, not excluding Hebrew etymological aspects. Most of all, see below (ch. 6, "Demythologizing the Thamūd"), the validation of etymology in the "historicity" of *qudār*/Qudār.

24. The formulaic character of such essentially ideological "in-text" hermeneutics is also evident in the other Genesis "pairing" of Cain and Abel (Gen. 4), or in the ideologically even more transparent distribution of patrimony and curse among the sons of Noah (Gen. 9:24–26). The

Romulus and Remus parallel is also obvious. In its myth-making and ideological aspects the latter receives its perhaps most comprehensive treatment in T. P. Wiseman, *Remus: A Roman Myth* (Cambridge: Cambridge University Press, 1995).

25. *Wa kāna fī ʿaynayhi zurqatun ka anna humā ʿadasatāni.* Al-Nuwayrī, *Nihāyat al-Arab* 13:83.

26. *Mithla zujājatin.* See al-Nābighah al-Dhubyānī, *Dīwān,* redaction of Ibn al-Sikkīt, ed. Shukrī Fayṣal (Beirut: Dār al-Hāshim, 1968), pp. 14–16 (rhymed in *dāl,* esp. v. 28). See further ʿAmr Ibn Baḥr al-Jāḥiẓ, *Kitāb al-Ḥayawān,* 8 vols., ed. ʿAbd al-Salām Muḥammad Hārūn (Cairo: Dār al-Maʿārif, 1938) 6:331.

27. Of importance to us primarily is Cassandra's role in *Aeneid* 2:246–49. In myth to be a "seer," or to become a "seer," comes, unavoidably, very dearly. Through her preference of a mortal over a god—in this case termed mythographically as "unfaithfulness"—Cassandra, for having thus defied Apollo, who had given her the gift of prophecy, has to live with the agony of ignored prophecy and, ultimately, of witnessing the destruction of Troy. To expatiate further on Cassandra's Arabian analogue: Zarqāʾ al-Yamāmah, alienated from her kin by being married into a clan (Jadīs) hostile to her own (Ṭasm), although she detects the camouflaged advancing Ḥimyarites from a distance of three days' march, is not believed by the Jadīs. Yamāmah falls, the Jadīs are put to the sword, and Zarqāʾ al-Yamāmah's eyes are plucked out by the king of the conquering Ḥimyarites. See Abū al-Ḥasan ʿAlī Ibn al-Ḥusayn Ibn ʿAlī al-Masʿūdī, *Murūj al-Dhahab wa Maʿādin al-Jawhar,* 4 vols., ed. Yūsuf Asʿad Dāghir (Beirut: Dār al-Andalus li al-Ṭibāʿah wa al-Nashr wa al-Tawzīʿ, 1401/ 1981) 2:117–19.

28. *Macbeth,* Act IV Scene 1 and Act V Scene 5.

29. Qurʾān 27:48.

30. To "hock" or "hamstring" *(ʿaqara)* an animal, especially a camel, is not only a complex word in the Arabic lexicon; it is, above all, a complex *term* in the earliest Arabic language of ritual and sacrifice, for it is the first step in the procedure of slaughtering an animal which in some form, explicitly or implicitly, is offered, or consumed, in a ritualized manner. This applies most closely and most variedly to pre-Islamic Arabia. Thus also the subsequent Muḥammadan injunction against the pre-Islamic Arabian funerary and commemorative custom of slaughtering camels at the graves of kinsmen: "There shall be no slaughtering [i.e. hocking] of camels in Islam" *(lā ʿaqra fī l-islām).* The "hocking" *(ʿaqr)* was thus the bringing down of the animal (sacrificial), followed by the slaying (cutting of the throat). Terminologically, however, such "hocking" also took over the meaning of the full procedure of the killing of the animal. And, more than that, when employed, it gave the slaughtering of the animal the implicit sense of something endowed with "significance": sacrificial, ritual, or even figuratively related to sacrificial and ritual. For the broad semantic scope of the verb *ʿaqara,* albeit with tighter lexicographical focus and circumscription, see Edward William Lane, *Arabic-English Lexicon,* 8 vols. (New York: Frederick Ungar, 1958 [London, 1863]) 5:2107–08. See also below, ch. 4 n. 11.

31. Al-Nuwayrī, *Nihāyat al-Arab* 13:83.

32. Al-Nuwayrī, *Nihāyat al-Arab* 13:83.

33. Al-Thaʿlabī, *Qiṣaṣ al-Anbiyāʾ*, p. 60; al-Nuwayrī, *Nihāyat al-Arab* 13:84.

34. Qurʾān 11:65; and, in another version, 51:43.

35. There are differing translations of *wayyaqemū leẓaḥeq* (Exodus 32:6), such as "and rose up to play" (Revised Standard Version), or "and rose up to make merry" (The Holy Scriptures According to the Masoretic Text [Philadelphia: The Jewish Publication Society of America, 1955]). Not only is one uncomfortable with "playing" and "making merry" in this uncomplicated way, but the insistence on translating *wayyaqemū* as "and *rose*" seems hardly tenable, since this verb may function here only in a manner similar to that of the Arabic verbs of "beginning," "undertaking," as well as "occurring." In the translation of this verse, I diverge from both the RSV and the Masoretic Text translations.

36. This "forensic manner" of Moses reappears almost as a caricature in the Ḥadīth, when, in the story of Muḥammad's Night Journey and Ascension *(al-isrāʾ wa al-miʿrāj)*, the figure of Moses appears to Muḥammad, advising him how to bargain down with God the number of obligatory prayers. Thus the number of daily prayers required of Muslims was set at a merciful five rather than God's original imposition of fifty. See Abū al-Ḥusayn Muslim Ibn al-Ḥajjāj al-Qushayrī al-Naysābūrī, *Ṣaḥīḥ Muslim,* 6 vols. (Cairo: Dār Iḥyāʾ al-Kutub al-ʿArabīyah: ʿĪsā al-Bābī al-Ḥalabī wa Shurakāhu, 1955) 1:145–47 [*ḥadīth* no. 259].

37. In this scene even Pinehas's choice of a spear with which to transfix the Midianite woman's belly begs for a Freudian reading.

38. The sin of "putting the Lord to a test" is one of the most important motifs of the qurʾānic/Thamūdic story itself, where the "She-Camel of God" (and of Ṣāliḥ) is herself given as a *fitnah* ("test") (Qurʾān 54:27).

39. See Ḥassān Ibn Thābit, *Sharḥ Dīwān Ḥassān Ibn Thābit,* recension of ʿAbd al-Raḥmān al-Barqūqī (Cairo: Al-Maktabah al-Tijārīyah al-Kubrā, 1347/1929), p. 426. Concerning another biblical text, this intransigence in the service of a new, or renewed, "covenant" in the Israelite Yahwist case has, in the laconic wording of Bernard M. Levinson, "Understandably . . . long troubled scholars." For his discussion of Deuteronomy 13:6–11/13:7–12 see his "'But You Shall Surely Kill Him': The Text-Critical and Neo-Assyrian Evidence for MT Deuteronomy 13:10," in Georg Braulik, ed., *Bundesdokument und Gesetz: Studien zum Deuteronomium* (Freiburg, Basel, Vienna, Barcelona, Rome, New-York: Herder, 1995), pp. 37–63.

With textual references to Neo-Assyrian treaties, Levinson reaches the unavoidable conclusion that contextualizes the Deuteronomy text (as much as it does that of Ḥassān Ibn Thābit): "Absolute loyalty to the sovereign requires the sacrifice of all other loyalties. Anyone undermining that primary commitment must summarily be executed" (p. 60).

40. Abdullah Yusuf Ali, *The Holy Qurʾan. Text, Translation and Commentary*, 2d ed. (New York: Tahrike Tarsile Qurʾan, Inc., 1988), p. 30.

41. *Fa -qtulū anfusakum dhālikum khayrun lakum ʿinda bāriʾikum*. Qurʾān 2:54.

42. Qurʾān 2:59

43. The root *r-j-s*, in turn, has itself carried over from *r-j-z* the meaning of "commotion." Thus these two roots ended up developing their common, polysemically intertwined semantic field.

44. Wilhelm Gesenius, *Hebräisches und aramäisches Handwörterbuch über das Alte Testament* (Berlin, Göttingen, Heidelberg: Springer Verlag, 1954), p. 680 ("*liebkosen mit einem Weibe*"). See also the complete context of Genesis 39:14, as it, too, refers itself to "sexual advances." Cf. the Arabic Third Form of *laʿiba*.

45. It is for that reason that the problem of the semantics of *ẓaḥeq* has led Hebrew exegesis and lexicography to associating its root *ẓ-ḥ-q* with the root, and the semantics, of *s-ḥ-q*, to be taken, in Gesenius's coy phrasing, *im üblen Sinne*—which, equally *im üblen Sinne*, is also understandable in Arabic as *sāḥaqa*.

In her paper "Sara and the Hyena: Laughter, Menstruation, and the Genesis of a Double Entendre" (*Journal of the History of Religion* 36 no. 1 [Aug., 1996], pp. 13–41), Suzanne Pinckney Stetkevych has studied the semantic and exegetical problem of the Arabic verb *ḍaḥika* in its qurʾānic occurrence (11:69–74) in the episode of "the laughter of Sara" and the analogical hermeneutics it suggests concerning the Hebrew *ẓ-ḥ-q* in the biblical story of Sara (Genesis 18:9–15).

46. Al-Ṭabarī, *Tārīkh* 1:230.

47. This scene is chiefly according to Ibn Kathīr, *Al-Bidāyah wa al-Nihāyah* 1:136.

48. The image of the black, overcast sky and the departure of Ṣāliḥ to Palestine is given in al-Nuwayrī's version of the story (*Nihāyat al-Arab* 13:85).

Chapter 3

1. See the antiposition of Badr and Uḥud precisely in such anthropologically definable ritual and tribal respects in S. Stetkevych, *The Mute Immortals Speak*, pp. 199–205. This is already clearly reflected in al-Ṭabarī, *Tārīkh* 1:421–83 (Badr), 499–537 (Uḥud), 2:100–111 (Tabūk). In the latter, too, compare entries on Badr and Uḥud with the entry on Tabūk.

2. Ibn Hishām, *Sīrah* (Cairo) 4:1368–90.

3. Al-Wāqidī, *Maghāzī* 3:989–1025.

4. To this the Qurʾān refers in 9:49. In a similar vein is the story of the incontinence of the Andalusian Umayyad emir ʿAbd al-Raḥmān Ibn al-Ḥakam, incidentally also as a *ghāzi[n]*, who during one of his campaigns to the "frontier" had a nightly discharge while dreaming of one of his concubines. Excited further by some pertinent *ṭayf al-khayāl* (nightly phantom) verses which he exchanged with one of his courtiers, he left the command of his army, mounted a horse and galloped from Guadalajara back to Cordova to satisfy his desires. Further celebratory verses on that "gallant" incident followed upon the emir's return. Such admission of intemperance, certainly among princes, was very much part of the culture of the time. See Ibn al-Qūṭīyah al-Qurṭubī, *Tārīkh Iftitāḥ al-Andalus* (Madrid: Real Academia de la Historia, 1868 [Arabic text]), p. 60.

5. Thus in Qurʾān 9:82.

6. Qurʾān 9:48; see Ibn Hishām, *Sīrah* (Cairo) 4:1371–77, 1402; and A. Guillaume, trans., *The Life of Muḥammad: A Translation of Isḥāq's Sīrat Rasūl Allāh* (Lahore and Karachi/London and New York: Oxford University Press, 1955 [1974]), p. 604 (henceforth cited as *Sīrah* [English]).

7. Al-Ṭabarī, *Tafsīr* 12:539; Ibn Kathīr, *Al-Bidāyah wa al-Nihāyah* 1:138; al-Thaʿlabī, *Kitāb Qiṣaṣ al-Anbiyāʾ*, p. 61; al-Wāqidī, *Maghāzī* 3:1008.

8. The editors of al-Ṭabarī's text (*Tafsīr* 12:539) indicate with reference to *nafar* that it should mean "the nine men of the Thamūd" that conspired against Ṣāliḥ. This, to me, is not likely. With even more certainty it is possible to reject the word's strict reference to *yawm al-nafar*, which is the day of the pilgrims' departure from Minā to Mecca. Al-Wāqidī's *Maghāzī* (3:1008), on the other hand, has the valley as *wādī al-nafr*, thus as the valley of "separation." As such it refers itself more strongly to the circumstances of al-Ḥijr.

9. The story of the asphyxiated man is nothing short of hilarious. In its context it would even be embarrassing, were it not such pure Bedouin folklore. The unfortunate man died of asphyxiation while attending to his bodily needs in an "outhouse." See al-Wāqidī, *Maghāzī* 3:1006; and al-Nuwayrī, *Nihāyat al-Arab* 17:358.

10. *Sīrah*, p. 605 (English); (Cairo) 4:1375.

11. *Sīrah* (Cairo) 4:1375.

12. *Sīrah* (Cairo) 4:1375–76.

13. Whereas Montgomery Watt (*Muḥammad at Medina* [Oxford: The Clarendon Press, 1956], pp. 189–91) seems oblivious to the legendary and mythopoeic factors in Muḥammad's march on Tabūk and in his passage by al-Ḥijr, D. S. Margoliouth notes, and comments on, the "wondrous soil" of legend that al-Ḥijr and the Thamūd represented to Muḥammad. In Margoliouth's words,

> The expedition was of interest to the Prophet as leading them past those ruined cities of whose history the Koran was so full; the rock-dwellings, as he supposed them to be, of the Thamud, who, having refused the voice of the prophet, had been destroyed, their rock-mansions remaining as a monument and a warning. . . . Mohammed, passing by this notorious country, could not fail to take some notice of the fact that they were in the presence of the great theatre of the divine vengeance. The Moslems were to pass by those deserted habitations with veiled faces, spurring their steeds: they were to eat and drink nothing that was to be found there, and after nightfall when they encamped they were to keep together. Fables were afterwards invented showing the need for these orders by the fate that befell those who violated them. Many years had elapsed since Mohammed had first heard the thrilling story of the fate of the Thamud from some storytellers attached to a caravan: and truly the seed had been sown on wondrous soil.

See his *Mohammed and the Rise of Islam* (London and New York: G. P. Putnam's Sons, 1927), pp. 420–21.

14. Abū ʿUbaydah Maʿmar Ibn al-Muthannā al-Taymī, *Majāz al-Qurʾān*, 2 vols., ed. Fu'ād Sazkīn (Cairo: Maktabat al-Khānjī, 1988 [photo offset 1954 ed.]) 1:207. It is furthermore to be noted that, as his philological "support" (*shāhid*) for the meaning (and connotation) of *ḥijr*, Abū ʿUbaydah quotes a verse from the pre-Islamic poet al-Mutalammis, in which *ḥijrun ḥarāmun* leads to "misfortune" *(al-dahārīsu).*

15. How intertwined, and interchangeable, the "figural" symbiosis of the personae of Ṣāliḥ and Muḥammad is, is shown further by Ibn Qutaybah in his *Al-Maʿārif (Things to Know).* There he ends his almost "shorthand" entry on the Thamūd and Ṣāliḥ with Ṣāliḥ's migration from the

city that had displeased God to Mecca, where the few Thamūdic faithful that accompanied him "lie buried in the western side of the Kaᶜbah." Then he concludes the entry with this, to us, significant statement: "And Ṣāliḥ was a merchant" *(Wa kāna Ṣāliḥun tājiran)* [Ibn Qutaybah (Abū Muḥammad ᶜAbd Allāh Ibn Muslim), *Al-Maᶜārif*, ed. Tharwat ᶜUkāshah, 2d ed. (Cairo: Dār al-Maᶜārif bi Miṣr, 1969), pp. 29–30]. This, obviously, does not mean that Mecca was a town of merchants—but that Ṣāliḥ had become like Muḥammad.

On the term and concept of "figura," see Erich Auerbach, *Scenes from the Drama of European Literature*, foreword by Paolo Valesio (Minneapolis: University of Minnesota Press, 1984), pp. 11–76. The German text of the essay "Figura" appeared first in *Neue Dantestudien* (Istanbul 1944). See also Auerbach's *Mimesis: The Representation of Reality in Western Literature*, trans. Willard R. Trask (Princeton, New Jersey: Princeton University Press, 1968), pp. 73–75, 116. To carry further the argument of Ṣāliḥ as the personification, indeed the allegory, of the archetypal prophetic, and even messianic, epithet, one can hardly avoid turning to Plato's *Republic* (Book II, 362 [Loeb Classical Library, pp. 124/125]), where Glaucon responds to Socrates, describing the fate of the *righteous man*, whom in Arabic we would necessarily call *al-rajul al-ṣāliḥ:* ". . . that such being his disposition the just man will have to endure the lash, the rack, chains, the branding-iron in his eyes, and finally, after every extremity of suffering, he will be crucified [or strictly, 'impaled']. . . ." Just as writers on Plato and Christianity have often compared the fate of Plato's "just" or "righteous" man with the Crucifixion, in order to maintain an analogy between the fate of the "just" and that of the Thamūdic-Islamic Ṣāliḥ, we must realize that in the Islamic case the prophetic agony and ultimate sacrifice have been "transferred" from the person of Ṣāliḥ to the she-camel, his agonistic-sacrificial extension, or substitute.

The pervasiveness with which the mythopoeia of Tabūk, or of the "march on Tabūk," bears the imprint of the identification of Muḥammad's persona with the persona of the mythical Ṣāliḥ is evident further from the fact that even to the present day Tabūk retains alive the legend of Muḥammad's acting, as it were, as an analogue-executor of a curse of extermination cast there upon an unfaithful people—only that the abomination committed is in the case of this surviving legend the perverse tribe's having refused to give Muḥammad and his army access to their well during the Raid on Tabūk. For that it was Muḥammad himself who pronounced the curse on the tribe. Accordingly, the tribe became annihilated, save for twenty women and twenty men and one sole child. Like this they would remain, bearing only one surviving offspring, till the Day of Resurrection, for, whenever a further offspring was born, that offspring had to die. This legend came to me from the modern Egyptian novel *Al-Baldah al-Ukhrā* (London/Cyprus: Riad el-Rayyes Books, 1991, pp. 77–78), by Ibrāhīm ᶜAbd al-Majīd. I also reconfirmed the "nonfictionality" of the story with the author himself.

Note that in this "secondary" myth, too, the cause behind the "abomination" is *water,* and the survival of the tribe through one sole child is semiotically reechoing the single camel-colt of the Thamūdic she-camel. A further interpretation of this myth of "curse and limited survival" could also be the need to limit population in a waterless place: a policy, or destiny, of "no growth" within a specific economy. What is most salient in this enduring myth, however, is its unflagging confirmation of the survival of the mythogenic environment left behind residually by the fall of the Thamūd.

16. The *ʿanazah* was a short spear which, beginning with the second year of the Hijrah, Bilāl, the Prophet's devoted "adjutant," used to carry before the Prophet and plant into the ground during prayers. It was originally a gift from the Najāshī of Abyssinia to Zurayb Ibn al-ʿAwwām, who then offered it to Muḥammad. See George C. Miles, "Miḥrāb and ʿAnazah: A Study in Early Islamic Iconography," in George C. Miles, ed., *Archaeologica Orientalia in Memoriam Ernst Herzfeld* (Locust Valley, New York: J. J. Augustin Publisher, 1952), pp. 159-68; also Franz Altheim and Ruth Stiehl, *Die Araber in der Alten Welt. Erster Band: Bis zum Beginn der Kaiserzeit* (Berlin: Walter de Gruyter & Co., 1964), esp. pp. 584ff; also *The Encyclopaedia of Islam*, 2d ed., 1:482 ("ʿAnaza"). Al-Jāḥiẓ, who in the third volume of his *Al-Bayān wa al-Tabyīn* has an extensive and thematically detailed essay on the staffs and scepters of early Arabia, nevertheless apportions only one sentence to the *ʿanazah,* assuring us that to him it was too famous and too much referred-to to need further attestation. He merely mentions that it "was carried in front of the Prophet, and perhaps they had it pointing out the direction to be assumed in prayers *(jaʿalūhā qiblatan)*." Al-Jāḥiẓ, *Al-Bayān wa al-Tabyīn* 3:95.

17. *Sīrah* (Cairo) 4:1476-77.

18. *Wa āyatu dhālika annahu dufina maʿahu ghuṣnun min dhahabin.* Ibn Kathīr, *Al-Bidāyah wa al-Nihāyah* 1:137.

19. See my discussion of this dimension of the Sūrat al-Shuʿarāʾ in J. Stetkevych, "Arabic Hermeneutical Terminology: Paradox and the Production of Meaning," *Journal of Near Eastern Studies* 40 no. 2 (April 1989), p. 84.

Chapter 4

1. The clear reference comes from Abū al-ʿAbbās Aḥmad Ibn ʿAlī al-Qalqashandī, *Ṣubḥ al-Aʿshā fī Ṣināʿat al-Inshā,* 14 vols. (Cairo: Al-Muʾassasah al-Miṣrīyah al-ʿĀmmah li al-Taʾlīf wa al-Tarjamah wa al-Ṭibāʿah wa al-Nashr, 1383/1963) 5:432. A construable assumption based on a piecing together, or contextualization, of consecutively used *ḥadīth* references is possible through Ibn Kathīr, *Qiṣaṣ al-Anbiyāʾ,* pp. 122-23. Otherwise we are left with the all-too-easy mechanical assignation of every *ḥaram* to Mecca. This, we know historically, was not the case.

2. Al-Wāqidī, *Maghāzī* 3:1007-08. M. Watt's (*Muḥammad at Medina,* pp. 89, 107, 110, 189, 252-254, 259) reconstruction of the fiscal atmosphere in Muḥammad's "camp" of the period immediately before, during, and immediately after the Tabūk campaign may help us, albeit no more than speculatively, to understand the reason behind the curious narrative "inventiveness" and seeming naïveté of al-Wāqidī's Abū Righāl story and, as we shall see, of its other related variants. For it was in that period that Muḥammad was most directly and insistently concerned with the question, and "institution," of the *ṣadaqāt* ("prescribed alms tax," "charitable

almsgiving"), which basically, at that time, equalled a tax levied to provide for the needs of the existing "proto-state." The duly salaried or recompensed office of the collector of the *ṣadaqāt,* the *muṣaddiq,* was then established, and the harshness of those tax impositions, precisely at that still unaccustomed stage of Islamic fiscal institutionalization, was strongly felt by some of the recent converts and affiliates; it was at this time, therefore, that the *muṣaddiq* must have become a most unwelcome if not altogether despicable figure. It is thus easily imaginable that such characteristics of the *muṣaddiq* may consequently have found their projection backwards, into the otherwise "condemned" era of the Thamūd, where it would be attached to Abū Righāl, "the last of the Thamūd."

3. Abū al-Faḍl Jamāl al-Dīn Muḥammad Ibn Mukarram Ibn Manẓūr al-Ifrīqī al-Miṣrī, *Lisān al-ʿArab,* 15 vols. (Beirut: Dār Ṣādir/Dār Bayrūt, 1375/1956) s.v. *r-j-m.*

4. Compare Ibn Hishām, *Sīrah* (Cairo) 1:59 with Ibn Manẓūr, *Lisān al-ʿArab,* s.v. *r-j-m.* For a discussion of this subject, see below (pp. 42–48).

5. Qurʾān, The Sura of the Elephant (no. 105), 5 vv. (Meccan).

6. Ibn Manẓūr, *Lisān al-ʿArab,* s.v. *r-j-m.*

7. The legend of a bough of gold buried in a grave on the road between Mecca and Ṭāʾif, in the land of the Banū Thaqīf, and of its recovery in the days of the Prophet Muḥammad as the golden bough of the Thamūd, may have been influenced, or reinforced, by an actual event that had occurred in Ṭāʾif at that last period of Muḥammad's life. Thus when, following the Thaqafites' conversion, or hesitant submission, to Islam, their idols that were found in the sanctuary of their principal goddess Al-Lāt were being destroyed, there was also found a substantial treasure buried under the white stone that represented the goddess herself. The treasure of the goddess, consisting of coins and jewels, was taken by Abū Sufyān, himself newly converted, who, supposedly, was accountable for it to the Prophet. See Julius Wellhausen, *Reste arabischen Heidentums,* 2d ed. (Berlin: Georg Reimer, 1897), p. 31; and Margoliouth, *Mohammed,* pp. 428–30.

8. Ibn Kathīr, *Al-Bidāyah wa al-Nihāyah* 1:137.

9. *Idhā th-Thaqafiyu fākharakum fa qūlū*
halumma fa ʿudda shaʾna Abī Righāli

Ḥassān Ibn Thābit, *Dīwān,* eds. Sayyid Ḥanafī Ḥasanayn and Ḥusayn Kāmil al-Ṣīrafī (Cairo: Al-Hayʾah al-Miṣrīyah al-ʿĀmmah li al-Kitāb, 1974), pp. 256–58.

10. Ḥassān Ibn Thābit, *Dīwān* (1974), pp. 256–57.

11. It may be important at this point to insist further, also with an eye to clarification, on the reason for the significance of the semantics/semiotics in pre-Islamic Bedouin Arabic of the verb *ʿaqara,* with its morphological variants presently relevant to us, such as the verbal noun *ʿaqr,* or the passive participle *maʿqūr* ("he hocked"/"hamstrung"; "hocking"/"hamstringing"; "hocked"/"hamstrung"). "Hocking" in Arabic must not be understood as merely a form of mutilation. Hocking always represents the first step in the slaughtering of an animal (sheep, camel). It is not properly used in speaking of the slaying of animals that are neither consumed nor sacrificed—except, as we have seen in the case of the Abyssinian elephant, allusively; and, especially communal consumption then implies sacrificial slaughtering. Furthermore, a more specifically sacrificial slaughtering then becomes *cultic* slaughtering. All such forms

of the killing of an animal were in the Arabic word and deed initiated by "hamstringing," that is, by incapacitating the animal, and it was such a ritualized usage which produced the term's semantic broadening and development: to kill/slaughter.

We acquire further understanding of the Arabic *ʿaqara* as we move into the semiotic sphere of the Hebrew Bible. It is true that there, in scenes of warfare (2 Sam 8:4/1Chron 18:4; Josh 11:6, 9), the Arabic term's precise Hebrew equivalent, *ʿiqqer,* also applies to "hamstringing" chariot battle horses—which, if nothing else, would bring its surface meaning close to the surface meaning of *maʿqūr* in the qurʾānic scene of the Abyssinian elephant. In its other, to us more significant occurrence, in Gen 49:6, however, its context is that of Jacob's patriarchal *curse* uttered against his two sons, Simeon and Levi, for having *hamstrung* steers/oxen in a manner, or for reasons, that the text calls *birẓonam,* and which comes translated (Revised Standard Version) as "in their wantonness." Such a translation strikes me as inadequate, however, inasmuch as it does not take into account the strong cultic underpinning of Gen 49:6-7, something close to abomination, through which condemnation becomes a curse. For not only does the Hebrew root *r-ẓ-w/y* carry the meaning of "pleasure in, or appeasement through, sacrificial offerings," but the very textuality of the noun *raẓōn* (v. 6) reflects the same cultic semiotics as its Arabic qurʾānic equivalent, *riḍwān* "[God's] pleasure."

12. *Ḥubisa l-filu bi l-Mughammasi ḥattā*
ẓalla yaḥbū kaʾannahū maʿqūru

Ibn Hishām, *Sīrah* (Beirut) 1:180; Umayyah Ibn Abī al-Ṣalt, *Dīwān,* ed. ʿAbd al-Ḥāfiẓ al-Salṭī (Damascus: Al-Maṭbaʿah al-Taʿāwunīyah, 1974), p. 392.

13. The Sura of the Elephant (105), of only five verses, makes a legend-clad, mythopoeic reference to the Abyssinian campaign under the command of Abraha against Mecca. It was during that campaign that, according to further legend, the role of the Banū Thaqīf is introduced—either merely as submissive to the might of the alien invader, or as pursuing their own "treacherous" designs. In that "atmosphere," quite in a manner in which ill fortune befalls a cursed individual, the choice is then made that Abū Righāl (of the beleaguered/treacherous Banū Thaqīf) serve as guide to the Abyssinians.

14. Al-Qalqashandī, *Ṣubḥ al-Aʿshā* 5:432.

15. Al-Qalqashandī, *Ṣubḥ al-Aʿshā* 5:432.

16. *Innā mursilū n-nāqati fitnatan lakum,* Qurʾān 54:27.

17. See above, pp. 37-38, Ibn Manẓūr's variant story concerning this "other" Abū Righāl.

18. Qurʾān 105:1.

19. Al-Masʿūdī, *Murūj al-Dhahab* 2:53-54.

20. Ibn Hishām, *Sīrah* (Beirut) 1:166.

21. Al-Masʿūdī, *Murūj al-Dhahab* 2:54. For the story of ʿUmar Ibn al-Khaṭṭāb threatening that the grave of a certain Ghaylān Ibn Salamah, a minor poet, would be stoned by everyone that should pass by it, "as the grave of Abū Righāl is stoned," see Muḥammad Ibn Sallām al-Jumaḥī, *Ṭabaqāt Fuḥūl al-Shuʿarāʾ,* 2 vols., ed. Maḥmūd Muḥammad Shākir (Cairo: Maṭbaʿat al-Madanī, 1393/1974) 1:269-70; and for a reference to the "grave of Abū Righāl" in the rather scabrous story of Ashʿab, the buffoon

of Sukaynah Bint al-Ḥusayn, Sukaynah, and the great singer of the Ḥijāzī school, Ibn Surayj, see Abū al-Faraj al-Iṣbahānī, *Kitāb al-Aghānī,* 31 vols., ed. Ibrāhīm al-Abyārī (Cairo: Dār al-Shaᶜb, 1969–79) 18:6314.

22. *Idhā māta l-Farazdaqu fa-rjumūhu*
kamā tarmūna qabra Abī Rughāli

Al-Masᶜūdī, *Murūj al-Dhahab* 2:53.

23. *Arjumu qabrahū fī kulli ᶜāmin*
ka rajmi n-nāsi qabra Abī Rughāli

Al-Masᶜūdī, *Murūj al-Dhahab* 2:54.

24. *La aᶜẓamu fajratan min Abī Rughālin*
wa ajwaru fī l-ḥukūmati min Sadūmi

Al-Masᶜūdī, *Murūj al-Dhahab* 2:54.

25. *Sīrah,* p. 50 (English); *Sīrah* 1:250–51 (Beirut).

26. For the Hebrew meanings of "excommunication" and "anathema" of the root *ḥ-r-m,* see Gesenius, *Handwörterbuch,* pp. 259–60; and Walter Burkert, *Greek Religion,* trans. John Raffan (Cambridge, Massachusetts: Harvard University Press, 1985), pp. 93 and 384, n. 96.

27. W. Robertson Smith, *The Religion of the Semites: The Fundamental Institutions* (New York: Meridian Books, 1957), p. 202.

28. Robertson Smith, *The Religion of the Semites,* p. 155.

29. Maḥmūd Shukrī al-Ālūsī, *Bulūgh al-Arab fī Maᶜrifat Aḥwāl al-ᶜArab,* 3 vols., ed. Muḥammad Bahjat al-Atharī, 2d ed. (Beirut: Dār al-Kutub al-ᶜIlmīyah, n.d. [1st ed. A.H. 1314]) 1:189–90.

30. Al-Ālūsī, *Bulūgh al-Arab* 1:189–90.

31. Ibn Hishām, *Sīrah* (Cairo) 2:454, 456, 462–64, 474.

32. A. F. L. Beeston et al., *Sabaic Dictionary (English-French-Arabic)* (Louvain-la-Neuve: Peeters; Beirut: Librairie du Liban, 1982), p. 166.

33. For a discussion of *erma/herm,* see G. B. Frazer ("stones") [*Taboo and the Perils of the Soul,* pp. 101–116].

34. Al-Ālūsī, *Bulūgh al-Arab* 3:145–46.

35. Lane, *Lexicon,* s.v. *j-m-r.*

36. See Jaroslav Stetkevych, "Toward an Arabic Elegiac Lexicon: The Seven Words of the *Nasīb,*" in Suzanne Pinckney Stetkevych, ed., *Reorientations/Arabic and Persian Poetry* (Bloomington and Indianapolis: Indiana University Press, 1994), pp. 89–105.

37. Walter Burkert, *Greek Religion,* p. 136.

38. This apotropaic aspect is also reflected in Hermes as Pylaios, who, in the *Homeric Hymn* no. 4 ("To Hermes"), line 15, stands at the gates of houses, "a watcher by night and a gate-keeper. . . ." *The Homeric Hymns,* trans., introduction, and notes by Apostolos N. Athanassakis (Baltimore and London: The Johns Hopkins University Press, 1976), p. 31.

39. Norman O. Brown draws the right conclusion from the role Hesiod assigns to Hermes in the myth of Pandora [*Works and Days,* 320–25]. Thus Hermes, who in his "gift" to Pandora represents the opposite of that which is "god-given," is in Hesiod's dualistic philosophy "the symbol of the immoral reality" and "is reduced to the rank of satan." See his *Hermes the Thief: The Evolution of a Myth* (Great Barrington, Massachusetts: Lindisfarne Press, 1990 [first published 1947]), p. 62.

40. The square base—and with it the whole shaft—of the herm/Hermes-pillar, together with its essential liminality, that means, its standing outside, its demarcation of spaces, and its apotropaic guardianship of gates—especially the latter placement and function—, all these aspects

are also proper of the ancient Egyptian obelisks. The factor of the basic anthropological and symbolic liminality of the obelisk has been rather studiously avoided, or plainly ignored, by philologically focused Egyptology. Reflecting that focus, there have been put forward diverse theories, prevalent among them being the cosmological-"solar" and "geodesic" ones, all that without drawing the anthropologically dictated consequences from the factor of the primary placement of obelisks: at gates. Only in our more contemporary confusion of symbolic forms and archetypal functionalities have we been led to place obelisks centrally instead of marginally—as, for instance, in the case of the Place de la Concorde of Paris. There the confusion arises from the interference of the rivaling form-function of the cylindrical column. The obelisk installed on the London Strand, however, has received a distinctly "liminal" placement; and the gigantic modern obelisk of the Washington Memorial in Washington, D.C., too, remains clearly "liminal" for its implicit closeness to being a mausoleum.

41. Georg Wissowa (et al.), *Paulys Real-Encyclopädie der classischen Altertumswissenschaft*, ed. Wilhelm Kroll (Stuttgart: J. B. Metzlerscher Verlag, 1894-) 15 [1912]:697–98 (from the entry on "Hermai" [15:696–708]). Also see the concise but insightful and broadly documented discussion of the significance of the archaic "herm" in Brown, *Hermes the Thief*, pp. 32–37. To be noted here is also James G. Frazer's extensive list of stoned cairns and analogical heaps of sticks. His theory is that such stoning represents transference of evil to the cast stone—or material substance. Thrown at cairns, stones mark scenes of great crime or great misfortune, "where something has happened or evil deeds have been done." See an extensive listing of the existence of such cairns and of their ritualized stoning, in his *The Golden Bough: A Study in Magic and Religion*. Part VI *The Scapegoat*, 3d ed. (London: The Macmillan Press Ltd., 1980 [first ed. 1913]), pp. 8–30, esp. pp. 13, 15–17, 19, 24.

Chapter 5

1. Ḥassān Ibn Thābit, *Dīwān* (1974), p. 197. It is to be noted further that not only verse 25 but also verses 26–28 constitute a *hijāʾ* (invective) application of the Thamūdic tragedy. These lines do not appear in *Sharḥ Dīwān Ḥassān Ibn Thābit* (1929).

2. With slight variations, this *ḥadīth* is retold in the context of the story of the Thamūd in Ibn Kathīr, *Al-Bidāyah wa al-Nihāyah* 1:135; and al-Thaʿlabī, *Kitāb Qiṣaṣ al-Anbiyāʾ*, p. 62.

The early pathos of the taboo characteristic of this motif is, however, at times dispelled and banalized in later Arabic verse. Thus when the Umayyad poet Jarīr uses it in his exchange of invective *(naqāʾiḍ)* with his rival al-Farazdaq:

Wa shabbahta nafsaka ashqā Thamūda
fa qālū ḍalilta wa lam tahtadi

You brought yourself to the likeness
of the most wretched of the Thamūd,
So they said: You went astray
and did not take the right way!

(al-Jumaḥī, *Ṭabaqāt Fuḥūl al-Shuʿarāʾ* 1:373). In the commentary upon the above verse, the editor M. M. Shākir quotes another verse from Jarīr's *naqāʾiḍ* against al-Farazdaq, in which al-Farazdaq, quite as Abū Righāl (Qudār?), shall be expelled from the (implied) *ḥaram,* that is, safe precinct or sanctuary, of the mosque, and perish (1:374)—for, as we remember, Abū Righāl was struck down with the punishment of the Thamūd upon stepping outside of the *ḥaram.*

3. The interesting addition to the motival repertory in Ibn Abī al-Ṣalt is the appearance of another "sole survivor" of the destruction—this time not Qudār/Abū Righāl himself but another she-camel, bearing here the epithet of *al-dharīʿah* (a camel used as a screen by a hunter). She became "restive" *(jarūr),* or "run-away," and escaped, as messenger, to the neighboring Qarḥ (or Qurḥ), where she died. See Ibn Abī al-Ṣalt, *Dīwān,* (1974), pp. 405–07; see also Friedrich Schultheiss, ed. and trans., *Umajja ibn Abi ṣṢalt: Die unter seinem Namen überlieferten Gedichtfragmente* (Leipzig: J. C. Hinrichs'sche Buchhandlung, 1911) [(Baltimore: Johns Hopkins Press), pp. 44–45 Arabic text, pp. 101–02 German text]. Concerning Qarḥ/Qurḥ, see Ḥusayn Muʾnis, *Aṭlas Tārīkh al-Islām* (Cairo: Al-Zahrāʾ li al-Iʿlām al-ʿArabī, 1407/1987), p. 57.

Ibn Abī al-Ṣalt's verses (29–32) that tell the story of *al-dharīʿah* are, to say the least, difficult to accept as a "stable" text capable of yielding a "stable" reading. This becomes even more so when one compares them with their textual variants in the prose of al-Ṭabarī's *Tafsīr* (vol. 12, p. 536), where the name/epithet of the escapee, or messenger, is a "putative" *al-zurayʿah,* i.e., the diminutive of "a plot of land fit to be sown." Also, in al-Ṭabarī the escapee-messenger is a *woman.* She is a crippled maidservant, but on that occasion, after she had witnessed the calamity that had befallen the Thamūd, God straightened out her crippled legs and she ran out at a speed never seen before. At Qurḥ she told what she had witnessed, asked to be given drink, drank and died. This would be the end of the story of al-Zurayʿah/al-Dharīʿah, only that al-Ṭabarī takes pains to tell us that this al-Zurayʿah, this "little plot of land ready to be sown," "was a godless woman, very hostile toward Ṣāliḥ!" Together with Ṣadūf and ʿUnayzah, there are thus three named women among the Thamūd who are very hostile to Ṣāliḥ. All three, too, are "godless." Especially this last case, thrown in quite as a reflex, should have its semiotic aspects. Al-Thaʿlabī [*Kitāb Qiṣaṣ al-Anbiyāʾ,* p. 61], too, gives the story as being that of al-Dharīʿah, although without dwelling on her godlessness and hatred of Ṣāliḥ. In *Al-Bidāyah wa al-Nihāyah* [vol. 1, p. 136], Ibn Kathīr, too, calls the *"jāriyah"*—a term that means both "maidservant" and "(fast and steady) runner"—al-Dharīʿah. But there God does not intervene "to straighten her legs."

4. Abū Tammām, *Dīwān,* recension al-Khaṭīb al-Tabrīzī, 4 vols. ed. Muḥammad ʿAbduh ʿAzzām, 4th ed. (Cairo: Dār al-Maʿārif bi Miṣr, 1976) 2:206. See also Suzanne Pinckney Stetkevych, *Abū Tammām and the Poetics of the ʿAbbāsid Age* (Leiden: E. J. Brill, 1991), p. 227.

5. Al-Qāḍī al-Fāḍil [ʿAbd al-Raḥīm Ibn ʿAlī al-Baysānī] *Dīwān,* 2 vols., ed. Aḥmad Aḥmad Badawī (Cairo: Dār al-Maʿārif, 1961) 1:162 [poem no. 241].

6. Abū al-ʿAbbās al-Mufaḍḍal Ibn Muḥammad al-Ḍabbī, *Dīwān al-Mufaḍḍalīyāt,* commentary by Abū Muḥammad al-Qāsim Ibn Muḥammad

Ibn Bashshār al-Anbārī, Vol. 1 Arabic Text, ed. Charles James Lyall (Beirut: Maṭbaʿat al-Ābāʾ al-Yasūʿīyīn, 1920), p. 784. For a modern comment see Aḥmad Kamāl Zakī, "Al-Tafsīr al-Usṭūrī li al-Shiʿr al-Qadīm," *Fuṣūl,* vol. 1, no. 3 (April 1981), p. 118. The somewhat cryptic *li ṭayrihinna dabību* of the poem's v. 37 (our v. 3) is, according to the wider context of pre-Islamic heroic poetry, a reference to vultures feasting upon the fallen enemy after the battle. Their "creeping on the ground" is because of their oversatiation and their inability to take off. See this subject discussed by Suzanne P. Stetkevych, *The Mute Immortals Speak,* pp. 67-70; and her "Pre-Islamic Panegyric and the Poetics of Redemption: *Mufaḍḍalīyah 119* of ʿAlqamah and *Bānat Suʿād* of Kaʿb Ibn Zuhayr," p. 14, in Stetkevych, ed., *Reorientations.*

7. Imruʾ al-Qays, *Dīwān,* 5th ed., ed. Muḥammad Abū al-Faḍl Ibrāhīm (Cairo: Dār al-Maʿārif, 1990), p. 208 [poem no. 43]. My reading in v. 3 of "hyenas" stems from the redaction of al-Sukkarī. See ibid., p. 208, note.

8. Abū Zayd Muḥammad Ibn Abī al-Khaṭṭāb al-Qurashī, *Jamharat Ashʿār al-ʿArab fī al-Jāhilīyah wa al-Islām,* 2 vols., ed. *ʿAlī Muḥammad al-Bijāwī* (Cairo: Dār Nahḍat Miṣr li al-Ṭibāʿah wa al-Nashr, 1387/1967) 2:625.

9. Al-Qurashī, *Jamharat Ashʿār al-ʿArab* 2:734.

10. See in Abū al-ʿAbbās Ibn Muḥammad Yazīd al-Mubarrad, *Kitāb al-Taʿāzī wa al-Marāthī,* ed. Muḥammad al-Dībājī (Damascus: Maṭbaʿat Zayd Ibn Thābit, 1396/1976), p. 17.

11. Abū Bakr Muḥammad Ibn Qāsim al-Anbārī, *Sharḥ al-Qaṣāʾid al-Sabʿ al-Ṭiwāl al-Jāhilīyāt,* ed. ʿAbd al-Salām Muḥammad Hārūn, 2d ed. (Cairo: Dār al-Maʿārif bi Miṣr, 1969), p. 269 [v. 32]. The blending together into one Qudār myth of Thamūd, Iram, and ʿĀd should be viewed as a poetic amalgam, not as a "mistake."

12. Muṣṭafā Nāṣif, *Dirāsat al-Adab al-ʿArabī* (Cairo: Dār al-Qawmīyah li al-Ṭibāʿah wa al-Nashr, [n.d.]), p. 251.

13. ʿUrwah Ibn al-Ward, *Dīwānā ʿUrwah Ibn al-Ward wa al-Samawʾal* (Beirut: Dār Ṣādir/Dār Bayrūt, 1384/1964), p. 36 [I have opted for the genitive reading: *fajūʿin/mazallatin/makhūfin*]. Note here, too, the she-camel's epithet *ṣarmāʾ,* translated by me (more traditionally) as "ill-tempered," but actually implying the cutting of bonds and permanent separation. Cf. vv. 39 and 40 of the *Lāmīyat al-ʿArab* by al-Shanfarā, where the people (as tribesmen) are *aḍāmīm* (those that band together), whereas the she-camels are *al-aṣārīm.* See Muḥammad Ibn ʿAmr al-Zamakhsharī, *Kitāb Aʿjab al-ʿAjab fī Lāmīyat al-ʿArab* (Istanbul: Maṭbaʿat al-Jawāʾib, A.H. 1300), p. 52.

14. Abū Tammām, *Dīwān* 2:460 [poem no. 101]. Does Abū Tammām intend here a further reference to the cryptic qurʾānic passages of *tamattuʿ,* the respite which the people of Thamūd received after killing the she-camel, before they themselves were destroyed? See Qurʾān, Hūd, v. 65; Tawbah, v. 68; al-Dhārīyāt, v. 43; also al-Ṭabarī, *Tafsīr* 12:525, 527, 537; Ibn Kathīr, *Al-Bidāyah wa al-Nihāyah* 1:136; al-Thaʿlabī, *Kitāb Qiṣaṣ al-Anbiyāʾ,* p. 60.

15. Dhū al-Rummah, *Dīwān,* 2d ed. (Damascus: Al-Maktabah al-Islāmīyah li al-Ṭibāʿah wa al-Nashr, 1384/1964) p. 339 [poem no. 32, v. 56]. Indeed, in Dhū al-Rummah's present poem there also surfaces the motif of the slaughter of the she-camel (p. 430, v. 61). Such an indictment of the Bedouin poet's she-camel also links up with the motif of the "crow

of separation" *(ghurāb al-bayn),* in which, however, that bird is only a harbinger, not the executor, of ill fortune.

16. Usāmah Ibn Munqidh, *Dīwān,* eds. Aḥmad Aḥmad Badawī and Ḥāmid ʿAbd al-Majīd ([Cairo?]: n.p., n.d.), pp. 70–72 [poem no. 143].

17. ʿAdī Ibn Zayd al-ʿIbādī, *Dīwān,* ed. Muḥammad Jabbār al-Muʿaybid (Baghdad: Dār al-Jumhūrīyah li al-Nashr wa al-Ṭabʿ, 1965), p. 159.

18. Al-Kisāʾī, *Qiṣaṣ al-Anbiyāʾ,* p. 37 [English translation, p. 38]; Al-Nuwayrī, *Nihāyat al-Arab* 13:16.

19. Ibn Qutaybah, *Al-Maʿārif,* p. 15. In Ibn Qutaybah's phrasing the connection between the snake-camel of Paradise and the biblical/qurʾānic Satan/Shayṭān is very strongly suggested, too.

20. Al-Jāḥiẓ, *Kitāb al-Ḥayāwān* 1:152–55. See also al-Damīrī, *Ḥayāt al-Ḥayawān* 1:32. The Qurʾān's own condemnation of the *baḥīrah/sāʾibah,* the ritually tabooed she-camel (Al-Māʾidah [5], v.103), should be mentioned here as well—inasmuch as this condemnation presents us with grave hermeneutical questions once we attempt to draw an equation between the tribal taboo *(baḥīrah/sāʾibah)* and that of "divine" provenance (nāqatu l-Lāhi). See further, below, pp. 60–61.

Chapter 6

1. See S. Stetkevych, *The Mute Immortals Speak,* pp. 27–28.
2. Al-Ṭabarī, *Tafsīr* 12:531.
3. Al-Ṭabarī, *Tafsīr* 12:531.
4. Al-Ṭabarī, *Tafsīr* 12:532.
5. Al-Ṭabarī, *Tafsīr* 12:531.
6. Al-Ṭabarī, *Tafsīr* 12:527.
7. Maçoudi, *Les prairies d'or,* ed. and trans. C. Barbier de Meynard and Pavet de Courteille, 9 vols. (Paris: Imprimerie Imperiale, 1861–1917) 3:84–87.
8. Al-Thaʿlabī, *Kitāb Qiṣaṣ al-Anbiyāʾ,* p. 58. If the size of the She-Camel of Ṣāliḥ is said to have been gigantic, so too, according to legend, would have been the size of the Thamūd themselves—and even more so that of the ʿĀd. To this Alfred von Kremer remarks that "indeed, the ʿĀd, especially in later Arabic tradition, played the role of the Nefilim of the Hebrews, and the Giants and the Cyclopes of the Greeks." Von Kremer quotes the anecdote of the "trousers of Qays Ibn Saʿd," the giant champion of Muʿāwiyah against the Byzantines. These trousers of Qays Ibn Saʿd were like "the trousers of a giant [ʿĀdite jinn] woven by Thamūd." See Alfred von Kremer, *Über die südarabische Sage* (Leipzig: F. A. Brockhaus, 1866), p. 21. See the Qays Ibn Saʿd anecdote further in Ibn Qutaybah, *Al-Maʿārif,* p. 593.
9. Al-Nuwayrī, *Nihāyat al-Arab* 13:81–82.
10. Ibn Kathīr, *Al-Bidāyah wa al-Nihāyah* 1:134.
11. See above, chapter 5.
12. See further in Lane, *Lexicon,* s.v. *b-ḥ-r, s-y-b;* and Maḥmūd Salīm al-Ḥūt, *Fī Ṭarīq al-Mīthūlūjiyā ʿind al-ʿArab wa huwa Baḥth Mushab fī al-Muʿtaqadāt wa al-Asāṭīr al-ʿArabīyah qabl al-Islām* (Beirut: n.p., 1955), pp. 105–06.

13. *Mā ja'ala l-Lāhu min baḥīratin wa lā sā'ibatin wa lā waṣīlatin wa lā ḥāmin wa lākinna l-ladhīna kafarū yaftarūna 'alā l-Lāhi l-kadhiba* . . . , Qur'ān 5:103.

14. This "rivalry" is not unlike the rivalry between the "prophet" and the "antiprophet/sorcerer/poet" which characterizes and, indeed, patterns the cyclic prophetic agon in the Sura of the Poets (26). See my "Arabic Hermeneutical Terminology: Paradox and the Production of Meaning," *Journal of Near Eastern Studies* 48, no. 2 (April 1989): 84.

15. Lane, *Arabic-English Lexicon*, s.v. *s-y-b*.

16. M. B. Piotrovskyj, *Koranicheskye Skazania* (Moscow: Nauka, 1991), p. 66.

17. Piotrovskyj, *Koranicheskye Skazania*, p. 66. Undoubtedly the Thamūdic slaying of the she-camel was an "abomination." But it was one not only to the "encroaching" nomadic camel-breeders. Indeed, according to the law of the totem, it had to be an abomination to the Thamūd in the first place. For the Thamūd to be exterminated for having killed the she-camel, that she-camel had to be their own totem—not just that of a camel-breeding invader, as Piotrovskyj seems to propose. A "bedouinization" of the Thamūd themselves, although closer to the historical conditions and possibilities, ought to have created its own symbolic relationships, their explanations, and totemic "requirements." There, too, it would still be applicable to follow Robert Fraser's paraphrase of W. Robertson Smith that the "life of the clan literally inhered in the totem." See, Robert Fraser, *The Making of the Golden Bough: The Origins and Growth of an Argument* (New York: St. Martin's Press, 1990), p. 93.

18. More to the point is Suzanne P. Stetkevych's discussion of the slaying of the She-Camel of Ṣāliḥ as "improper sacrifice." See her *The Mute Immortals Speak*, pp. 28-29:

> The she-camel here [that is, in the qur'ānic conception] functions as a symbol of fecundity and prosperity, a sign of divine blessing whose improper or forbidden sacrifice marks the disintegration, indeed, extermination, of the polity. . . . The point, with respect to the argument at hand, is that the she-camel is the preeminent symbol of prosperity and fecundity and, in particular, of human culture. The proper sacrifice of the she-camel thus constitutes a commensal meal that defines and consolidates the kin group, just as, conversely, her improper sacrifice signals the disintegration and destruction of the polity.

19. There is a record of the presence of the camel, or of camel figurines, in Nabataean worship as far as the mercantile port of Puteoli [Nelson Glueck, *Deities and Dolphins: The Story of the Nabataeans* (New York: Straus and Giroux, 1965), pp. 379-80]. Also see Robertson Smith, *The Religion of the Semites*, p. 168. Consider also the fact that Parthian Hatra, a polity that was also commercially camel-dependent, although without being, in a stricter sense, a "caravan empire," had, and still has, on the façade of one of its largest temples prominently sculptured representations of nursing she-camels.

20. *Aeneid* 2:49.

21. See Christopher A. Faraone, *Talismans and Trojan Horses: Guardian Statues in Ancient Greek Myth and Ritual* (New York and Oxford: Oxford University Press, 1992), esp. Chapter 6, pp. 94-112. On the other hand, for the possible reason of the absence of particular topical linkage between the *Odyssey* and the *Iliad*, see Gregory Nagy, *The Best of the Achaeans:*

Concept of the Hero in Archaic Greek Poetry (Baltimore and London: The Johns Hopkins University Press, 1981), pp. 20–22. For a discussion of Vergil's indebtedness to the Hellenistic poetic tradition of the Trojan Horse, see Wendell Clausen, *Virgil's Aeneid and the Tradition of Hellenistic Poetry* (Berkeley, Los Angeles, London: University of California Press, 1987), pp. 29–39.

22. C. M. Bowra, *Homer* (New York: Charles Scribner's Sons, 1972), pp. 20–21.

23. Gilbert Murray, *The Rise of the Greek Epic, Being a Course of Lectures Delivered at Harvard University*, 4th ed. (London, Oxford, New York: Oxford University Press, 1967), p. 36. For the importance of the she-camel in pre-Islamic Arabic poetry, with that animal's more than one thousand epithetic names, see Jaroslav Stetkevych, "Name and Epithet: The Philology and Semiotics of Animal Nomenclature in Early Arabic Poetry," *Journal of Near Eastern Studies* 45, no. 2 (1986), pp. 112–25; See also S. Stetkevych, *The Mute Immortals Speak*, pp. 26–31, 207–10.

24. In his *Kitāb Luṭf al-Tadbīr fī Ḥiyal al-Mulūk*, Abū ʿAbdallāh al-Khaṭīb (d. 420/1029) of the court of al-Ṣāḥib Ibn ʿAbbād includes a curious retelling of the story of the Trojan Horse. At first, Odysseus is totally absent from that story, however. Instead, the story revolves around Achilles entirely. The main ingredients of the Homeric Achilles are present in it. Thus Achilles quarrels with "his king," his friend Patrocles falls in combat with the Trojan Hector, then Achilles falls into rage and slays Hector. From there onward, however, the story becomes that of Odysseus. Phrased very much in the manner of an Arabic story of blood vengeance, Achilles swears to destroy Troy. For that he conceives of the ruse of the large, hollow wooden horse, with room inside for one hundred Greek warriors. The ruse succeeds, the horse is brought into Troy through a torn-open gate, and Achilles breaks out and secures the entry of the Greeks into the city. Thus Troy, the city of Africa [Phrygia], falls and is destroyed completely. See the full text of this anecdotal retelling of the "Homeric" story, which has probably gone through various previous Arabic versions, in Franz Rosenthal, "From Arabic Books and Manuscripts VII: Some Graeco-Arabica in Istanbul," *Journal of the American Oriental Society* 81, no. 1 (March 1961): 11–12.

25. The exception of the "ritual" epithet, thus not a "direct" one, of al-Masīḥ, "the anointed one," as qualifying ʿĪsā, is essentially (in the Qurʾān) a secondary epithet (3:45; 4:157).

26. Thus see the qurʾānic *wa lā tufsidū fī l-arḍi baʿda iṣlāḥihā* ("and do not corrupt the earth after it has been set right" [7:56, 85]). Particularly pertinent to the Thamūdic conspiracy against Ṣāliḥ in these terms is Sura 27:48.

27. On the term and concept of "figura," see above, pp. 123–24, n. 15.

28. Al-Ṭabarī, *Tārīkh* 1:226.

29. Qurʾān, trans. Abdullah Yusuf Ali, p. 1596. For the classical *tafsīr* literature concerning Sūrat al-Aʿrāf, vv. 75–76, see, for instance, al-Ṭabarī, *Tafsīr* 12:542; Abū al-Faraj Jamāl al-Dīn ʿAbd al-Raḥmān Ibn ʿAlī Ibn Muḥammad al-Jawzī al-Qurashī al-Baghdādī [Ibn al-Jawzī], *Zād al-Masīr fī ʿIlm al-Tafsīr* (Damascus/Beirut: Al-Maktabah al-Islāmīyah li al-Ṭibāʿah wa al-Nashr, 1385/1965) 3:225; Muḥammad ʿAbduh, *Tafsīr al-Qurʾān al-Ḥakīm*, 2d ed. (Cairo: Maṭbaʿat al-Manār, 1347/1929) 8:504.

30. Regarding the nature of Thamūdic economy, the Iraqi historian Jawād ʿAlī observes that "from the Thamūdic inscriptions it appears that the Thamūdeans were both agriculturalists and owners of herds, and that they were closer to being sedentary than Bedouin tent-dwellers." See his *Al-Mufaṣṣal fī Tārīkh al-ʿArab qabl al-Islām,* 10 vols. (Beirut: Dār al-ʿIlm li al-Malāyīn/Baghdad: Maktabat al-Nahḍah, 1968) 1:330.

31. Qurʾān 22:45. It would appear that the independent story invented around *biʾr muʿaṭṭalah*—as being another place in another "prophetic" scheme of time—is merely an awkward attempt to explain something that ought to be sufficiently clear and simple in the qurʾānic context itself. For this, see al-Nuwayrī, *Nihāyat al-Arab* 13:88-89.

32. Lane, *Arabic-English Lexicon,* s.v. *th-m-d.*

33. Sorting out the historical circumstances of the downfall of the Thamūd, Alfred von Kremer draws the conclusion that "the Thamūd perished—as did their mother-city Petra—through war or through penury that resulted in more and more neglect of commerce, not at all through a direct divine intervention, as told in the Qurʾān." See von Kremer, *Über die südarabische Sage,* pp. 17-19. See also A. Kammerer, *Petra la Nabatène: L'Arabie Pétrée et les Arabes du Nord—Dans leurs rapports avec la Syrie et la Palestine jusqu'à l'Islam. Atlas* (Paris: Librairie Orientale Paul Geuthner, 1930). For more on the mercantile and caravan cultures of the Nabataeans and the Thamūd, see M. Rostovtzeff, *Caravan Cities,* trans. D. and T. Talbot Rice (Oxford: The Clarendon Press, 1932), esp. pp. 50-51. Glueck (*Deities and Dolphins,* p. 9), however, notes that "for a considerable period thereafter [i.e., after the Roman conquest] no perceptible deterioration in the Nabataean economy" took place. Thus, too, Albertus van den Branden, *Histoire de Thamoud,* Publications de l'Université Libanaise Section des Études Historiques, VI (Beirut: 1960); and idem, *Les textes thamoudéens de Philby* (Louvain: Publications universitaires, Institute orientaliste, 1956). On the related subject of Liḥyān, see Werner Caskel, *Lihyan und Lihyanisch* (Cologne and Opladen: Westdeutscher Verlag, 1954); and idem, *Das altarabische Königreich Lihyan* (Krefeld: Scherpe Verlag, 1950), p. 42.

34. Fergus Millar, *The Roman Near East 31 BC-AD 337* (Cambridge, Massachusetts/ London: Harvard University Press, 1993), p. 140. Millar, who gives to SRKT the meaning of "confederation," follows in this, it appears, J. T. Milik ("Inscriptions grecques et nabatéennes de Rawwafah," *Bulletin of the Institute of Archaeology* [University of London], 10 [1971], pp. 54-58), who suggests that *SRKT* means "federation," although Millar makes primary reference to G. W. Bowersock, "The Greek-Nabataean Bilingual Inscription at Ruwwāfa, Saudi Arabia," in *Le monde grec: Hommages à Claire Préaux* (1975), p. 513 = *Année épigraphique* (1977), no. 834. Irfan Shahîd, however, offers a philologically more complex discussion of that undoubtedly significant term. See his *Rome and the Arabs: A Prolegomenon to the Study of Byzantium and the Arabs* (Washington, D.C.: Dumbarton Oaks Research Library and Collection, 1984), pp. 123-41. See also Shahîd's *Byzantium and the Arabs in the Fourth Century* (Washington D.C.: Dumbarton Oaks Research Library and Collections, 1984, pp. 29, 399), where the author discusses the two ways of referring to the Thamūd in the *Notitia Dignitatum,* i.e. "the two Thamudi units in Palestine and Egypt" other than the Saraceni in Phoenicia—namely, the Thamudeni referred to one time as "Saraceni" and on another occasion simply as Thamudeni.

Furthermore, Millar himself admits, with reference to *Notitia Dignitatum* (p. 140) that "It is only in the late fourth century that we know that the Roman army included units of 'Equites Saraceni Thamudeni'." For a pertinent discussion of the *Notitia Dignitatum*, see Shahîd, *Rome and the Arabs*, pp. 51-63.

35. Shahîd, *Byzantium and the Arabs in the Fourth Century*, p. 385.

36. Shahîd, *Byzantium and the Arabs in the Fourth Century*, p. 385.

37. Here Shahîd (*Byzantium and the Arabs in the Fourth Century*, p. 385) bases himself on O. Blau, "Arabien im sechsten Jahrhundert," *ZDMG*, 23 (1869), p. 565, n. 3.

38. Shahîd, *Byzantium and the Arabs in the Fourth Century*, p. 385 (note), and p. 400, n. 194.

39. See above, pp. 22-23, 119 n. 23.

40. Al-Masᶜūdī, *Murūj al-Dhahab* 2:16.

41. Jawād ᶜAlī, *Al-Mufaṣṣal* 1:298-385.

42. Genesis 10:25.

43. *Wa min Nābit wa Qīdar nashara Allāh al-ᶜArab* ("And out of Nābit and Qaydar God propagated the Arabs"), al-Ṭabarī, *Tārīkh* 1:314. The genealogical dilemma here is that, taking this *khabar* literally, it would seem to obliterate the distinction between the first and most prevalent Arabic traditional genealogical principle, namely, the assignation of Arab autochthony to the line of Qaḥṭān alone. Further on ᶜAdnān, see "ᶜAdnān," *Encyclopaedia of Islam*, New Edition.

44. The translations which I introduce in what follows are, if not otherwise indicated, those of the Revised Standard Version. I have, however, consistently used the spelling of Qedar rather than that of Kêʾdār. Also, instead of the generic scriptural "Lord," I have made clear which apellation is relevant and appropriate.

45. Ernst Axel Knauf already suggests that Qedar and Nebayot in Isaiah 60:7 are in themselves a reference to the Nabataeans and to the Nabataean-Qedar kinship ties. See his *Ismael: Untersuchungen zur Geschichte Palästinas und Nordarabiens im 1. Jahrtausend v. Chr.*, 2d ed. (Wiesbaden: Otto Harrassowitz, 1989), p. 109; as well as his article on Kedar in *The Anchor Bible Dictionary*, 6 vols., David Noel Freedman et al., editors (New York: Doubleday, 1992) 4:9.

46. Isidore Epstein, *Judaism: A Historical Presentation* (Harmondsworth, Middlesex: Penguin Books Ltd., 1959), p. 53.

47. Inasmuch as the maid of the opening "stanza" of the Song of Songs describes herself as being "dark" "like the curtains of Solomon," and inasmuch as the imaged darkness of the curtains makes them clearly of the black tents of Qedar, that is, of the Bedouin Ishmaelite tent-dwellers, we are presented with a definite difficulty of interpretation. Are we supposed to understand here that Solomon, the temple-builder, was equally a Bedouin tent-dweller, quite as the Qedar? Especially considering the rest of the "Solomonic" poem, full of "streets and squares" and "city watchmen," such an interpretation becomes careless at best. Furthermore, the time of composition/redaction within the biblical corpus of this formally eclogue-like, or epithalamium-like, poem ought to be very late indeed. Or was this belated Solomon already stylizing himself in this "mannered," bedouinizing fashion?

Within the scholarly and otherwise many-faceted literary fascination with the Song of Songs, stanza 1 verse 5 of this poetic cluster has begotten its particular share of concern, precisely because of the ambiguity of the name "Shalomoh" in it. Julius Wellhausen observes that this name's pre-exegetic reference is actually not to King Solomon but to a tribe, or people, known as the Salmaeans, who appear in "Canticles (i. 5, the tents of Kedar, the curtains of *Salmah* [my italics]), and also as the name of a Nabataean tribe in Pliny. Among the families of the Nethinim enumerated in Neh. vii. 46-60 the B'ne Salmah also occur, along with several other names which enable us distinctly to recognize (Ezek. xliv.) the non-Israelite and foreign origin of these temple slaves." See his *Prolegomena to the History of Ancient Israel,* with a reprint of the article *Israel* from the *Encyclopaedia Britannica,* preface by Prof. W. Robertson Smith (New York: Meridian Books, 1957), p. 218. So too, Wilhelm Wittekindt (*Das Hohe Lied und seine Beziehungen zum Istarkult* [Hannover: Orient-Buchhandlung Heinz Lafaire, 1925], pp. 21-22), to whom 1:5-6 is a "much disputed and difficult text," unreservedly insists that the presently current reading "like the tent-sheets of Solomon" is an exegetically motivated misreading of *slmh*/"Salmaeans." For the Song's exegetical history, as well as for its genre-critical overview, see Friedrich Ohly, *Hohelied-Studien: Grundzüge einer Geschichte der Hoheliedauslegung des Abendlandes bis um 1200* (Wiesbaden: Franz Steiner Verlag GMBH, 1958); and Walter Woodburn Hyde, "Greek Analogies to the Song of Songs," pp. 31-42, in Wilfred H. Schoff, ed., *The Song of Songs: A Symposium* (Philadelphia: The Commercial Museum, 1924).

The fact should also be considered here that the conspicuously "formulaic" *yerīʿot shelomoh/shalmoh/shalmah* of Song 1:5 occurs nowhere else in the Hebrew text [see Ariel Bloch and Chana Bloch, *The Song of Songs,* a new Translation with an Introduction and Commentary by Robert Alter (New York: Random House, 1995), p. 140]. Rather, *yerīʿot,* as we already know from Jer. 49:29, are the booty taken from Qedar; or, in the word's other biblical loci—Exodus 26:1ff., 36:8ff., and Numbers 4:25—their context is that of the drapings of the tabernacle. In this latter case, too, the word bears the strong imprint of bedouinity, as it does in the ceremonial function in Exodus and Numbers. This becomes clear in the manner in which David refers to the tabernacle (2 Samuel 7:2).

48. Al-Anbārī, *Sharḥ al-Qaṣāʾid al-Sabʿ,* pp. 48-51.

It may be a mere coincidence of "topic construction," but just as in Song of Songs 1:5 the mention of Qedar is followed by a mention of "curtains," so, too, in the earliest Arabic poetry, both pre-Islamic and Mukhaḍram (of the generation that was poetically active between the two ages, the pre-Islamic one and the Islamic), the mention of *khidr* is followed by a mention of "curtains." Thus, aside from the aforementioned lines by Imruʾ al-Qays, see the Mukhaḍram Suḥaym ʿAbd Banī al-Ḥasḥās's poem rhyming in *mā* (Muḥammad Khayr al-Ḥalwānī, *Suḥaym ʿAbd Banī al-Ḥasḥās: Shāʿir al-Ghazal wa al-Ṣūrah* [Beirut: Maktabat Dār al-Sharq, 1972], p. 145). On the other hand, this Qedar/*khidr*/curtains interdependence that seems to cross from late biblical poetry over to early Arabic poetry may have noteworthy hermeneutical implications in both directions.

49. The standard dictionary definitions of *khidr* itself are that it means "a curtain that is extended for a girl in a part of a house, or chamber, or

tent"; as well as "a chamber, or house, or tent that conceals a person (woman)." But the substantive/verbal noun *khadar* means "darkness" (of night), or "darkness" (absolutely); furthermore, *khudrah* means "intense darkness"; and the adjectival forms *khudrī/khudārī* mean "dark" (as night, or hair). Related are: *kadira/kadura* ("to be turbid"), with the verbal noun *kadar* ("turbidness"); and *qadhura/qadhira* ("to be, or become, unclean, dirty, filthy"); and *khaḍara/khaḍira* ("to be, or become, of a dark, ashy, dust-color"; "to be, or become, of a tawny, brownish, blackish color"; "to be of a blackish hue inclining to green or black"; or "to be black," "intensely black"). For the above, see Lane, *Arabic-English Lexicon,* s.v. *kh-d-r, k-d-r, q-dh-r, kh-ḍ-r.*

50. It is highly questionable whether it is possible to deduce, as does Ernst Axel Knauf, merely on the basis of the great prominence of the tribe of Qedar within the Šumuʾil confederacy, that that tribe's name would *ipso facto* derive from the (no doubt important) alternate etymological shed of the root *qadara* in Arabic, with its meaning of "to ordain," "to have power" ["Der Name gehört zu arab. *qadara* 'beschließen; Macht haben' und paßt zu der Rolle, die der Stamm in der Konföderation Šumuʾil spielte"]. See his *Ismael,* p. 66.

51. *Wa ana l-akhḍaru man yaʿrifunī*
akhḍaru l-jildati fī bayti l-ʿArab

See Lane, *Arabic-English Lexicon,* s.v. *kh-ḍ-r.* I have "unburdened" the translation of the verse somewhat of its philological encumbrance. Also the literal "who knows me?" appears too unidiomatic, and thus unclear.

52. Also compare the aforementioned Hebrew and Arabic motif of the erotically envisioned feminine (tribal, pastoral, or bucolic) with the same motif's "northern" Hesiodic *(Works and Days)* variant:

> And it [the wind] does not blow through
> the tender maiden
> who stays indoors with her dear mother,
> unlearned as yet in the works of golden Aphrodite,
> and who washes her soft body and anoints herself
> with oil and lies down in an inner room
> within the house,
> on a winter's day . . .

Hesiod: The Homeric Hymns and Homerica, trans. Hugh G. Evelyn-White (Cambridge, Massachusetts: Harvard University Press, 1959 [The Loeb Classical Library]), pp. 40/41 (lines 519-24).

53. See Gesenius, *Handwörterbuch,* s.v. *ḥ-ẓ-r.* For archaeological documentation of Ḥaẓōr of Naphtali, see Amihai Mazar, *Archaeology of the Land of the Bible, 10,000-586* B.C.E. (New York: Doubleday, 1992, esp. pp. 335, 380, 412, 414, 481, 546.

54. Cf. also in 1 Kings 18:5 and Isaiah 34:13 the Hebrew *ḥaḍīr* ("grass") as connoting "greenness." See Gesenius, *Handwörterbuch,* s.v. *ḥ-ẓ-r.*

55. See my "Toward an Arabic Elegiac Lexicon," in S. Stetkevych, ed., *Reorientations,* pp. 61-74.

56. Gesenius, *Handwörterbuch,* s.v. *q-d-r (qedar);* and Knauf, *Ismael,* p. 66. With reference to E. Ebeling's "Neubabylonische Briefe" (ABAW.PH NF 30; Munich, 1949), Knauf remarks that "the <*u*> in *Qu-da-ri* may represent the *shwā* standing for /i/" (*Ismael,* p. 75 [n. 393]).

57. Pliny, *Natural History*, trans. H. Rackham (Cambridge, Massachusetts: Harvard University Press, 1942 [Loeb Classical Library]), pp. 268/269 (Book V, lines 71-72).

58. Knauf, *Ismael*, pp. 1-2.

59. Knauf, *Ismael*, p. 5 (n. 20). Knauf makes the reservation, however, that "The description 'king' does not say anything about the self-characterization of the leader of the Ishmaelite coalition, nor anything at all about his functions. We have already noted that in the case of the queens they [the functions] were in part of a cultic nature."

60. Knauf, *Ismael*, p. 49.

61. Knauf's *Ismael* is almost too densely packed with historical and philological Qedar documentation to go into detailed quotation. I shall limit myself presently to main page references only: 2, 4-5, 9 (n. 42), 66, 72, 74-75, 88-91, 93, 95, and especially 96-108.

Chapter 7

1. The association of the "scream" with an earthquake may nevertheless be well supported by the actual experience of anyone who has ever lived through a powerful earthquake; for such an earthquake comes announced by the most ghostly rumbling sound—certainly a voice like no other voice, or, as in al-Thaᶜlabī's dramatization, "the voice of every thing that has voice." See below, n. 14.

2. Qurʾān 15:83.

3. Qurʾān 54:31.

4. Qurʾān 11:67. Not only the Thamūd heard the "scream," but also, with an exact phrasing later in the same sura (v. 94), the Madyan.

5. Qurʾān 41:13, where the word occurs twice: "We warn you of a *ṣāᶜiqah* like the *ṣāᶜiqah* of ᶜĀd and Thamūd"; or Qurʾān 51:44; and Qurʾān 2:55.

6. Qurʾān 69:5.

7. Qurʾān 7:78. Here *al-rajfah* also belongs in an unmediated way to the Thamūdic context; and Qurʾān 29:37, where the Thamūd (and the ᶜĀd) are only implied, the direct reference being to Madyan.

8. Al-Ṭabarī, *Tafsīr* 12:528, 536-37, 545.

9. *Ar-rajfatu hāhunā ṣ-ṣayḥatu -llatī zaᶜzaᶜathum wa ḥarrakathum li l-halāki liʾanna Thamūda halakat bi ṣ-ṣayḥati fī mā dhakara ahlu l-ᶜilmi.* See al-Ṭabarī, *Tafsīr* 12:545.

10. A further exegetic question mark is introduced by al-Ṭabarī into the understanding of the qurʾānic phrasing of Thamūd contextuality *wa hum yanẓurūna/wa antum tanẓurūna* [Qurʾān 51:44/2:55], where the customary understanding/translation is that of "while they/you were looking on" as the cataclysmic *al-ṣāᶜiqah* struck them. Applicable to this, al-Ṭabarī adds a hermeneutically and, to my mind, philologically corrective sense of the Thamūd "*awaiting* the 'scream' [of death]" *(yantaẓirūna ṣ-ṣayḥata)* in full ritual readiness [*Tafsīr* 12:528]. For the meaning of *naẓara* as "waiting for," see in Arabic poetry Kuthayyir ᶜAzzah: *wa lam yanẓur il-ghādī -lladhī huwa rāʾiḥu* ("and he that departed in the early morning did not *wait for* him that departed at evening-time"). See Ibn Qutaybah, *Al-Shiᶜr wa al-Shuᶜarāʾ*, 2 vols., ed. Aḥmad Muḥammad Shākir (Cairo: Dār al-Maᶜārif bi Miṣr,

1966) 1:13; and Maḥmūd Ibn ʿUmar al-Zamakhsharī, *Asās al-Balāghah* (Cairo: Dār wa Maṭābiʿ al-Shaʿb, 1960), p. 21 [where the author is not given]. In the *Dīwān* of Kuthayyir ʿAzzah [ed. Iḥsān ʿAbbās (Beirut: Dār al-Thaqāfah, 1971), p. 525] the verse, considered by the editor as being of unclear authorship, offers the reading of *wa lā yaʿlamu* instead.

11. See above, pp. 24-28.

12. Al-Nuwayrī, *Nihāyat al-Arab* 13:85.

13. See above, p. 28 n. 46.

14. Al-Thaʿlabī, *Kitāb Qiṣaṣ al-Anbiyāʾ*, p. 61. Ibn Kathīr, however [*Al-Bidāyah wa al-Nihāyah* 1:137], speaks of a "scream" without a further literary concern, but at the same time without introducing semantic ambiguities regarding *al-ṣayḥah.*

We note, furthermore, that, even if we take into account clearly derivative lexicographical and exegetical tendencies to interpret the term *ṣayḥah* as a "storm," and thus as "wind," the only clear reference to a "destructive wind" occurs in the Sura of al-Dhāriyāt, and then, too, with reference to the ʿĀd. In the same sura (v. 44), however, the Thamūd are, nonetheless, destroyed by the *ṣayḥah*. Also, that sura, by its first verse, *Wa dh-dhāriyāti dharwan* ("By the scatterers wide and high"), already announces itself semiotically as the Sura "of the wind."

15. Werner Caskel, *Lihyan und Lihyanisch* (Köln and Opladen: Westdeutscher Verlag, 1954), p. 42. See the review of Liḥyān scholarship in *Encyclopaedia of Islam* (New Edition), art. "Liḥyān."

16. Werner Caskel, *Lihyan und Lihyanisch*, pp. 108-09.

17. Werner Caskel, *Lihyan und Lihyanisch*, p. 109.

18. See F. V. Winnett and W. L. Reed, with contributions by J. T. Milik and J. Starcky, *Ancient Records of North Arabia* (Toronto: University of Toronto Press, 1970), pp. 39 and 43.

Chapter 8

1. James George Frazer, *The Golden Bough: A Study in Magic and Religion*, 3d ed., 12 vols. (London: Macmillan and Co., Limited, 1907-15 [1st ed. 1890]).

2. Christopher Pitt, *The Aeneid of Virgil* (London, 1743), I, 177. See Robert Fraser, *The Making of the Golden Bough*, pp. 190-91, 229.

3. James Sowerby, *English Botany*, xxi. (London, 1805), p. 1470, as referred to by Frazer himself in *Balder the Beautiful: The Fire-Festivals of Europe and the Doctrine of the External Soul*, 2 vols., 1:248n. [= *The Golden Bough*, vols. 10 and 11 (1913)].

4. See the note to *Aeneid* VI, 137 by T. E. Page, *The Aeneid of Virgil, Books I-VI*, Edited with Introduction by T. E. Page (London, Toronto: Macmillan and Co., Ltd., 1967 [1st ed. 1894]), p. 455.

It is Vergil himself, too, who, through the popular etymology of his name as *virga*/bough, fitted smoothly into a twofold "prophetic" role: once as the ideological visionary of the Empire in the *Aeneid*, and again in his fourth eclogue, sometimes referred to as the Messianic Eclogue, which, with its vaguely mystical and strongly oracular pronouncements, was interpreted as prophetic of Christianity.

5. Hesiod, *The Homeric Hymns and Homerica,* trans. Hugh G. Evelyn-White (Cambridge, Massachusetts: Harvard University Press/London: William Heinemann Ltd., 1959 [Loeb Classical Library]), pp. 400/401-402/403 (vv. 529, 539).

6. Homer, *The Odyssey,* trans. A. T. Murray, 2 vols. (Cambridge, Massachusetts/London: Harvard University Press, 1984/1991 [Loeb Classical Library]) 2: 402/403 (XXIV, 1-5). For a remarkably comprehensive and detailed exposition of "The Staff of Hermes from Homeric Times till the 5th Century," see F. J. M. de Waele, *The Magic Staff or Rod in Graeco-Italian Antiquity* (Ghent: Drukkerey Erasmus, 1927), pp. 33-69, 77-79.

7. De Waele, *The Magic Staff,* p. 145.

8. De Waele, *The Magic Staff,* pp. 82-83. See further, *Archaeologischer Anzeiger,* XXVII (1912), p. 238.

9. De Waele, *The Magic Staff,* pp. 25-26. For more on the etymological dimensions of "the willow," see Paul Friedrich, *Proto-Indo-European Trees: The Arboreal System of a Prehistoric People* (Chicago and London: The University of Chicago Press, 1970), pp. 53-57.

10. De Waele, *The Magic Staff,* pp. 26, 32 (n. 6).

11. De Waele, *The Magic Staff,* p. 35.

12. Thus Walter Burkert, following H. Frankfort (*Iraq* I [1934]: 10) and E. D. van Buren (*Archiv für Orientforschung* 10 [1935-36]: 53-65): ". . . the *kerykeion,* which is really the image of copulating snakes taken over from ancient Near Eastern tradition." See his *Greek Religion,* p. 158.

13. Patrick Boylan, *Thoth: The Hermes of Egypt* (Chicago: Ares Publishers, Inc., 1987), pp. 139-40.

14. Ali Hassan, *Stöcke und Stäbe im Pharaonischen Ägypten bis zum Ende des Neuen Reiches* (Munich/Berlin: Deutscher Kunstverlag, 1976), p. 96.

15. Hassan, *Stöcke und Stäbe,* pp. 63-64, 89, 131.

16. Hassan, *Stöcke und Stäbe,* pp. 98ff.

17. Joseph L. Henderson and Maud Oaks, *The Wisdom of the Serpent: The Myth of Death, Rebirth, and Resurrection* (Princeton, New Jersey: Princeton University Press: 1990), p. 111.

18. Hassan, *Stöcke und Stäbe,* pp. 6-9, Plates (Appendix). The Arabic word *ʿaṣā* (staff) is so close to the ancient Egyptian *uas/w3s* as to suggest an etymological connection.

19. Based on John Layard's researches of Malekulan mortuary beliefs and practices, W. F. Jackson Knight, in his *Cumaean Gates,* points to the fact that on two small islets, Atchin and Wala, off the northeastern coast of the island of Malekula in the archipelago of the New Hebrides, by the side of the buried dead man on Atchin there is laid "a cane cut to the length of his body." On Wala the cane laid in the grave "is also cut to the length of the dead man's body" and "is called *ne-row,* translated 'measuring stick.' . . . The dead man at his departure slings a sacrificial fowl on the cane. He then gnaws the bark of a certain magic tree, walks straight through the Cave of the Dead to the shore, and crosses a river by *striking it with the cane, and thus parting the waters*" [ital. mine]. See W. F. Jackson Knight, *Vergil: Epic and Anthropology. Comprising Vergil's Troy, Cumaean Gates, and The Holy City of the East,* ed. John D. Christie (New York: Barnes and Noble, Inc., 1967), pp. 152-53 [*Cumaean Gates* first published in 1936]. I was reminded of this now rarely cited but still altogether fascinating work by Professor Michael Beard.

20. As represented in a relief from Thebes, Tomb 312, reign of Psammetichus I, ca. 664–610 B.C. (Oriental Institute, Chicago, # OI M 18236). Representations analogous to the one above are to be considered standard, and are valid more for the Old Kingdom than for the subsequent periods.

21. Hassan, *Stöcke und Stäbe,* pp. 191–92.

22. Oriental Institute, # OI M 1836. This being the same relief in which the *user* is also borne by Anubis, the difference is, however, that the fieldworker's *user* is coarse and knotty, whereas that of Anubis is of fine workmanship.

23. Hassan, *Stöcke und Stäbe,* 192–93. Here, too, the *user* is rough and knotty.

24. Hassan, *Stöcke und Stäbe,* p. 192. See also C. G. Seligman, "The Was Sceptre as a Beduin Camel Stick," *Journal of Egyptian Archaeology* 3 (1916): 127; G. Daressy, "L'Origine du Sceptre Uas (w3s)," *Annales du Service des Antiquités de l'Egypte* (Cairo) 17 (1917): 183ff.; W. Helck, "Herkunft und Deutung einiger Züge des frühägyptischen Königsbildes," *Anthropos* 49 (1954): 971.

25. The *mikhṣarah* may also be viewed as the "staff of oratory," as, according to a *ḥadīth,* the Prophet held it in his hand, poking about in the dust at the cemetery of Medina, and delivering one of his concise pronouncements on heaven and hell. See al-Jāḥiẓ, *Al-Bayān wa al-Tabyīn,* 3:11.

26. Al-Jāḥiẓ, *Al-Bayān wa al-Tabyīn,* 3:11–12.

27. The semantics of duration of *iqāmah* go indeed as far as "permanent" duration, thus "lying in the grave." Thus *muqīm* may mean "lying in one's grave," and *muqām* "a grave," or "a place of final repose."

28. See al-Jāḥiẓ, *Al-Bayān wa al-Tabyīn* 3:40, 124; and Zuhayr's *Muʿallaqah,* v. 15:

Fa lammā waradna l-māʾa zurqan jimāmuhu
waḍaʿna ʿiṣiyya l-ḥāḍiri l-mutakhayyimi

[Al-Anbārī, *Sharḥ al-Qaṣāʾid al-Sabʿ,* pp. 251–52].

29. Qurʾān 27:10.

30. Qurʾān 7:107, 117; 26:32.

31. 3) *Fa in yaku fīkum ifku firʿawna bāqiyan*
fa inna ʿaṣā Mūsā bi kaffi khaṣībi
4) *Ramākum amīru l-muʾminīna bi ḥayyatin*
akūlin li ḥayyāti l-bilādi sharūbi

[al-Ḥasan Ibn Hāniʾ] Abū Nuwās, *Dīwān,* ed. Aḥmad ʿAbd al-ʿAzīz al-Ghazālī (Beirut: Dār al-Kitāb al-ʿArabī, 1402/1982), p. 484. Also see al-Jāḥiẓ, *Al-Bayān wa al-Tabyīn* 3: 31–32.

32. As part of the exegetic mythopoeia spun out of the qurʾānic apocalyptic hermeticism of Qurʾān 27:82, which speaks of the "beast out of the earth," a curious further reference to the "staff of Moses" is introduced from a *ḥadīth* by Abū Hurayrah and used exegetically by al-Ṭabarī (*Tafsīr* 20:15): "The Beast shall come out, with it the seal of Solomon and the staff of Moses, and it shall rub [polish] the face of the believer with the staff and stamp the nose of the infidel with the seal. . . ." Furthermore, the characteristic of this Beast is that, in its mythopoeia, it comes out of the sacred Mount al-Ṣafā, splitting it in half. Compare this Beast, which also "utters words," not only with the miraculous production of the She-Camel of Ṣāliḥ, but note equally Revelation 13:5: "And the beast was given

a mouth uttering haughty and blasphemous words" [Revised Standard Version]. The staff appears again in the Qur'ān in a manner interesting to us when it symbolizes the life force and the life span of Solomon. Upon it Solomon must lean to sustain himself. When the staff is eaten away by "the worm"—here also *dābbatu l-arḍi*—Solomon dies (Qur'ān 34:14).

33. As the tree—both "own" and "alien" to the golden bough that resembles a mistletoe—must be understood to be the oak, it is of interest to look into the diversely branched-out nomenclature, etymology, and anthropology of that tree, which, among other indicators, points to light, fire, the thunderbolt, the Slavic "thunder god" Perun, and the Late Sanskrit "sacred fig tree." See Friedrich, *Proto-Indo-European Trees,* pp. 129–49.

34. Servius, *Commentarii in Virgilium Serviani sive Commentarii in Virgilium qui Mauro Servio Honorato tribuuntur,* 2 vols., ed. H. Albertus Lion (Göttingen: Vandenhoeck and Ruprecht, 1826) 1:363. See the discussion of the pertinent passage from Servius on the *Aeneid,* VI, 136, in Fraser, *The Making of the Golden Bough,* pp. 191, 229n.

In quoting, or paraphrasing, Servius's gloss, Frazer does not even insist further on the specifying epithet "golden" while speaking of the bough of the Rex Nemorensis. We are only told that "In the sacred grove there grew a certain tree . . . ," and that "Within the sanctuary at Nemi grew a certain tree of which no branch might be broken. Only a runaway slave was allowed to break off, if he could, one of its boughs. Success in the attempt entitled him to fight the priest in single combat, and if he slew him he reigned in his stead with the title of King of the Wood *(Rex Nemorensis).*" Only then, with clearly excessive faith in the evidence on which his argument rests, does Frazer add that "According to the public opinion of the ancients the fateful branch was the Golden Bough which, at the Sibyl's bidding, Aeneas plucked before he essayed the perilous journey to the world of the dead." This claim to "the public opinion of the ancients" is, to say the least, an awkward exaggeration. See J. G. Frazer, *The Magic Art and the Evolution of Kings,* 2 vols., 1:8 and 11.

35. Concerning this mistake of identification, see Fraser, *The Making of the Golden Bough,* pp. 190–91.

36. Frazer, *Balder the Beautiful* 2:294 [*The Golden Bough,* Vol. 11].

37. Far be it from me to be thus belatedly joining in the tearing down of the monumental scholarly and cultural-historical figura of Frazer—as this has been a rather sorry fashion in more particularized gremial circles. My intention is only to facilitate for my own purposes a less obstructed access to the Vergilian golden bough against, or despite, the mediation of Frazer, a mediation which, indeed, is tantamount to being an impediment.

38. Pausanias, *Description of Greece,* Vol. IV, Books VIII-X, trans. W. H. S. Jones, Loeb Classical Library (London: William Heinemann/Cambridge, Massachusetts: Harvard University Press, 1935), pp. 544/545 [X. xxx. 6].

39. Thus in barely one printed page Frazer sums up (and disposes of) the Vergilian meaning of Aeneas's golden bough. See *Balder the Beautiful* 2:294–95.

40. Frazer, *Balder the Beautiful* 2:293–94.

41. Frazer, *Balder the Beautiful* 1:2.

42. Robert Fraser, *The Making of the Golden Bough,* p. 191.

43. For more on the *nekyia* in *Odyssey* XI, see below, n. 73.

44. Odysseus's "questioning" of the spirit of Teiresias, his *puthéstai* (XI, 50), strikes an intriguing echo, full of Orphic overtones, to those familiar with the classical Arabic (pre-Islamic) poets' "questioning" of their *aṭlāl,* the ruins of their abandoned habitation sites or encampments. The Orphism of those poets' questioning is then only a potentiality of the revelation of some unarticulatable truth. As such, questioning is also the potentiality of a prophecy. Thus, too, Odysseus's calling up of the spirit of Teiresias in order to "question" him is Orphic—while Teiresias's response is prophetic. Knowledge of the unknown is Orphic in intent and prophetic in realization. See an extensive discussion of the Arabic poetic Orphic "question" in my essay, "Toward an Arabic Elegiac Lexicon," pp. 105–19. Aside from its usefulness for the understanding of the Arabic elegiac *suʾāl* (question), some of the complexity present in the Homeric meaning of *puthéstai* as "to inquire (of the dead)" and its usefulness in the exegesis of 1 Samuel 28:3–20 of the meaning of the Hebrew Hades/*Sheôl* has already been pointed out by Cyrus H. Gordon (*The Common Background of Greek and Hebrew Civilizations* [New York: W. W. Norton and Company, Inc., 1965], p. 86n).

45. *Odyssey* XI, 568–71. It ought to be of significance that immediately following the scene of Minos sitting in judgment with the golden scepter in his hand, there is placed in the Hades sequence the scene of Orion holding a club of bronze: "And after him I marked huge Orion driving together over the field of asphodel wild beasts which himself had slain on the lonely hills, and in his hands he held a club all of bronze, ever unbroken" (vv. 572–75). Different symbolic attributes and characteristics of endowed, differentiated power are thus formulaically remembered and associated with "signifying" metals in the *Odyssey*'s Hades.

46. In his formidable commentary on the Sixth Book of the *Aeneid,* Eduard Norden stresses, on the one hand, that "the Misenus episode, that is, verses 149–52, 156–89, 212–36 . . . is, in a manner externally not separable, most closely tied in with the obtaining of the golden bough." Vergil "lets for that purpose the burial be the pre-condition of the journey into Hades (vv. 149–52)." On the other hand, all this said, Norden also admits that in the properly ritual sense one could view the "condition" of the burial of Misenus to be superfluous, since it is the golden bough *(der Zweig)* which gives the right to the *katabasis* (vv. 140ff.). He thus asks: "Why, then, is there a further sacrifice offered as expiation for something in itself forbidden?" Norden's simplest answer is that in the textual sense of sources and compositional design this is due to "the contamination of two versions not invented by Vergil, but merely appropriated: the Homeric version that knows no golden bough, and the version of the golden bough that knows no sacrifice. Vergil ties these two together." See Eduard Norden, *P. Vergilius Maro Aeneis Buch VI,* 2d ed. (Leipzig/Berlin: Druck und Verlag B. G. Teubner, 1916): 180–81, 198, 352. Having thus faced the problem, Norden nevertheless leaves the "gap of significance" of the Misenus episode ultimately unfilled—the greatest stumbling block being his reduction of every act leading to Aeneas's *nekyia* to the formalism of "sacrifice," never considering deeper levels of significance, namely, the symbolic and the magic acts.

47. Furthermore, as far as the archaic Greek, and rather circumstantially "Arian," requirement to bury the body in the sense of "to lay to rest" the

spirit/soul, we shall be reminded of the essentially almost identical Arabian Bedouin requirement to bury and avenge the fallen kinsman. See S. Stetkevych, *The Mute Immortals Speak,* p. 131.

48. Literary criticism of all periods has had considerable difficulty with the labored intertextuality and source problem of the trio of Elpenor/ Misenus/Palinurus. Beyond the great philological effort exemplified by Eduard Norden's commentary *(P. Vergilius Maro Aeneis Buch VI),* scholarship and criticism have paid them no more than limited attention. This stance may have been facilitated (quite handily) by that distinct air of "underplay" characteristic of the style, between humorous and insouciant, by virtue of which the three companion-heroes appear almost incidentalized in their respective scenes and in the broader flow of the two respective narratives. Thus, for example, all W. B. Stanford (*The Ulysses Theme: A Study in the Adaptability of a Traditional Hero* [Dallas: Spring Publications, 1992 (first published 1954)], p. 61) cares to tell us about Elpenor is that "To his [Odysseus's] surprise the ghost of Elpenor, the companion accidentally killed in Cyrce's palace, meets him first, and after that Anticleia's [i.e., Odysseus's mother's]." Reflecting no more than the linearity of the narrative, this hardly needs retelling, however. Cedric H. Whitman (*Homer and the Heroic Tradition* [New York: W. W. Norton and Company, Inc., 1965 (first published 1958)], p. 292), too, hardly goes farther than observing that Elpenor is one of the two companions of Odysseus—the other being Eurylochus—who, aside from being named, "emerge as people" (p. 292); although, quite pertinently, he also notices the element of "geometric design," that is, a formalist and aesthetic aspect of structure, albeit not a symbolic and semiotically effective one, as being evident in the fact that the two episodes (XI, 51-83 and XII, 9-15) of Elpenor appear to have their specific (formalist, balancing) connection to the prophecy of Teiresias. Whitman's subsequent chart in which he views these Elpenor episodes as actually "framing" the central episode of *nekyia* (p. 292), however, should be of an almost independent validity. What interests us here is that Whitman, in his own "non-structural" way, sees the importance of Elpenor, an importance that can then be "structurally" reinforced.

49. Norden, *P. Vergilius Maro Aeneis Buch VI,* p. 181.

50. Norden, *P. Vergilius Maro Aeneis Buch VI,* p. 184.

51. Norden, *P. Vergilius Maro Aeneis Buch VI,* p. 181. Here to note further is the distinction between the Homeric and the Vergilian heroic graves. Thus, whereas the Roman imperial poet's graves of Misenus (effectively) and Palinurus (as Sibylline promise) are monumental mounds to be remembered and venerated by generations, the grave of Homer's Elpenor is no more than a "mound . . . on the shore of the grey sea, in memory of an unhappy man" (*Odyssey* XI, 76-78). His, however, will more truly be a sailor's tomb, for his last request to Odysseus is: "Fulfil this my prayer, and fix upon the mound my oar wherewith I rowed in life when I was among my comrades" (79-80); and, of the three, only Elpenor and Misenus are explicitly burned, or to be burned, on pyres.

Keeping in mind Elpenor's oar fixed upright upon his grave, it then becomes of further interest to note that, subsequently, but still in the same scene (*Odyssey* XI, 123-34), Odysseus himself, as an obligatory step toward the fulfillment of his prophecy, receives from Teiresias the instruction that, upon his return to Ithaca and upon slaying Penelope's wooers, Odysseus must carry his oar inland, away from the sea, until he reaches people that no longer know the sea and do not recognize the shape and use of the oar but think it to be a winnowing shovel. Then he must fix the oar in the ground, sacrifice to Poseidon, and return home, where—or rather whereupon—his "people shall dwell in prosperity around" him.

Does Teiresias try here to tell Odysseus, in a way that is more quaint than prophetic, that he had sailed enough, that his seafaring days are over? Is the "oar of Odysseus" altogether a folkloric vestige in the Homeric narrative scheme and, above all, style? The likelihood of the latter has been entertained by recent folklorists—in our specific case, by William F. Hansen ("Odysseus and the Oar: A Folkloric Approach," in Lowell Edmunds, ed., *Approaches to Greek Myth* [Baltimore and London: The Johns Hopkins University Press, 1991], pp. 241-42). Drawing upon Roderick Beaton ("The Oral Traditions of Modern Greece: A Survey," *Oral Tradition* [1986] 1:110-33), Hansen notes that "Countless mountaintops in present-day Greece are crowned by a chapel dedicated to St. Elias" (p. 256), and that in the story of St. Elias, in its numerous retellings and variants, the saint figures as a seaman who, tired of his endless rowing, shouldered his oar and went in search of a place where no one would know the oar. He found such a place in a village on top of a mountain. There he settled down, and "from that time the chapels of St. Elias have always been built on mountain tops" (Hansen, p. 243). Thus in one version. In another version, St. Elias "sets the oar straight up, builds a hut, and resolves to remain there [on the mountaintop] for the rest of his life" (p. 243). So far the St. Elias hagiographic folklore does not differ in substance from the "oar test" imposed by Teiresias upon Odysseus—except for the mountaintop in the St. Elias stories and its total absence in the Homeric narrative. Hansen does not seem to achieve clarity on that point, even with his reference to a shrine of Poseidon and Athena, "said to have been built by Odysseus after his return from Troy" (p. 249). The site of the shrine being land-locked Arcadia, there seems to be a double paradox, and even a triple one, in this tradition, first for placing Odysseus in Arcadia, second for his building there a shrine for Poseidon, and third for devoting the shrine in part at least to Athena, a goddess not known for any measure of kinder sentiments toward Odysseus.

This latter aspect has been properly addressed and at least partly clarified, also with reference to Hansen, by Gregory Nagy in his *Greek Mythology and Poetics* (Ithaca and London: Cornell University Press, 1990) p. 214. Of further, and more direct, interest to us is Nagy's discussion of Elpenor's request to have his oar planted on the mound of his grave—and of its analogue in the condition imposed by Teiresias on Odysseus. Here Nagy focuses on the meaning of the Greek *sêma* as both "sign" and "tomb" and tries to answer the question: "why should the *sêma* 'sign' (xi 126) given by Teiresias to Odysseus take the form of a stylized tomb?" (p. 215). With such an approach, and understanding, of the planting of Odysseus's oar as a sign of a kind of "closure," a further connection becomes apparent between the request of Elpenor and the act of Odysseus. As a variant of the symbolic planting of the oar may here also be considered the hanging up of the seaman's oar upon returning from the sea, or upon withdrawal from the sea—as in Schubert's "Lied eines

Schiffers an die Dioskuren" (poem by J. Mayrhofer): *Dieses Ruder, das ich schwinge, / Meeresfluten zu zerteilen, / Hänge ich, so ich geborgen, / Auf an eures Tempels Säulen.*

I should add here an Arabic comment to Nagy's highly cogent discussion of the Greek *sêma,* namely, that the word for, and concept of, a very particular "sign" in Arabic equally means "grave," or rather, the "mound of a grave," usually in the form of rocks piled up on top of a hill or mountain. Such a "grave mound"/"sign" then becomes a marker by which travelers in the desert guide themselves. See Lane, *Arabic-English Lexicon* 4: 1739 (entry on *ṣuwwah [aṣwāʾ]*).

It should also be possible to clarify—beyond the scope of Hansen's interpretation—the reason for St. Elias's predilection for hills and mountains. Thus already one of the versions of the St. Elias anecdote, while still insisting that St. Elias was a seaman, concludes that "all the churches of the *prophet* Elias [my ital., J.S.] that exist are also on mountains" (p. 243). This should put us on the right interpretive source-track, making it quite clear that here we have a conflation of folklore and hagiography with the Old Testament persona and narrative of the prophet Elijah of 2 Kings 1:9, 11, 13; for he, equally invariably, "was sitting on the top of a hill." So too the prophet Elisha, himself not easily differentiable from Elijah, is to be found on a mountaintop—Mount Carmel (2 Kings 4:25). All of these connections and circuities are, despite the danger of falling into casuistic argumentation, connections of symbols trying to reach out for each other.

For a more detailed exposition of Homeric/Trojan and Vergilian/Latin burial rites, see Maria Alessio, *Studies in Vergil, Aeneid Eleven: An Allegorical Approach* (Laval, Québec: Montfort & Villeroy, Inc., 1993), pp. 65-74 ["Trojan and Latin Burial Rites (11. 182-202; 203-24)"].

52. Commenting directly on the ceremonial burial of Misenus ("Aeneas heaps over him a massive tomb, with the soldier's own arms, his oar and trumpet" [*Aeneid* VI, 232-35]), Knight (*Cumaean Gates,* p. 171) considers the oar as the instrument "to cross the waters of death," and goes as far as to exclaim: "Here is one of the surprises: the oar of Misenus is part of the golden bough."

53. This affinity has not only been observed, but, at times, carried to casuistic overstatement. Characteristic here, although oftentimes highly enlightening—as in his recognition of the *Verschmelzung* of the Siduri episode with the Circe episode—is Peter Jensen in his *Gilgamesch-Epos: judäische Nationalsagen, Ilias und Odyssee* (Leipzig: Verlag von Eduard Pfeiffer, 1924), p. 33 (but also the entirety of this brief essay [66 pp.]). Jensen's above material is then incorporated into the second volume (1928) of his monumental work, *Das Gilgamesch-Epos in der Weltliteratur,* 2 vols. (Strassburg: Verlag von Karl J. Trübner, 1906 [Vol. 1]/Marburg a. L.: Verlag von Adolf Ebel, 1928 [Vol. 2]) 2:176-226. More strictly dealing with the *Epic of Gilgamesh* and *Aeneid* VI, and also more imaginatively—or idiosyncratically—and less casuistically, is W. F. Jackson Knight in his *Cumaean Gates* (1936), reedited in *Vergil: Epic and Anthropology, Comprising Vergil's Troy, Cumaean Gates and The Holy City of the East,* ed. John D. Christie (New York: Barnes and Noble, Inc., 1967). See esp. pp. 155ff.

54. This perception of closure is then contradicted by the subsequent Tablet XII, which, although closely reflecting an old Sumerian Gilgamesh text, finds itself translated and attached to the "late," Assyrian Version of

Tablet XI. "Lacking the end of the Old Babylonian version," writes Jeffrey H. Tigay, "we cannot document a claim that it lacked the equivalent of the late version's Tablet XII, but everything argues against the presence of that episode in the original Old Babylonian version: The episode contradicts the rest of the epic in having Enkidu still alive at its beginning and in describing him as Gilgamesh's servant, and it is, unlike the rest of that version, a literal translation from the Sumerian, rather than a creative adaptation. It was probably added to the epic at a later date." See Jeffrey H. Tigay, *The Evolution of the Gilgamesh Epic* (Philadelphia: University of Pennsylvania Press, 1982), p. 49. See also Alexander Heidel, *The Gilgamesh Epic and Old Testament Parallels* (Chicago and London: The University of Chicago Press, 1965 [first ed. 1946]), p. 15.

55. Homer, *The Odyssey*, 2 vols., trans. A. T. Murray [Loeb Classical Library] (Cambridge, Massachusetts: Harvard University Press/London: William Heinemann, Ltd., 1984/1991) 1:380/381-382/383-384/385 [vv. 507–540, 565]. Circe assures Odysseus that the North wind will carry his ship to where he will find "the dank house of Hades." There Odysseus is to set foot and "dig a pit of a cubit's length this way and that"; and there he will "consult the Theban Teiresias."

56. Thus Aeneas turns to the Sibyl: "You, O most holy prophetess, foreseeing the outcome . . ."; upon which follows her prophecy of the Trojans' coming to "Lavinia's realm"; and this, in turn, is followed by the Sibyl's instructions to Aeneas on how he shall enter "the hidden world beneath the mortal world" (*Aeneid* VI, vv. 65–76, 83–97, 125–55).

57. Here I shall throughout be making reference to the text as arranged and translated by Heidel in *The Gilgamesh Epic*. I shall, however, avoid the awkwardness of the translation's antiquarian "scriptural" English.

58. Heidel, *The Gilgamesh Epic,* p. 71 (v. 4). It may be of further significance to note that "she is covered with a veil." It is a rather unfortunate term, that of "divine barmaid," which the philological Gilgamesh scholarship has imposed on us and which we, willy-nilly, find ourselves adhering to. That she is another aspect, or facet, of the figura of Ishtar—as well as a Sibyl—seems to be closer to her textual performance. She is clearly not the Sumerian/Babylonian version of the "divine cup-bearer," Ganymedes.

59. Heidel, *The Gilgamesh Epic,* p. 70 (Tablet X, Column iii).

60. Heidel, *The Gilgamesh Epic*, pp. 12–13.

61. Rivkah Schärf Kluger, *The Archetypal Significance of Gilgamesh: A Modern Ancient Hero,* edited by H. Yehezkel Kluger (Einsiedeln, Switzerland: Daimon Verlag, 1991), p. 171.

62. Joseph Campbell, *The Hero with a Thousand Faces* (Princeton: Princeton University Press, 1973), p. 186n.

63. Other aspects of the *ʿādhilah* motif are discussed in my *The Zephyrs of Najd*, pp. 14 and 244 (n. 48).

64. ʿAntarah Ibn Shaddād, *Dīwān* (Beirut: Dār al-Kutub al-ʿIlmīyah, 1405/1985), p. 99 (rhyming in *lām*).

65. The soul of the Bedouin warrior who fell in battle and lies unavenged was believed to assume the form of an owl that circled over the grave, calling for the blood of vengeance. See al Masʿūdī, *Murūj al-Dhahab* 2:132–33; al-Damīrī, *Ḥayāt al-Ḥayawān* 2:375; al-Alūsī, *Bulūgh al-Arab* 2:311

-13; Ignaz Goldziher, "Der Seelenvogel im islamischen Volksglauben," in J. Desomogyi, ed., *Gesammelte Schriften* (Hildesheim: G. Olms, 1970) 4:403-06; Th. E. Homerin, "Echoes of a Thirsty Owl," *Journal of Near Eastern Studies* 44, no. 3 (1985): 165-84.

66. ʿUrwah Ibn al-Ward, *Dīwān*, p. 35 (rhyming in *rāʾ*).

67. Ḥātim al-Ṭāʾī, *Dīwān Shiʿr Ḥātim Ibn ʿAbd Allāh al-Ṭāʾī wa Akhbāruh*, recension of Hishām Ibn Muḥammad al-Kalbī, ed. ʿĀdil Sulaymān Jamāl, 2d ed. (Cairo: Maktabat al-Khānjī, 1411/1990), p. 288 (poem no. 123). See also other examples of the *ʿādhilah* motif in Ḥātim al-Ṭāʾī's *Dīwān*, pp. 218-19, 221-22, 245, 292.

68. Abū Tammām, *Dīwān*, 1:218-20.

69. Heidel, *The Gilgamesh Epic*, pp. 73-77.

70. Gregory Crane, *Calypso: Backgrounds and Conventions of the Odyssey* (Frankfurt am Main: Athenäum), 1988. From the point of view of the structure of the narrative in the *Odyssey*, it is of interest to note that here Calypso makes her appearance before Circe, although she follows her in the actual sequence of Odysseus's adventures. This "device," a narratological flashback, as it were, makes it possible for the story to accommodate Odysseus's recounting of his reversals, as well as his *nekyia*, to his Phaeacian host, Alcinous (himself quite Utnapishtim-like). Furthermore, the figures of Calypso and Circe thus obtained and narratively "accommodated" are allowed to supplement and reinforce each other precisely because of the transparency of their "similarity." They represent not so much a repetitive layering for the purposes of a merely horizontal drawing out of the tale, as an "extended persona."

71. Circe, too, is "veiled" as she receives Odysseus: "and upon her head she put a veil" (*Odyssey* X, 545). Quite hypothetically, the name Siduri, too, might suggest a Semitic root meaning of *s-t-r* ("to veil").

72. Arthur Ungnad, "Gilgamesch-Epos und Odyssee," in Karl Oberhuber, ed., *Das Gilgamesch-Epos*, pp. 129-37 (Darmstadt: Wissenschaftliche Buchgesellschaft, 1977). The recent attempt by William L. Moran at establishing contacts and relationships between *Gilgamesh* material (Enkidu) and Ovid's *blanda voluptas* strikes me as much less felicitous, since it is not concerned with structure but merely with the deferalizing power of sexual love. Such approaches take us too far out into all too common places and overworked grounds, becoming thus neither historically nor literarily useful. See his "Ovid's *Blanda Voluptas* and the Humanization of Enkidu," *Journal of Near Eastern Studies* 50, no. 2 [April 1991]: 121-27.

73. Already in antiquity scholiast-commentators had observed that Odysseus's *nekyia* had not been an entry, or descent, into Hades, that is, that it was not properly a *katabasis*, and that the Homeric hero had merely called up the spirits of the dead to the sacrificial pit which he had dug with his sword. His *nekyia* was thus only limited to the stylistically fixed and formulaic "questions-and-answers" between him and the upcoming spirits—foremost among them Teiresias, who "went back into the house of Hades, when he had declared his prophecies" (XI, 150-52), while Odysseus "remained there steadfastly" (XI, 152). On the other hand, however, introducing an element of ambiguity, in the scene with the spirit of Odysseus's mother, that spirit asks him—in the true style of the *nekyia*—how he had "come beneath the murky darkness, being still

alive" (XI, 155-56). This ambiguity is then resolved when, at the end of the same scene, spirits of women, "wives and daughters of chieftains," came up sent by Persephone. They "flocked in throngs about the dark blood"—of the pit, we ought to be reminded—and Odysseus considered how he "might question each" (XI, 226-30). This ambiguity, arguably an aspect of stylistic indebtedness to oral-formulaism, repeats itself in the scene with the spirit of Achilles ("How didst thou dare to come down to Hades?" XI, 475-76). The actual *katabasis,* or descent into Hades, appears likely only in XI, 565-627, a passage athetized by scholars of antiquity, beginning with Aristarchus (second century B.C.). This latter aspect of Odysseus's *nekyia* is reviewed and properly weighed as to its critical merit by Crane, *Calypso: Backgrounds and Conventions of the Odyssey,* pp. 87-90. Otherwise, the *Odyssey* is quoted from the Loeb Classical Library edition.

74. Heidel, *The Gilgamesh Epic,* pp. 69-70 (Old Babylonian Version, Tablet X ii); and p. 73 (Assyrian Version, Tablet X i, vv. 24-25; X ii, vv. 6-13; X iii, vv. 20-31).

75. To achieve this structural proximity and its symbolic sense one does not have to go as far as does Knight (*Cumaean Gates,* pp. 154-59), who sees a connection between Palinurus's "lost tiller" (*Aeneid* VI, 349-54) and the *Gilgamesh* references to the "stone things," or, more literally, "those of stone," or, as in the Hittite version, the "two images of stone," which, Siduri advises Gilgamesh, he will find with Urshanabi, the boatman of Utnapishtim, and with the help of which he will cross the sea of death (Heidel, *The Gilgamesh Epic,* p. 74 [Tablet X, Column ii, vv. 28-29]). Gilgamesh, however, destroys the "stone things" and, instructed by Urshanabi, has to cut in the forest one hundred and twenty punting-poles, each sixty cubits in length. With the help of these he crosses the waters (Heidel, p. 76 [Tablet X, Column iii, vv. 36-41]). It is thus this destruction of the "stone things" that Knight equates with Palinurus's loss of the tiller. Furthermore, Knight also sees in Gilgamesh's one hundred and twenty punting-poles the Sumerian hero's "golden bough." Quite strangely, Knight completely passes over—in this connection—Gilgamesh's obtaining the "wondrous plant" that was also Utnapishtim's "secret of the gods." Here it would be more advisable, therefore, to rethink the iconography of the Early-Dynastic II Mesopotamian cylinder seal representing Gilgamesh, the plant of immortality in his hand, seated in a boat opposite Utnapishtim, with the boatman (Urshanabi [?]) at the stern. See above, Chapter 2 n. 10.

76. Heidel, *The Gilgamesh Epic,* Tablets VIII and IX, p. 68; John Gardner, John Maier, *Gilgamesh. Translated from the Sîn-leqi-unninnī version* (New York: Vintage Books, Random House, 1984), pp. 183-208.

77. Heidel, *The Gilgamesh Epic,* p. 80 (Assyrian Version, Tablet XI, vv. 7, 9-10).

78. Heidel, *The Gilgamesh Epic,* p. 88.

79. Heidel, *The Gilgamesh Epic,* p. 88.

80. Heidel, *The Gilgamesh Epic,* p. 91.

81. Heidel, *The Gilgamesh Epic,* p. 91.

82. Heidel, *The Gilgamesh Epic,* p. 92.

83. Very much in the manner of medieval Christian "figural" hermeneutics there existed, and in the literary realm still exists, a pronouncedly

tiresome school of approaching the historicity of Near Eastern antiquity not only *ab urbe condita* forwards but, above all, backwards—the *urbs* being here the Old Testament. Within such historicity that knows only one point of departure and one center of the value of time, in the case that concerns us presently the *Gilgamesh Epic* becomes merely a prefiguration of the Noah story, and the important hermeneutics of that epic, as a result, is bent to conform to the comfortably entrenched exegesis of the biblical Noah text. In a way that should embarrass a rigorous literary critic, or rather as a custom not easily broken, this exegesis is rarely prepared to speak with consistency and unencumbered understanding of Noah as symbolically and mythopoeically dependent on, not just narratively "overlapping" with, Utnapishtim. As a result, Gilgamesh himself will then not easily be left out of such interdependence. Correcting such a situation with laudable clarity of textual-historical and literary perspective, Bernard F. Batto sums up the philological results of Sumerian/Old Babylonian/Assyrian scholarship on our subject in his recent book of lucid synthesis, *Slaying the Dragon.* Above all, his understanding of the biblical narrative tradition as falling methodologically centrally into "mythmaking" makes room for the establishment of a refreshing common denominator of ancient Near Eastern lore and textuality without the customary extraliterary scriptural "priorization." To Batto the biblical Yahwist's primeval narrative is an example of "mythmaking based on prior Mesopotamian myths, notably *Atrahasis* and *Gilgamesh*" (p. 14)—in its Assyrian version, *Gilgamesh* itself being here an intermediate narrative stage in more than one respect. Batto thus observes that in *Gilgamesh* "the flood story is clearly retold from *Atrahasis,* merely by changing the third-person account into the first person to better fit the narrative structure" of the epic (pp. 23–24). Furthermore, what is more important to us is that any scripturally Noah-centered exegesis is methodologically readily disposed toward merely glossing over key symbolic, semiotic, and plainly narratological elements in the *Gilgamesh Epic,* thus underinterpreting or misinterpreting them whenever, or to the extent to which, the biblical Noah story lacks such elements or is not sufficiently transparent regarding their integration and contextuality. Altogether, we have here a residual problem in our understanding of both texts and of both textualities.

84. Myths, of course, speak to us in many ways. In the way in which they are encumbered by hermeneutics and exegesis, as well as in their ability to generate their webs of mythopoeia, myths possess the rare supratemporal ability to address themselves to any given, or any changing, cultural-historical expectations, or to any individual states of mind. Facing this mutability of the "matter of myth," which even goes so far as to place itself outside all that is historically temporal, the discomforting characteristic of much of contemporary hermeneutics seems to be a well-intentioned, almost "liberal," I might say, tendency toward banalization—or say, toward a forced psychological, temporal "humanization" of archaic heroic matter. This is very clearly reflected in Thorkild Jacobsen's assessment of that which *is* the "matter" of *Gilgamesh*. He concludes that "The Gilgamesh Epic is a story about growing up," and that the loss of the "plant" "brings home the necessity of growing up, of facing and accepting reality." Gilgamesh "has at last become mature." See Thorkild

Jacobsen, *The Treasures of Darkness: A History of Mesopotamian Religion* (New Haven and London: Yale University Press, 1976), p. 219. Such a conclusion is all too easy to accept. It brings Gilgamesh so close to us that we could almost touch him, and this pleases us and comforts us. He is like us, after all. He is "ours," just as Goethe's Faust in *Faust II* has ultimately been brought down to earth and, in leaving myth, his to us unreachable realm of pathos, has become "ours"; for he has "grown up" as all of us must. Our own values—and fears—have thus been reaffirmed. The "growing up" of the tragic, or epic, hero is, however, by the same token presented as a reversal: as a submission to one of the voices of Siduri, and to that of the *ʿādhilah*. Paul Diel, therefore, has properly characterized such reversals as the banalization of the myth, as well as a banalization in the myth—and these lead to a banalization of the hermeneutics of myth. See his *Symbolism in Greek Mythology: Human Desire and Its Transformation*, preface by Gaston Bachelard, trans. by Vincent Stuart, Micheline Stuart, and Rebecca Folkman (Boulder and London: Shambhala, 1980), esp. pp. 85–87, 99, and 101–44.

Conclusion

1. Al-Thaʿlabī, *Kitāb Qiṣaṣ al-Anbiyāʾ*, p. 50.

2. In its psychology and symbolism, Muhammad's situation is here quite compellingly comparable to the biblical Saul's anguished turning to the Sibyl at the omphalos of ʿEn Dor. Thus texts have changed, but roles are played out nonetheless. Cf. my discussion (within an Arabic mythopoeic context) of Saul and the Sibyl of ʿEn Dor, "Toward an Arabic Elegiac Lexicon," pp. 117 and 127–28 (n. 169).

3. In mythical and anthropological terms, to be a "hero," especially to be a culture hero, is of a piece with being "marked." The hero's mark, however, is necessarily also a sign of dramatic, and even tragic, nature and consequence. Above all it indicates inherent ambiguity and even polarity of personal, social, and moral behavior. Such is the marking of Cain, the "first" murderer and the first civilizer-culture hero. His punishment for the murder was that of being marked and made recognizable for his deed—according to scriptural mythopoeia, by growing one horn, or two, from his forehead. But the very mark he bore also carried in it "sevenfold vengeance" that would fall upon anyone who were to slay him (Genesis 4: 8–24). Thus Cain's mark/horn of the murderer would be in an equal measure a kind of "apotropaic device." There being no reference in Genesis to his death, this was interpreted by exegetes that he indeed did not die—thus by the Alexandrian Jewish allegorizer of the Hebrew Bible, Philo (d. after 39 C.E.). A further interpretation would then lead to the connection between his mark and his indestructibility, if not eternity. Ultimately, however, Midrashic anecdotal exegesis solved the dilemma strictly within the logic of archaic symbolism by letting Cain be mistakenly killed by Lamech—as though he were a hunted horned animal, not a human. See the broader discussion of the anthropological and symbolic phenomenon of "the mark of Cain" by Ruth

Mellinkoff, *The Mark of Cain* (Berkeley, Los Angeles, London: University of California Press, 1981), esp. pp. 15–40. See also the discussion of the ambiguity/polarity that constitutes the makeup of the sacred and the heroic, in René Girard, *Violence and the Sacred* (Baltimore and London: The Johns Hopkins University Press, 1977), 250–53.

BIBLIOGRAPHY

ʿAbd al-Ḥakīm, Shawqī. *Mawsūʿat al-Fulklūr wa al-Asāṭīr al-ʿArabīyah*. Beirut: Dār al-ʿAwdah, 1982.

ʿAbd al-Majīd, Ibrāhīm. *Al-Baldah al-Ukhrā*. London/Cyprus: Riad el-Rayyes Books, 1991.

ʿAbduh, Muḥammad. *Tafsīr al-Qurʾān al-Ḥakīm*. 8 vols. 2d ed. Cairo: Maṭbaʿat al-Manār, 1347/1929.

Abū Tammām. *Dīwān*. 4 vols. Recension of al-Khaṭīb al-Tibrīzī. Ed. Muḥammad ʿAbduh ʿAzzām. 3d ed. Cairo: Dār al-Maʿārif bi Miṣr, 1970.

Abū ʿUbaydah Maʿmar Ibn al-Muthannā al-Taymī. *Majāz al-Qurʾān*. 2 vols. Ed. Fuʾād Sazkīn. Cairo: Maktabat al-Khānjī, 1988.

Alessio, Maria. *Studies in Vergil, Aeneid Eleven: An Allegorical Approach*. Laval, Québec: Montfort and Villeroy, Inc., 1994.

ʿAlī, Jawād. *Al-Mufaṣṣal fī Tārīkh al-ʿArab qabl al-Islām*. 10 vols. Beirut: Dār al-ʿIlm li al-Malāyīn/Baghdad: Maktabat al-Nahḍah, 1968.

Ali, Yusuf Abdullah, trans. *The Holy Qurʾan. Text, Translation and Commentary*. Elmhurst, New York: Tahrike Tarsile Qurʾan, Inc., n.d.

Altheim, Franz, and Ruth Stiehl. *Die Araber in der Alten Welt. Erster Band: Bis zum Beginn der Kaiserzeit*. Berlin: Walter de Gruyter and Co., 1964.

al-Ālūsī, Maḥmūd Shukrī. *Bulūgh al-Arab fī Maʿrifat Aḥwāl al-ʿArab*. 3 vols. Ed. Muḥammad Bahjat al-Atharī. 2d ed. Beirut: Dār al-Kutub al-ʿIlmīyah, n.d. [1st ed. 1314 H.].

al-Anbārī, Abū Bakr Muḥammad Ibn Qāsim. *Sharḥ al-Qaṣāʾid al-Sabʿ al-Ṭiwāl al-Jāhilīyāt*. Ed. ʿAbd al-Salām Muḥammad Hārūn. 2d ed. Cairo: Dār al-Maʿārif bi Miṣr, 1969.

Anchor Bible Dictionary. 6 vols. David Noel Freedman et al., eds. New York: Doubleday, 1992.

ʿAntarah Ibn Shaddād. *Dīwān*. Beirut: Dār al-Kutub al-ʿIlmīyah, 1405/1985.

Arberry, A. J. *The Koran Interpreted*. 2 vols. New York: Macmillan, 1969.

Athanassakis, Apostolos N. *The Homeric Hymns*. Translation, Introduction, and Notes. Baltimore and London: The Johns Hopkins University Press, 1978.

Auerbach, Erich. *Mimesis: The Representation of Reality in Western Literature*. Trans. Willard R. Trask. Princeton, New Jersey: Princeton University Press, 1968.

———. *Scenes from the Drama of European Literature*. Foreword by Paolo Valesio. Minneapolis: University of Minnesota Press, 1984.

Batto, Bernard F. *Slaying the Dragon: Mythmaking in the Biblical Tradition*. Louisville, Kentucky: Westminster/John Knox Press, 1992.

Beeston, A. F. L. et al. *Sabaic Dictionary (English - French - Arabic)*. Louvain-la-Neuve: Peeters/Beirut: Librairie du Liban, 1982.

Bible [*The Holy Bible. Revised Standard Version*]. Cleveland and New York: The World Publishing Company, 1962.

———. *The Holy Scriptures According to the Masoretic Text*. Philadelphia: The Jewish Publication Society of America, 1955.

Bloch, Ariel, and Chana Bloch. *The Song of Songs*. Translation, Introduction, and Commentary. Afterword by Robert Alter. New York: Random House, 1995.

Bowersock, G. W. *Roman Arabia*. Cambridge, Massachusetts and London: Harvard University Press, 1983.

Bowra, C. M. *Homer*. New York: Charles Scribner's Sons, 1972.

Boylan, Patrick. *Thoth: The Hermes of Egypt*. Chicago: Ares Publishers, Inc., 1987.

Branden, Albertus van den. *Histoire de Thamoud*. Publications de l'Université Libanaise Section des Études Historiques, VI. Beirut: 1960.

———. *Les textes thamoudéens de Philby*. Louvain: Publications universitaires, Institute orientaliste, 1956.

Brown, Norman O. *Hermes the Thief: The Evolution of a Myth*. Great Barrington, Massachusetts: Lindesfarne Press, 1990.

Bürgel, Johann Christoph. *Allmacht und Mächtigkeit: Religion und Welt im Islam*. Munich: Verlag C. H. Beck, 1991.

Burkert, Walter. *Greek Religion*. Trans. John Raffan. Cambridge, Massachusetts: Harvard University Press, 1985.

Campbell, Joseph. *The Hero with a Thousand Faces*. New York: Pantheon Books, 1949.

Caskel, Werner. *Das altarabische Königreich Lihyan*. Krefeld: Scherpe Verlag, 1950.

———. *Lihyan und Lihyanisch*. Cologne and Opladen: Westdeutscher Verlag, 1954.

Clausen, Wendell. *Virgil's Aeneid and the Tradition of Hellenistic Poetry*. Berkeley, and Los Angeles, London: University of California Press, 1987.

Crane, Gregory. *Calypso: Backgrounds and Conventions of the Odyssey*. Frankfurt am Main: Athenäum, 1988.

Cumont, Franz. *The Mysteries of Mithra*. Trans. Thomas J. McCormack. New York: Dover Publications, Inc., 1956.

al-Damīrī, Kamāl al-Dīn. *Ḥayāt al-Ḥayawān al-Kubrā wa bi Hāmishihā Kitāb ʿAjāʾib al-Makhlūqāt wa al-Ḥayawānāt wa Gharāʾib al-Mawjūdāt li Zakariyā Muḥammad Ibn Maḥmūd al-Qazwīnī*. Cairo: Maṭbaʿat al-Istiqāmah, 1963.

Dhū al-Rummah. *Dīwān*. 2d ed. Damascus: Al-Maktabah al-Islāmīyah li al-Ṭibāʿah wa al-Nashr, 1384/1964.

Diel, Paul. *Symbolism in Greek Mythology: Human Desire and Its Transformation*. Preface by Gaston Bachelard. Trans. Vincent Stuart, Micheline Stuart, and Rebecca Folkman. Boulder, Colorado and London: Shambhala, 1980.

The Encyclopaedia of Islam. New Edition. 8 vols. Eds. H. A. R. Gibb et al. Leiden: E. J. Brill/London: Luzak and Co., 1960–95.

Epstein, Isidore. *Judaism: A Historical Presentation*. Harmondsworth, Middlesex: Penguin Books Ltd., 1959.

Faraone, Christopher A. *Talismans and Trojan Horses: Guardian Statues in Ancient Greek Myth and Ritual*. New York and Oxford: Oxford University Press, 1992.

Fraser, Robert. *The Making of the Golden Bough: The Origins and Growth of an Argument*. New York: St. Martin's Press, 1990.

Frazer, James George. *The Golden Bough: A Study in Magic and Religion*. 3d ed. 12 vols. London: Macmillan and Co., Limited, 1907-15 [1st ed. 1890].

Friedrich, Paul. *Proto-Indo-European Trees: The Arboreal System of a Prehistoric People*. Chicago and London: The University of Chicago Press, 1970.

Frye, Northrop. *The Great Code*. New York and London: Harcourt Brace Jovanovich, 1982.

Gesenius, Wilhelm. *Hebräisches und aramäisches Handwörterbuch über das Alte Testament*. Berlin, Göttingen, Heidelberg: Springer Verlag, 1954.

Girard, René. *Violence and the Sacred*. Trans. Patrick Gregory. Baltimore and London: The Johns Hopkins University Press, 1977.

Glueck, Nelson. *Deities and Dolphins: The Story of the Nabataeans*. New York: Straus and Giroux, 1965.

Goldziher, Ignaz. *Gesammelte Schriften*. Ed. Joseph Desmogyi. Hildesheim: G. Olms, 1970.

———. *Muslim Studies*. Ed. S. M. Stern. Trans. by C. R. Barber and S. M. Stern. Albany: State University of New York Press, 1967.

Gordon, Cyrus H. *The Common Background of Greek and Hebrew Civilizations*. New York: W. W. Norton and Company, Inc., 1965.

Guillaume, A. *The Life of Muḥammad: A Translation of Isḥāq's Sīrat Rasūl Allāh*. With Introduction and Notes by A. Guillaume. Lahore and Karachi/London and New York: Oxford University Press, 1955 [1974].

al-Ḥalwānī, Muḥammad Khayr. *Suḥaym ʿAbd Banī al-Ḥasḥās: Shāʿir al-Ghazal wa al-Ṣabwah*. Beirut: Maktabat Dār al-Sharq, 1972.

Hansen, William F. "Odysseus and the Oar: A Folkloric Approach." In Lowell Edmunds, ed. *Approaches to Greek Myth*, pp. 241-72. Baltimore and London: The Johns Hopkins University Press, 1991.

Hassan, Ali. *Stöcke und Stäbe im Pharaonischen Ägypten bis zum Ende des Neuen Reiches*. Münchner Ägyptologische Studien, Heft 33. Munich/Berlin: Deutscher Kunstverlag.

Ḥassān Ibn Thābit. *Dīwān*. Eds. Sayyid Ḥanafī Ḥasanayn and Ḥusayn Kāmil al-Ṣīrafī. Cairo: Al-Hayʾah al-Miṣrīyah al-ʿĀmmah li al-Kitāb, 1974.

———. *Sharḥ Dīwān Ḥassān Ibn Thābit*. Recension of ʿAbd al-Raḥmān al-Barqūqī. 2d ed. Cairo: Al-Maktabah al-Tijārīyah al-Kubrā, 13471929.

Ḥātim al-Ṭāʾī. *Dīwān Shiʿr Ḥātim Ibn ʿAbd Allāh al-Ṭāʾī wa Akhbāruh*. Recension of Hishām Ibn Muḥammad al-Kalbī. Ed. ʿĀdil Sulaymān Jamāl. Cairo: Maktabat al-Khānjī, 1411/1990.

Heidel, Alexander. *The Gilgamesh Epic and Old Testament Parallels*. Chicago and London: The University of Chicago Press, 1965.

Henderson, Joseph L., and Maud Oaks. *The Wisdom of the Serpent: The Myth of Death, Rebirth, and Resurrection*. Princeton, New Jersey: Princeton University Press, 1990.

Hesiod. *The Homeric Hymns and Homerica*. Trans. Hugh G. Evelyn-White. Loeb Classical Library. Cambridge, Massachusetts: Harvard University Press/London: William Heinemann, Ltd., 1959.

Homer. *The Odyssey*. Trans. Robert Fitzgerald. Garden City, New York: Doubleday and Company, Inc., 1961.

———. *The Odyssey*. Trans. A. T. Murray. 2 vols. Loeb Classical Library. Cambridge, Massachusetts: Harvard University Press, 1984/1991.

Homerin, Th. E. "Echoes of a Thirsty Owl." *Journal of Near Eastern Studies* 44, no. 3 (1985): 165–84.

Huber, P. Michael. *Die Wanderlegende von den Siebenschläfern*. Leipzig: Otto Harrassowitz, 1910.

al-Ḥūt, Maḥmūd Salīm. *Fī Ṭarīq al-Mīthūlūjiyā ʿind al-ʿArab wa huwa Baḥth Mushab fī al-Muʿtaqadāt wa al-Asāṭīr al-ʿArabīyah qabl al-Islām*. Beirut: n.p., 1955.

Ibn ʿAbd Rabbih al-Andalusī, Abū ʿUmar Aḥmad Ibn Muḥammad. *Kitāb al-ʿIqd al-Farīd*. 7 vols. Eds. Aḥmad Amīn, Aḥmad al-Zayn, Ibrāhīm al-Abyārī. Cairo: Maṭbaʿat Lajnat al-Taʾlīf wa al-Tarjamah wa al-Nashr, 1367/1948.

Ibn Abī al-Ṣalt, Umayyah. *Dīwān*. Ed. ʿzbd al-Ḥafīẓ al-Salṭī. Damascus: Al-Maṭba ʿah al-Taʿāwunīyah, 1974.

Ibn Hishām, Abū Muḥammad ʿAbd al-Malik. *Al-Sīrah al-Nabawīyah*. 4 vols. Cairo: Dār al-Fikr li al-Ṭibāʿah wa al-Nashr wa al-Tawzīʿ, 1980.

———. *Al-Sīrah al-Nabawīyah li Ibn Hishām*. 6 vols. Ed. Ṭāhā ʿAbd al-Raʾūf Saʿd. Beirut: Dār al-Jīl, 1411/1991.

———. *The Life of Muhammad, Apostle of Allah*. Adapted by Ibn Hishām. Trans. Edward Rehatsek. Ed. Michael Edwards. London: Folio Society, 1964.

Ibn Kathīr, ʿImād al-Dīn Abū al-Fidā Ismāʿīl Ibn ʿUmar al-Qurashī al-Dimashqī. *Al-Bidāyah wa al-Nihāyah fī al-Tārīkh*. 14 vols. Cairo: Maṭbaʿat Kurdistān al-ʿIlmīyah li Nashr al-Kutub al-ʿĀliyah al-Islāmīyah, 1348–58/1929–39.

———. *Qiṣaṣ al-Anbiyāʾ*. [Cairo?]: Dār Nahr al-Nīl, n.d. [1981?].

Ibn Khurdādhbih, Abū al-Qāsim ʿUbayd Allāh Ibn ʿAbd Allāh. *Kitāb al-Masālik wa al-Mamālik*. Ed. M. J. De Goeje. Leiden: E. J. Brill, 1306/1889.

Ibn Manẓūr al-Ifrīqī al-Miṣrī, Abū al-Faḍl Jamāl al-Dīn Ibn Mukarram. *Lisān al-ʿArab*. 15 vols. Beirut: Dār Ṣādir/Dār Bayrūt, 1375/1956.

Ibn Muḥammad al-Jawzī al-Qurashī al-Baghdādī, Abū al-Faraj Jamāl al-Dīn ʿAbd al-Raḥmān Ibn ʿAlī. *Zād al-Masīr fī ʿIlm al-Tafsīr*. Damascus/Beirut: Al-Maktabah al-Islāmīyah li al-Ṭibāʿah wa al-Nashr, 1385/1965.

Ibn Munqidh, Usāmah. *Dīwān*. Eds. Aḥmad Aḥmad Badawī and Ḥāmid ʿAbd al-Majīd. [Cairo?]. No publisher, n.d.

Ibn Qutaybah, Abū Muḥammad ʿAbd Allāh Ibn Muslim. *Al-Maʿārif*. Ed. Tharwat ʿUkāshah. 2d ed. Cairo: Dār al-Maʿārif bi Miṣr, 1969.

———. *Al-Shiʿr wa al-Shuʿarāʾ*. 2 vols. Ed. Aḥmad Muḥammad Shākir. Cairo: Dār al-Maʿārif bi Miṣr, 1966.

Ibn al-Qūṭīyah al-Qurṭubī. *Tārīkh Iftitāḥ al-Andalus*. Madrid: Real Academia de la Historia, 1868.

Ibn Wāqid, Muḥammad Ibn ʿUmar. *Kitāb al-Maghazī li al-Wāqidī*. 3 vols. Ed. Mārisdin Jūns [Marsden Jones]. Oxford: Oxford University Press, 1966.

Ibn Zayd al-ʿIbādī, ʿAdī. *Dīwān*. Ed. Muḥammad Jabbār al-Muʿaybid. Baghdad: Dār al-Jumhūrīyah li al-Nashr wa al-Ṭabʿ, 1965.

Imruʾ al-Qays. *Dīwān*. 5th ed. Ed. Muḥammad Abū al-Faḍl Ibrāhīm. Cairo: Dar al-Maʿārif, 1990.

al-Iṣbahānī [al-Iṣfahānī], Abū al-Faraj. *Kitāb al-Aghānī*. 31 vols. Ed. Ibrāhīm al-Abyārī. Cairo: Dār al-Shaʿb, 1969-79.

Jacobsen, Thorkild. *The Treasures of Darkness: A History of Mesopotamian Religion*. New Haven and London: Yale University Press, 1976.

al-Jāḥiẓ, ʿAmr Ibn Baḥr. *Al-Bayān wa al-Tabyīn*. 4 vols. 5th ed. Ed. ʿAbd al-Salām Muḥammad Hārūn. Cairo: Maktabat al-Khānjī, 1405/1985.

———. *Kitāb al-Ḥayawān*. 8 vols. Ed. ʿAbd al-Salām Muḥammad Hārūn. Cairo: Dār al-Maʿārif, 1938.

Jensen, Peter. *Gilgamesch-Epos: judäische Nationalsagen, Ilias und Odyssee*. Leipzig: Verlag von Eduard Pfeiffer, 1924.

———. *Das Gilgamesch-Epos in der Weltliteratur*. Zweiter Band: Die israelitischen Gilgamesch-Sagen in den Sagen der Weltliteratur. Mit einem Ergänzungsheft, worin unter anderem vier Kapitel über die Paulus-Sage. Marburg a. L.: Verlag von Adolf Ebel, 1928.

al-Jumaḥī, Muḥammad Ibn Sallām. *Ṭabaqāt Fuḥūl al-Shuʿarāʾ*. 2 vols. Ed. Maḥmūd Muḥammad Shākir. Cairo: Maṭbaʿat al-Madanī, 1394/1974.

Kammerer, A. *Petra la Nabatène: L'Arabie Pétrée et les Arabes du Nord—Dans leurs rapports avec la Syrie et la Palestine jusqu'à l'Islam. Atlas*. Paris: Librairie Orientale Paul Geuthner, 1930.

Keel, Othmar. *Vögel als Boten: Studien zu Ps 68, 12-14, Gen 8, 6-12, Koh 10, 20 und dem Aussenden von Botenvögeln in Ägypten. Mit einem Beitrag von Urs Winter zu Ps 56, 1 und zur Ikonographie der Göttin mit der Taube*. Freiburg Schweiz: Universitätsverlag/Göttingen: Vandenhoeck und Ruprecht, 1977.

al-Kisāʾī, Muḥammad Ibn ʿAbd Allāh. *Qiṣaṣ al-Anbiyāʾ*. 2 vols. Ed. Isaac Eisenberg. Leiden: E. J. Brill, 1923.

———. *The Tales of the Prophets of al-Kisaʾi*. Trans. W. M. Thackston, Jr. Boston: Twayne Publishers/G. K. Hall and Co., 1978.

Knauf, Ernst Axel. *Ismael: Untersuchungen zur Geschichte Palästinas und Nordarabiens im 1. Jahrtausend v. Chr.* 2d ed. Wiesbaden: Otto Harrassowitz, 1989.

Knight, W. F. Jackson. *Vergil: Epic and Anthropology. Comprising Vergil's Troy, Cumaean Gates, and The Holy City of the East*. Ed. John D. Christie. New York: Barnes and Noble, Inc., 1967.

Kremer, Alfred von. *Über die südarabische Sage*. Leipzig: F. A. Brockhaus, 1866.

Kuthayyir ʿAzzah. *Dīwān*. Ed. Iḥsān ʿAbbās. Beirut: Dār al-Thaqāfah, 1971.

Lane, Edward William. *Arabic-English Lexicon*. 8 vols. New York: Frederick Ungar, 1958 [London, 1863].

Levinson, Bernard M. "'But You Shall Surely Kill Him!': The Text-Critical and Neo-Assyrian Evidence for MT Deuteronomy 13:10." In Georg Braulik, ed. *Bundesdokument und Gesetz: Studien zum Deuteronomium,* pp. 37-63. Freiburg, Basel, Vienna, Barcelona, Rome, New York: Herder, 1995.

Margoliouth, D. S. *Mohammed and the Rise of Islam*. London and New York: G. P. Putnam's Sons, 1927.

al-Masʿūdī, Abū al-Ḥasan ʿAlī Ibn al-Ḥusayn Ibn ʿAlī. *Murūj al-Dhahab wa Maʿādin al-Jawhar*. 4 vols. Ed. Yūsuf Asʿad Dāghir. Beirut: Dār al-Andalus li al-Ṭibāʿah wa al-Nashr wa al-Tawzīʿ, 1401/1981.

——— [Maçoudi]. *Les prairies d'or*. Ed. and trans. C. Barbier de Meynard and Pavet de Courteille. 9 vols. Paris: Imprimerie Imperiale, 1861–1917.

Mazar, Amihai. *Archaeology of the Land of the Bible, 10,000–586 B.C.E.* New York: Doubleday, 1992.

Mellinkoff, Ruth. *The Mark of Cain*. Berkeley, Los Angeles, and London: University of California Press, 1981.

Miles, George, C. "Miḥrāb and ʿAnazah: A Study in Early Islamic Iconography." In George C. Miles, ed. *Archaeologica Orientalia in Memoriam Ernst Herzfeld*, pp. 156-71. Locust Valley, New York: J. J. Augustin Publisher, 1952.

Millar, Fergus. *The Roman Near East 31 BC–AD 337*. Cambridge, Massachusetts and London: Harvard University Press, 1993.

Moran, William L. "Ovid's *Blanda Voluptas* and the Humanization of Enkidu." *Journal of Near Eastern Studies* 50, no. 2 (April 1991): 121-27.

al-Mubarrad, Abū al-ʿAbbās Ibn Muḥammad Yazīd. *Kitāb al-Taʿāzī wa al-Marāthī*. Ed. Muḥammad al-Dībājī. Damascus: Maṭbaʿat Zayd Ibn Thābit, 1396/1976.

al-Mufaḍḍal Ibn Muḥammad al-Ḍabbī, Abū al-ʿAbbās. *Dīwān al-Mufaḍḍalīyāt*. Commentary by Abū Muḥammad al-Qāsim Ibn Muḥammad Ibn Bashshār al-Anbārī. Vol. 1 Arabic Text. Ed. Charles James Lyall. Beirut: Maṭbaʿat al-Ābāʾ al-Yasūʿīyīn, 1920.

Muʾnis, Ḥusayn. *Aṭlas Tārīkh al-Islām*. Cairo: Al-Zahrāʾ li al-Iʿlām al-ʿArabī, 1407/1987.

Murray, Gilbert. *The Rise of the Greek Epic, Being a Course of Lectures Delivered at Harvard University*. 4th ed. London, Oxford, and New York: Oxford University Press, 1967.

Muslim Ibn al-Ḥajjāj al-Qushayrī al-Naysābūrī, Abū al-Ḥusayn. *Ṣaḥīḥ Muslim*. 6 vols. Cairo: Dār Iḥyāʾ al-Kutub al-ʿArabīyah: ʿĪsā al-Bābī al-Ḥalabī wa Shurakāhu, 1955.

al-Nābighah al-Dhubyānī. *Dīwān*. Redaction of Ibn al-Sikkīt. Ed. Shukrī Fayṣal. Beirut: Dār al-Hāshim, 1968.

Nagy, Gregory. *The Best of the Achaeans: Concept of the Hero in Archaic Greek Poetry*. Baltimore and London: The Johns Hopkins University Press, 1981.

———. *Greek Mythology and Poetics*. Ithaca and London: Cornell University Press, 1990.

Nāṣif, Muṣṭafā. *Dirāsat al-Adab al-ʿArabī*. Cairo: Dār al-Qawmīyah li al-Ṭibāʿah wa al-Nashr, n.d.

———. *Qirāʾah Thāniyah li Shiʿrinā al-Qadīm*. [Tripoli, Libya]: Manshūrāt al-Jāmiʿah al-Lībīyah, Kullīyat al-Ādāb, n.d.

Norden, Eduard. *P. Vergilius Maro Aeneis Buch VI*. 2d ed. Leipzig/Berlin: Druck und Verlag B. G. Teubner, 1916.

al-Nuwayrī, Shihāb al-Dīn Aḥmad Ibn ʿAbd al-Wahhāb. *Nihāyat al-Arab fī Funūn al-Adab*. 31 vols. Cairo: Dār al-Kutub al-Miṣrīyah, 1357/1938 [vols 1-18]; and Cairo: Al-Hayʾah al-Miṣrīyah al-ʿĀmmah li al-Kitāb, 1975-92 [vols. 19-31].

Ohly, Friedrich. *Hohelied-Studien: Grundzüge einer Geschichte der Hohelied-auslegung des Abendlandes bis um 1200*. Wiesbaden: Franz Steiner Verlag GMBH, 1958.

Ovid [Publius Ovidius Naso]. *Metamorphoses*. Trans. Rolfe Humphries. Bloomington: Indiana University Press, 1964.

Pausanias. *Description of Greece*. Trans. W. H. S. Jones. Vol. IV, Books viii-x. London: William Heinemann/Cambridge, Massachusetts: Harvard University Press, 1935. Loeb Classical Library.

Piotrovskyj, M. B. *Koranicheskye Skazania*. Moscow: Nauka, 1991.

Plato. *Republic*. Loeb Classical Library.

al-Qāḍī al-Fāḍil [ʿAbd al-Raḥīm Ibn ʿAlī al-Baysānī]. *Dīwān*. 2 vols. Ed. Aḥmad Aḥmad Badawī. Cairo: Dār al-Maʿārif, 1961.

al-Qalqashandī, Abū al-ʿAbbās Aḥmad Ibn ʿAlī. *Ṣubḥ al-Aʿshā fī Ṣināʿat al-Inshā*. 14 vols. Cairo: Al-Muʾassasah al-Miṣrīyah al-ʿĀmmah li al-Taʾlīf wa al-Tarjamah wa al-Ṭibāʿah wa al-Nashr, 1383/1963.

al-Qurashī, Abū Zayd Muḥammad Ibn Abī al-Khaṭṭāb. *Jamharat Ashʿār al-ʿArab fī al-Jāhilīyah wa al-Islām*. 2 vols. Ed. ʿAlī Muḥammad al-Bijāwī. Cairo: Dār Nahḍat Miṣr li al-Ṭibāʿah wa al-Nashr, 1387/1967.

Robertson Smith, W. *The Religion of the Semites: The Fundamental Institutions*. New York: Meridian Books, 1957.

———. *Kingship and Marriage in Early Arabia*. Osterhout N.B., Netherlands: Anthropological Publications, 1966.

Rosenthal, Franz. "From Arabic Books and Manuscripts VII: Some Graeco-Arabica in Istanbul." *Journal of the American Oriental Society* 81, no. 1 (March 1961): 7-12.

Rostovtzeff, M. *Caravan Cities*. Trans. D. and T. Talbot Rice. Oxford: The Clarendon Press, 1932.

Schärf Kluger, Rivkah. *The Archetypal Significance of Gilgamesh: A Modern Ancient Hero*. Ed. H. Yehezkel Kluger. Einsiedeln, Switzerland: Daimon Verlag, 1991.

Schoff, Wilfred H., ed. *The Song of Songs: A Symposium*. Philadelphia: The Commercial Museum, 1924.

Schultheiss, Friedrich. *Umajja ibn Abi ṣṢalt: Die unter seinem Namen überlieferten Gedichtfragmente*. Leipzig: J. C. Hinrichs'sche Buchhandlung, 1911.

Servius. *Commentarii in Virgilium Serviani sive Commentarii in Virgilium qui Mauro Servio Honorato Tribuuntur*. 2 vols. Ed. H. Albertus Lion. Göttingen: Vandenhoeck and Ruprecht, 1826.

Shahîd, Irfan. *Byzantium and the Arabs in the Fifth Century*. Washington, D.C.: Dumbarton Oaks Research Library and Collection, 1989.

———. *Byzantium and the Arabs in the Fourth Century*. Washington, D.C.: Dumbarton Oaks Research Library and Collection, 1984.

———. *Rome and the Arabs: A Prolegomenon to the Study of Byzantium and the Arabs*. Washington, D.C.: Dumbarton Oaks Research Library and Collection, 1984.

Shakespeare, William. *Macbeth*. Ed. John F. Andrews. London: J. M. Dent, 1993.

Somogyi, Joseph de. *Biblical Figures in ad-Damīrī's Ḥayāt al-Ḥayawān* [Reprint from the *Jubilee Volume Edward Mahler*]. Budapest, 1937.

Stanford, W. B. *The Ulysses Theme: A Study in the Adaptability of a Traditional Hero*. New Foreword by Charles Boer. Dallas: Spring Publications, 1992.

Stetkevych, Jaroslav. "Arabic Hermeneutical Terminology: Paradox and the Production of Meaning." *Journal of Near Eastern Studies* 48, no. 2 (April 1989): 81–95.

———. "Arabic Poetry and Assorted Poetics." In Malcolm H. Kerr, ed. *Islamic Studies: A Tradition and Its Problems*, pp. 103-23. Malibu, California: Undena Publications, 1980.

———. "Name and Epithet: The Philology and Semiotics of Animal Nomenclature in Early Arabic Poetry." *Journal of Near Eastern Studies* 45, no. 2 (April 1986): 89–124.

———. "Toward an Arabic Elegiac Lexicon: The Seven Words of the *Nasīb*." In Suzanne Pinckney Stetkevych, ed., *Reorientations/Arabic and Persian Poetry*, pp. 58–129. Bloomington and Indianapolis: Indiana University Press, 1994.

———. *The Zephyrs of Najd: The Poetics of Nostalgia in the Classical Arabic Nasīb*. Chicago: The University of Chicago Press, 1993.

Stetkevych, Suzanne Pinckney. "Intoxication and Immortality: Wine and Assocated Imagery in al-Maʿarrī's Garden." In Fedwa Malti-Douglas, ed., *Critical Pilgrimages: Studies in Arabic Literary Tradition* [=*Literature East and West* 25 (1989)], 29–48.

———. *Abū Tammām and the Poetics of the ʿAbbāsid Age*. Leiden: E. J. Brill, 1991.

———. *The Mute Immortals Speak: Pre-Islamic Poetry and the Poetics of Ritual*. Ithaca, New York: Cornell University Press, 1993.

———. "Pre-Islamic Panegyric and the Poetics of Redemption: *Mufaḍḍalīyah 119* of ʿAlqamah and *Bānat Suʿād* of Kaʿb Ibn Zuhayr." In Suzanne Pinckney Stetkevych, ed. *Reorientations/Arabic and Persian Poetry*, pp. 1-57. Bloomington and Indianapolis: Indiana University Press, 1994.

———. "Sara and the Hyena: Laughter, Menstruation, and the Genesis of a Double Entendre." *Journal of History of Religion* 36 no. 1 (Aug. 1996): 13–41.

al-Ṭabarī, Abū Jaʿfar Muḥammad Ibn Jarīr. *Tafsīr al-Ṭabarī: Jāmiʿ al-Bayān ʿan Taʾwīl Āy al-Qurʾān*. 16 vols. Eds. Maḥmūd Muḥammad Shākir and Aḥmad Muḥammad Shākir. Cairo: Dār al-Maʿārif bi Miṣr, 1954–69.

———. *Tārīkh al-Ṭabarī/Tārīkh al-Rusul wa al-Mulūk*. 11 vols. Ed. Muḥammad Abū al-Faḍl Ibrāhīm. Cairo: Dār al-Maʿārif, 1960–77.

al-Thaʿlabī, Ibn Isḥāq Aḥmad Ibn Muḥammad Ibn Ibrāhīm. *Kitāb Qiṣaṣ al-Anbiyāʾ al-Musammā bi al-ʿArāʾis*. Cairo: Al-Maṭbaʿah al-Kāstalīyah, 1298 H.

Tigay, Jeffrey. *The Evolution of the Gilgamesh Epic*. Philadelphia: University of Pennsylvania Press, 1982.

Ungnad, Arthur. "Gilgamesch Epos und Odyssee." In Karl Oberhuber, ed. *Das Gilgamesch Epos*, pp. 105–52. Darmstadt: Wissenschaftliche Buchgesellschaft, 1977.

ʿUrwah Ibn al-Ward. *Dīwānā ʿUrwah Ibn al-Ward wa al-Samawʾal*. Beirut: Dār Ṣādir/Dār Bayrūt, 1384/1964.

Vergil/Virgil. *The Aeneid of Virgil*. 2 vols. Ed. with introduction and notes by T. E. Page. London: Macmillan/New York: St. Martin's Press, 1967 [1st ed. 1894].

———. *Virgil: I, Eclogues/Georgics/Aeneid 1-6; II, Aeneid 7-12/The Minor Poems*. Trans. H. Rushton Fairclough. Loeb Classical Library. Cambridge, Massachusetts: Harvard University Press, 1984/1969.

Waele, F. J. M. de. *The Magic Staff or Rod in Graeco-Italian Antiquity*. Ghent: Drukkerey Erasmus, 1927.

Watt, Montgomery. *Muḥammad at Medina*. Oxford: The Clarendon Press, 1956.

Wellhausen, Julius. *Prolegomena to the History of Ancient Israel*. With a Reprint of the Article "Israel" from the *Encyclopaedia Britannica*. Preface by W. Robertson Smith. Translators Menzies and Black. New York: Meridian Books, 1957.

———. *Reste arabischen Heidentums*. 2d ed. Berlin: Georg Reimer, 1897.

Wensinck, A. J., J. P. Mensing, and J. B. Brugman. *Concordance et indices de la Tradition Musulmane: Le Six Livres, Le Musnad dʾal Dārimī, Le Muwattaʾ de Mālik, Le Musnad de Ahmad Ibn Hanbal*. 8 vols. Leiden, New York: E. J. Brill, 1962 [photo-offset of 1936-1943 edition].

Whitman, Cedric H. *Homer and the Heroic Tradition*. New York: W. W. Norton and Company, Inc., 1965.

Winnett, F. V., and W. L. Reed, with contributions by J. T. Milik and J. Starcky. *Ancient Records of North Arabia*. Toronto: University of Toronto Press, 1970.

Wisemann, T. P. *Remus: A Roman Myth*. Cambridge: Cambridge University Press, 1995.

Wissowa, Georg et al. *Paulys Real-Encyclopädie der classischen Altertumswissenschaft*. Ed. Wilhelm Kroll. Stuttgart: J. B. Metzlerscher Verlag, 1894-.

Wittekind, Wilhelm. *Das Hohe Lied und seine Beziehungen zum Istarkult*. Hannover: Orient-Buchhandlung Heinz Lafaire, 1925.

Zakī, Aḥmad Kamāl. "Al-Tafsīr al-Usṭūrī li al-Shiʿr al-Qadīm." *Fuṣūl* 1, no. 3 (April 1981): 115-26.

al-Zamakhsharī, Maḥmūd Ibn ʿAmr. *Asās al-Balāghah*. Cairo: Dār Maṭābiʿ al-Shaʿb, 1960.

———. *Kitāb Aʿjab al-ʿAjab fī Lāmīyat al-ʿArab*. Istanbul: Maṭbaʿat al-Jawāʾib, 1300 H.

INDEX

Jaroslav Stetkevych

is Professor Emeritus of Arabic Literature at the University of Chicago. He is the author of The Modern Arabic Literary Language: Lexical and Stylistic Developments *and* The Zephyrs of Najd: The Poetics of Nostalgia in the Classical Arabic Nasīb. *His articles on classical and modern Arabic literature have appeared in Spanish, English, Arabic, and Ukrainian.*